IMAGINING THE HEARTLAND

IMAGINING THE

HEARTLAND

**WHITE SUPREMACY AND
THE AMERICAN MIDWEST**

Britt E. Halvorson and Joshua O. Reno

 UNIVERSITY OF CALIFORNIA PRESS

University of California Press
Oakland, California

Library of Congress Cataloging-in-Publication Data

Names: Halvorson, Britt, author. | Reno, Joshua, author.
Title: Imagining the heartland : white supremacy and the American
    Midwest / Britt E. Halvorson and Joshua O. Reno.
Description: Oakland, California : University of California Press,
    [2022] | Includes bibliographical references and index.
Identifiers: LCCN 2021052447 (print) | LCCN 2021052448 (ebook) |
    ISBN 9780520387607 (cloth) | ISBN 9780520387614 (paperback) |
    ISBN 9780520387621 (epub)
Subjects: LCSH: Whites—Race identity—Middle West. | BISAC:
    SOCIAL SCIENCE / Anthropology / Cultural & Social |
    SOCIAL SCIENCE / Ethnic Studies / American / General
Classification: LCC HT1575 .H35 2022 (print) | LCC HT1575 (ebook) |
    DDC 305.809/077—dc23/eng/20211115
LC record available at https://lccn.loc.gov/2021052447
LC ebook record available at https://lccn.loc.gov/2021052448

Manufactured in the United States of America

31 30 29 28 27 26 25 24 23 22
10 9 8 7 6 5 4 3 2 1

For our siblings
   Bengt Halvorson
   Jen Kane
   Jay Parkman
   Zack Reno
   Sarah Westland
who taught us the skills of good collaboration

CONTENTS

ILLUSTRATIONS

ACKNOWLEDGMENTS

Our initial foray into the questions we explore in this book would not have been possible without the intellectual home of the Alfred P. Sloan Center for the Ethnography of Everyday Life (CEEL) and the University of Michigan's Department of Anthropology. We are especially grateful to CEEL director Tom Fricke for creating the space there for rigorous engagement with Midwestern history and ethnography and to Gillian Feeley-Harnik for mentorship and intellectual guidance with placing the Midwest in a critical global history. Our rich, wide-ranging conversations and friendships with fellow CEEL trainees, now faculty all over the country, laid the foundation for this book. We especially wish to thank Sallie Han, Cecilia Tomori, Jessica Smith, Rebecca Carter, and Brian Hoey for being inspiring and generous people whom we feel fortunate to know.

Several people supported the research and writing of this book in important ways and deserve special mention. Lena Hanschka, Colby College Class of 2021, played a critical role in the research for chapter 5 and is listed there as a coauthor of the text. As Britt's research assistant, she helped create the database of 125 media articles that the chapter relies on and identified a set of initial terms for the media content analysis. We are also thankful to Lena for reading the entire manuscript and offering incisive editing suggestions during the final stages of the project. Jada Basdeo, Binghamton University Class of 2020, was Josh's research assistant, whose crucial labor and critical eye were indispensable for the argument that developed into chapter 4 and is credited as a coauthor. Jada spent hours (which she can never get back) examining individual film profiles as listed in the American Film Institute (AFI) database online, trying to identify historical patterns in how films are regionally categorized.

We have also benefited tremendously from the generosity of students, friends, and colleagues who made reading recommendations, were curious about the project, or shared support in other ways. For comments on earlier writing that became part of this book, we would like to thank Debbora Battaglia, Emanuela Grama, Richard Handler, and Marcel LaFlamme. For directing us to key sources, we are grateful to Catherine Besteman, AB Brown, Nadia El-Shaarawi, Roy Grinker, Jemima Pierre, and participants of the Colby NEHC Race and Identity reading group. Britt would like to thank her colleagues Chandra Bhimull, Sarah Duff, Suzanne Menair, Mary Beth Mills, Maple Razsa, and Winifred Tate, who took the time for conversation about this project and provided insightful guidance and support. Molly Mullin also carefully read several initial chapters and offered important suggestions for how to strengthen the final draft of the manuscript. Britt is also grateful for conversations with Alyssa Lang, Colby College Class of 2018, on many different topics, including ethnography, white supremacy, American history, and the politics of place-making. Josh would like to thank his students and colleagues at Binghamton University for helpful conversations over the years on the relationship between field and study, including Doug Holmes, and members of the Ethnography Workgroup that formed during the COVID-19 pandemic (Gaby Hanley-Mott, Rae Jereza, Laura Johnsen, Raha Peyravi, Jessica Santos, and Rachael Sebastien) for helping to keep him sane, but especially Sabina Perrino, and Matthew Wolf-Meyer, who provided specific and helpful suggestions at an early stage of this project.

Writing a book is never easy, and, even under the best conditions, it takes years of effort and loads of support to make it happen. Britt would like to thank her parents, her mother, Berit, and her late father, Phillip, for their insistence on complex stories; her brother Bengt and sister-in-law Deena for their interest and encouragement; and Odessa for the wonderful break of spending hours together on adventures in Moomin Valley. Britt would like to thank her husband, Jonathan, who was intrigued by this project from the start and saw its potential before we did; he never wavered in his enthusiasm for the book and helped make it a reality through countless, quotidian acts of support. Josh would like to thank his wife and son, Jeanne and

Charlie, for tolerating him, especially during various coronavirus lockdowns and quarantines, while he obsessed over writing deadlines that were largely imaginary. We have chosen to dedicate this book to our siblings, and Josh would like to point out that one big reason for this, for him, is that growing up with Jen, Jay, Sarah, and Zack taught him how to share everything from clothes to toys, food, chores, rooms, and holiday rituals over the years. Writing a book with another person is not that different from temporarily sharing a house with a sibling before, eventually, your paths diverge.

We are grateful to Reed Malcolm, who saw the potential in this book early on and to the three anonymous reviewers for the University of California Press, who gave important feedback that strengthened the manuscript. Last but not least, Colby College provided research support that assisted us in completing the book.

Introduction

Narrative is radical, creating us at the very moment it is being created.
—Toni Morrison, celebrated Midwestern author

What is a region? Region is one of those spatial concepts, like place or com-munity, that seems to have self-evident meaning, yet comes apart as soon as one looks at it too closely. This is very clear when it comes to the Midwestern United States, which for over a century has had a strange relationship to actual space and actual people. Who or what qualifies as "really Midwest-ern" is an open question. People may not debate this with the same inten-sity as they might about whether someone is a "real New Yorker" or a "real Southerner," but this is partly because it seems almost banal by comparison. It is almost as if people are not *from* the Midwest as much as they are *merely from* there. Consider talk show host Dick Cavett's televised interview with director Orson Welles on May 14, 1970:

> *Cavett:* If you were to ask, I think, the average person "where is Orson Welles' hometown?" I have a feeling that you would get a guess that would go all over the globe, probably starting with Budapest or something, and the fact that it's Kenosha, Wisconsin . . .
> [light applause]
> *Welles:* [laughter]
> *Cavett:* . . . is one of the most startling. . . . That's the truth, isn't it?
> *Welles:* That's right, I was born in Kenosha.

Cavett was incredulous that such a global and cosmopolitan figure, a celeb-rity and man-of-the-world like Welles, was from such an underwhelming place. From their exchange it's clear that Kenosha is not a bad place to be born, just a painfully ordinary one.

In this book, we take issue with this underwhelming quality, this banality, and ask a series of questions that emerge from it: What are the conditions that make regions appear average, plain, and homogenous, and what are the social, political, and cultural consequences of this? Our central argument is that if one can understand the ways in which a region and its people do not seem to matter, then national and imperial projects of race and inequality can be understood and challenged in a new way. In the chapters that follow, we argue that the Midwest—as an imagined national middle, or average—is less a real place or collection of places and more a screen onto which various conceptions of middle-ness and average-ness are projected. Put differently, the Midwest serves as a standard and has for many years, one that allows for normative claims about the state of the nation and fosters projects of structural violence from white supremacy to imperialism and nativism.[1] And, most important of all, it has swept everyone up in its narrative, creating us as we create it, to paraphrase Toni Morrison, whether or not we identify as Midwestern.

This book started as a conversation between the two of us, both anthropologists, while we were on a Minneapolis/St. Paul light rail train in November 2016, two weeks after the election of Donald Trump. We were traveling to the annual meeting of the American Anthropological Association, from Maine and New York, respectively, and discussing the role "the Midwest" played in the election outcome. But we already had a shared language for thinking through this problem. Our conversation really began nearly twenty years prior when we were both graduate students at the University of Michigan. We were recruited for a special, newly formed research center called The Center for the Ethnography of Everyday Life; it aimed to place the Midwest in a critical global and historical context and use immersive, long-term cultural research—the hallmark of anthropology—to better understand issues of work and family in the region. There, we found a wonderful group of fellow students (all now scholar-teachers around the country), with whom we read, debated, and developed ways to think critically together about our research endeavors.

We each went on to pursue our own research projects in Midwestern communities, even as these experiences also built on earlier formative years in the Midwest. Britt was raised in Muskegon, Michigan, by parents who grew up in Madagascar and Sweden and, as a result, had from a young age a sense of the globalizing Midwest rarely portrayed in national media. In the metropolitan area of one hundred thousand where she was raised along Michigan's western edge, she and her brother were not alone among their young school friends in the 1980s in having family members in other parts of the world. Yet, because of her white middle-class upbringing, no one questioned whether she was a "real American" or "where she was from" and, though her parents' accents were sometimes remarked on in public spaces, her parents' ties elsewhere seemed alternately hidden and unknown or a source of occasional cultural capital. After living in the Midwest for over twenty years, she went on to conduct two years of research in Minneapolis/ St. Paul and in Madagascar with white American Christians and ethnically Merina Malagasy Christians who participate in a medical aid program. Though he grew up in upper New York State, Josh lived with his family for five years in Michigan, and did research in a southeast Michigan landfill on the periphery of Detroit. His later work involved an examination of military waste, including the bizarre impact of falling space debris on a small town in Wisconsin. Even though he was not from the Midwest originally, Josh is white and could live in and move about the overwhelmingly white communities within which he did research without anyone wondering if he really belonged for the most part (that is, until he opened his mouth).

These widely varying, long and complex experiences gave us a set of critical perspectives that we reactivated on that Minneapolis train and have been grappling with ever since. While the 2016 election of Donald Trump sparked scholars and journalists to ask important questions about whiteness, this moment of American cultural reflection led to some other problems. Notably, it produced considerable research about white people *over there*, magnifying the perceived gulf between liberal, middle-class, anti-racist whites and working-class, conservative (it is often assumed, more racist) whites.[2] Focusing on white working-class people in this way partly served the political and economic interests and cultural sensibilities of middle- and upper-class whites, creating social distance between themselves and the pernicious effects of structural racism. Post-2016 cultural reflection largely sidestepped the fact that white supremacy is not simply a matter of individual prejudice but an old, yet continuously transforming, global form of structural power that controls disproportionate access to resources. A second problem has therefore involved white people characterizing the Trump era as somehow new and

totally unprecedented. One way to challenge this tendency is to draw attention to the histories of white supremacy that inform the current era, illumi-
nating historical connections that have been erased or ignored. We seek to do
precisely that, not only historically but spatially, by tracing how the Midwest
has operated as a screen or stage on which to articulate whiteness and virtue,
or white virtue through non-virtuous whites, across different time periods in
US history. For this reason, while we touch on it briefly in what follows, it is
not until chapter 5 that we return to the 2016 election, and the relationship
of whiteness and the Midwest during this contest, after we have covered this
widespread historical and cultural terrain that came before it.[3]

As we argue, distinguishing virtuous from non-virtuous whiteness is an
old, long-standing component of white supremacy. It unwittingly recycles
a system in which good (often class-privileged) whites distance themselves
from the harms of racism by identifying a group of bad (often less class-
privileged) whites—what some scholars have called a group of "repugnant
others," offensive due to their retrograde political sensibilities.[4] Calling out
racism on the part of whites and developing anti-racist forms of whiteness
are critically important. But simplified ideas of white goodness and badness
are part of the same system and do not address the systemic problem of
racism, with its long and ongoing history of violence and disproportionate
distribution of resources and life itself. We need fresh, new ways of thinking
about and seeing what racism is and does in order to begin the multigenera-
tional, hard, and unglamorous work of dismantling white supremacy.

Though we focus extensively on familiar ideas about the Midwest, the
book uses this material in order to investigate something else: the often
taken-for-granted connection between this seemingly most ordinary of
American regions and whiteness, a connection that lends support to other
projects related to nation and empire, both historically and today. In fact,
that seeming ordinariness is at the crux of our argument. The fact that the
Midwest is often imagined as ordinary—and in so many different ways—
helps to conceal its relationship to whiteness and vice versa. Uncovering this
connection between ideas about the Midwest and whiteness does not rely
on unraveling a secret conspiracy or unearthing lost or forgotten materials.
Rather, regional narratives have both fully apparent and hidden dimensions
that work in tandem to fulfill a variety of cultural imperatives. Our object
of analysis is a bit like a well-tied knot—you may not know how to tie or
untie it and you may not be able to see every part of the knot, but that does

not stop it from holding firm. The Midwest is just such a knot, made up of a tangle of various threads. Looking into *and* looking through the widely circulated narratives of the Midwest shows what this knot holds in place, fleshing out what remains less openly articulated and what cultural values and interests are reinforced through the more visible elements. The looking-glass quality of these Midwestern common tropes—think of flat, verdant cornfields—does not make the trope itself irrelevant, but in fact reveals a more complex knot of threads, as the apparent elements make possible and relate to the more concealed cultural processes. Because they hold so many ideologies firmly in place, regionalizing knots are power relations that can serve intersecting projects of race, nation, and empire.[5]

One of our claims is that Midwest regional tropes are heavily invested in the imagination of whiteness, though they do not name it as such, and that whiteness actually does require a lot of creative imagery to exist and spread. As we will show, the work of signaling and consolidating whiteness often happens in the absence of white people and instead emerges through racialized white spaces, land, and labor. We are especially interested in how dynamic notions of white virtue and industry are smuggled into Midwest representations, in ways that help connect race, nation, and empire. We explore not only text, but also art and films, and their complex interrelations, which we suggest are central to publicizing whiteness and its many contradictions and inconsistencies. Altogether, this suggests that whiteness does not fly under the radar, per se, but hides in plain sight. Publicly circulating media, whether film, fiction, art, or the news, are a key channel for establishing these dominant visions of the world and we explore this extensively in the chapters to come.

What is true of public culture is also true of academic writing. Oftentimes people write academic texts in a third-person point of view with an objective authorial perspective, as if they are standing above it all, nowhere and everywhere. This is a problematic position that can reproduce forms of dominance, such as masculinity and whiteness. To counter this tendency, we have written a number of personal reflections on our experiences with and in Midwest communities that the reader will find between the chapters. The purpose of these reflections, in general and in our book, is to complicate the idea of a single and authoritative self by revealing the complexities of becoming a person in an unequal world.[6] Here we follow feminist writers about whiteness, who have suggested that "personal narratives provide a space in which theorists might expose our struggles with racial formation and racism."[7] We partook in and have been shaped by the projects of whiteness, nation, and empire that we describe, and are not separate from or outside of them; we consider our distinct life experiences a source of insight into the mundane work of regional tropes as complex signifiers of race, nation, and empire.

It is our hope that this book will not only challenge the Midwest as a racial trope but help readers to see themselves in what we write about. This brings us back to another meaning of Morrison's quotation with which we began this introduction: the radical power of narrative to enlist us all in the creation of more just worlds. Many approaches to race in the United States create distance between readers and the racist people *over there* who cause problems, but we want readers to see race and racism at work even in the most ordinary of things, like landscapes, paintings, poems, and films. Morrison's lesson is simple and powerful: when you hear or tell stories about "other" places and people, you're making them and yourself in the process.

REFLECTIONS I

I distinctly remember a late-night taxi ride in 2009 from the Phoenix airport to a downtown hotel. I was attending a conference, and it was convenient and economical to hop in the cab with another anthropologist heading to a different hotel a few blocks from mine, a fifty-something white man whom I had just met on the curb outside baggage claim. In the taxi, our conversation turned within a few moments to the usual question: "What do you work on?" I explained that I had been doing field research on historical and contemporary connections between Lutherans in the Midwest United States and Madagascar, particularly on a thirty-year-old medical aid program. My taxi companion responded: "Lutherans in Madagascar! Really? I mean, Lutherans in the Midwest I know, but in Madagascar?" I was prepared for his questions and explained why Lutherans in Madagascar did indeed exist—and composed one of the island's four largest Protestant churches, with over three million members. But I have often thought about the sequencing of his (and other people's) response and the difficulty for him of putting "Lutheran" and "Madagascar" together, along with the ease of thinking about "Lutherans" and the "Midwest." The difference could perhaps be explained by my companion's American upbringing and his lack of familiarity with Madagascar, or by the exotic way Madagascar is often viewed by Americans and Europeans. Looking back, I think his tone of incredulousness—which I have often heard—conveys something else too, something more inchoate and impactful: a deep yet often tacit sense of Midwestern Lutherans as prototypic whites, even hyper-whites that are the focus of satire and parody for their perceived lack of worldliness. To imagine Black Lutherans in Madagascar was humorous and dissonant because of the knot of white racial and cultural associations Midwestern Lutherans evoked, without race ever being mentioned.

—Halvorson

I have always had difficulty talking about where, exactly, I conducted my research and with whom. I've taken to saying, "with Americans" or "in the United States."—especially now that I've done research in several regions of the country. But those answers do not signal earned symbolic and cultural capital in the same way as they would if I were a more conventional anthropologist, one who, as a British friend liked to put it, does fieldwork "in the colonies" (a joke that is already quite telling on many levels, not least of which because the United States was of course a loose set of colonies originally). This existing difficulty, the problem of not having a rarefied "area" and therefore recognizable anthropological expertise, was compounded by the fact that my original informants in southeastern Michigan were Midwestern and white. What is curious to me now is not that scholars with whom I would discuss my research were uninterested in the Midwest or white people there, per se, but that they thought they already knew a lot about "them." If ostensibly anthropologists are meant to talk about people whose lives are thought to be less well known, this presents an interesting problem to the ethnographer of Midwestern white folks, because you have to convince your audience that they do not know as much as they think, that *your* white folks are especially unique, and/or that it's not the people but the unique circumstances they are facing that are worth investigating (e.g., neoliberalism or deindustrialization). In hindsight, I think I did both by focusing my doctoral research on landfill workers and local people who resented the presence of a transnational landfill near their homes.

—Reno

Challenging Ideas of the Midwest

The Midwest region was not discovered, as if it were some natural feature of the American landscape. It was invented. Over the years, it has been successively reinvented again and again. But invention does not mean creating something out of nothing. Like other US regions, such as Appalachia, the South, and New England, the Midwest is a cultural product shaped by multiple historical forces. To better understand them, we selectively trace over the first two chapters some of the events informing the region's invention in the late nineteenth and early twentieth centuries.

Popular imagery and narratives of the Midwest have bundled together whiteness, labor, and property—or a particular kind of racial capitalism—in ways that helped underwrite white political and economic interests. But it might not seem that way at first when we imagine Rust Belt cities, verdant cornfields, the quaint accent of the movie or television series *Fargo*, the Dust Bowl, and the meatpacking plants of Upton Sinclair's *The Jungle*. If these seem familiar, it is important to understand how they came to be so. All of these examples share unexamined, historically shaped associations between national belonging, race, and region.

The global rise of heartlands like the Midwest in the late nineteenth century occurred at a time of widespread urbanization and industrialism throughout the United States and similar parts of the world, from other settler colonies, like Australia and South Africa, to other emerging imperial powers, like Japan and Germany. Some regional narratives were invented to facilitate these dramatic transformations, while other conceptions of region emerged as a reaction to them. On the one hand, multinational regionalist discourse was on the rise in the nineteenth century in general as different parts of the world were increasingly incorporated into global capitalist markets.[1] On the other hand, regions could take on an altogether different meaning as places in need of protection against the transformations of urbanization and industrialization. Rural heartlands were a nationalist ideal promoted in contrast to the allegedly cosmopolitan and corrupt values and populations of the growing cities. In the more powerful countries of Europe, like France and Germany, the period prior to World War I saw regionalism officially subsumed within nationalist narratives of unity or, as in Sweden, a vehicle for locating and reproducing folkloric national heritage. At the same time, regional attachments could just as easily become mobilized in nationalist movements, as occurred during the Spanish Civil War. Sometimes regions were taken as antecedents to nations, as in the case of Poland and Czechoslovakia until independence in 1918, and they were thought to become something of the past or disappear as soon as political autonomy was achieved.[2]

Even where regional differences were reduced in favor of a singular nationalist identity, there is widespread evidence of a simultaneous revalorization of a particular regional cultural figure, the "traditional" rural citizen, family, and/or community. Rural folkways and political subjects, associated with particular regions of the nation-state, were critical for the support of right-wing populism in Weimar Germany and Japan during the late Meiji Restoration period. They also often served as a critical nationalist and nativist trope and standard in relation to which all others, whether citizens or enemies of the state, were unfavorably measured.[3] In this way, regionalisms became enrolled in the political forces of nationalism, which reified "rural" and "urban" into phantom cultural figures expressing opposed political sentiments and sensibilities. Regionalisms were thus used in order to respond to the destabilizing context of industrialization and the rise of new forms of economic and political authority, as well as rural-to-urban migration and increasing wage labor. Global projects of colonialism and white supremacy also enlisted some of these specific national regionalisms. Moving across different time periods in both chapters shows the enduring relationship of the Midwest and whiteness in US history. This relationship has not always existed, and when it has, it has not been plainly obvious, at least not to everyone affected by it. In fact, the association of whiteness with the Midwest becomes more or less apparent as a symbol of race and class under specific cultural conditions.

CHAPTER I

The Midwest and White Virtue

Local. Insulated. Exceptionalist. Isolationist. Provincial. The ultimate safe space. What if, instead of treating these components of the heartland myth as foregone conclusions, we approached them as questions, as invitations to explore.

—Kristin Hoganson (2019: xxiii)

I. INTRODUCTION

This is not a book about the Midwest, the place, or Midwesterners, the people. Our concern is less with specific places and people than with the cultural work of place-making. All places change over time as people dwell in them, imagine them, name and transform them. But in the case of the American Midwest, the cultural work of place-making is arguably even more pronounced, because there is not even shared agreement on what "its" literal boundaries are (i.e., which states are included and excluded in the region), making even the most banal statements about "Midwestern" places and people subject to dispute.[1] When Midwestern places and people are invoked, they are not only referred to, therefore, but are actually brought into being again and again. And it is not only to the people who "belong" to this eminently imagined region that such invocations and conjurings matter. Imagining the Midwest is a national and global pastime.

Why should it matter if people and places are labeled as being or not being "Midwestern"? Two protests that gained widespread national attention in 2020 were arguably covered by the mass media very differently. "Anti-lockdown" protests, in response to the coronavirus pandemic, began in Michigan in April 2020. They were quickly identified with "the Midwest," and were widely covered as white, with critics and supporters both signaling the racial composition and politics of those involved explicitly and implicitly. A month later, protests over the wrongful police killing of George Floyd had also broken out, beginning this time in Minneapolis where his murder occurred. These protests were instead generally coded as "urban" (not Midwestern) despite the fact that both they and the anti-lockdown protests took place primarily in cities and both started in the Midwest. The tendency to identify certain people and actions as regional (and especially as "Midwestern") tends to bring with it other identifications that might not be overt, but are easy to recognize.

The Midwest, as an idea, is a slippery concept: it encompasses a bewildering variety of figures, places, histories, and events, from the plains of North Dakota to the snowy fields of northern Minnesota and the nearly fifty-year-old baseball diamond of the Kansas City Royals, to the deindustrializing cities of the Rust Belt and the biennial Iowa political caucus. And, for individual people who live in or frequent these places, the Midwest may not even be a meaningful place association at all, as people identify more as from the Great Lakes, as Nebraskan, or as from Cincinnati. Our argument is that, by regionalizing an imagined and ever-shifting American heartland, many different people have been given a screen or tableau against which they could project, test, and reinforce tropes and values of whiteness with national and global significance. Perceiving and imagining the Midwest has contributed to the spread of white supremacy among all Americans, as well as people elsewhere in the world, not just Midwesterners. It may seem that the whiteness of the Midwest is quite obvious in the current moment, possibly even a given. But it was not always so, and today, ongoing cultural work is needed to make it seem to be so. Focusing on the Midwest's significance as an American heartland or a cultural idea consolidating dominant national values reveals how the region has at different times in US history enabled people to articulate and define exclusionary national narratives of race and belonging. This tendency was especially apparent in the 2016 presidential election. But the Midwest has in fact a long, often overlooked history serving exactly this role in the United States.

Widespread references to the insularity and whiteness of the Midwest during the 2016 presidential election, a time when whiteness was being reimagined as a force in US national politics, were neither coincidental nor new. A brief look at the history of the term *Midwest* can help bring to light some of these culturally forgotten histories. The term *Middle West* was initially used by the settler state to survey land and referred to a north-to-south ordering of space on the plains from the vantage point of Kansas and Nebraska. It was not until the late nineteenth and early twentieth centuries, however, that the Midwest regional label took on nationalist sentiments associated with the farming livelihood of white European settlers, as a counterpoint to the perceived changes wrought by rapid urbanization and industrialization. The widely popularized pastoral imagery of the Midwest, encapsulated in novels such as Willa Cather's 1918 *My Ántonia*, never actually reflected the existing economic diversity in the region. Dominant representations of the pastoral Midwest were thoroughly modern constructs that sought to present the region and its inhabitants through the lens of a selective tradition of Midwestern farming, as a foil to the technology and modernity of industrial labor as well as its toil, pollution, inequalities, workers of color, and forms of alienation. In remarkably parallel ways to today's uses of this trope, it began to function in the early twentieth century as an idealized representation of an imagined earlier form of economic production and social relations. An iconic and imagined place, the Heartland remains coded as white.

Since the 2016 election, a number of scholars have questioned stereotypical portraits of the Midwest, particularly those of parochialism, working-class whiteness, and insularity. Important works include historian Kristin Hoganson's *The Heartland: An American History*, anthropologist Sujey Vega's *Latino Heartland*, globalization scholar Faranak Miraftab's *Global Heartland*, journalist Sarah Smarsh's memoir *Heartland*, and literary scholar Adam Ochonicky's *The American Midwest in Film and Literature*. Still others have focused on white resentment and its role as a political and economic force in Midwest communities, as in political scientist Katherine Cramer's *The Politics of Resentment*, or as an embodied cause of affliction, as in medical sociologist Jonathan Metzl's *Dying of Whiteness*. We find these works extraordinarily valuable and build on them here. Yet a different set of questions can also be asked about the Midwest: What work do regional concepts perform and how and why do they get reproduced? Linking regionalism with nationalism and with globalized forms of racialization and even empire requires a kind of critical and creative analysis, of looking for nonobvious yet fully apparent connections. It also means seeking out "knots" of power, those nodes or sites of intersection where we see the work of empire, race, and nation being performed all at once through regional concepts.[2]

Regional concepts like that of the heartland Midwest have far greater purchase than they might seem to at first glance. They are not merely misrepresentations but ideological tropes that reproduce race and empire in both obvious and non-obvious ways. Yet it is precisely through the notion that they are benign misrepresentations, merely harmless stereotypes, that they do some of their most far-reaching cultural work, not simply for Midwesterners but for elite white Americans in general. As we will show, the iconic Midwest is essential for understanding white supremacy as it has been linked with nationalism and regionalism over the last century and a half.

There is an affinity, in fact, between whiteness, Midwestness, and Americanness, anchored in their shared emptiness or unmarked and homogenized qualities.[3] All three are touted as if they are ordinary, average, or even banal. At the same time, creating successful representations of ordinary Midwestness requires cultural expression through many diverse, publicly circulating media. Far from just another region among others, and what some imagine to be the least interesting one at that, the Midwest is a political and affective logic in racial projects of global white supremacy. Neglecting the Midwest means neglecting the production of white supremacist imaginings at their most banal and influential, their most locally situated and globally dispersed. For the rest of this chapter, we will first introduce white virtue as a key concept that links the Midwest to specific projects of nationalism and global white supremacy. We consider how the tacit whiteness of the Midwestern trope works in tandem with tensions and crises specific to capitalism and imperialism at the turn of the nineteenth century, which helps explain the continuing success of the Midwest as a cultural trope. In the second half of the chapter, however, we offer a counterpoint to both the white virtue model of Midwest labor and to the apparent stability of whiteness itself, derived on this basis.

II. REGION AND WHITE VIRTUE

Global historians suggest that a sharpened interest in whiteness emerged at the turn of the twentieth century as a reactionary mode in response to Black consciousness and, specifically, colonial rebellions (like the ones that occurred in the Dakotas during the Ghost Dance war in 1890–91, in the Philippines in 1896–1902, or southeast Madagascar in 1904–05). Writing in 1910, W. E. B. Du Bois observed, "Wave upon wave, each with increasing virulence, is dashing this new religion of whiteness on the shores of our time."[4] Du Bois saw increasing claims of whiteness to be "proprietary" or an ownership claim and alliance forged out of fear. Thus, though it is often assumed that whiteness has been unmarked historically, heightened articulations of whiteness were part of late nineteenth and early twentieth century globalized efforts of colonialism and imperialism that extended far beyond American borders.[5] This is of course apparent in the underpinning imperial rationale of the "white man's burden." Yet, as we point out, the narrative outline of the white man's burden or the notion of the white ability to self-govern and promote industry, in contrast with colonized people's presumed inability to do so, was echoed and expressed in many non-juridical forms that seemed to bear little relation to them, including regional Midwestern tropes of vitality, strength, and labor and their prevalent iconography.[6] This imagined figure of the white man came about as a global and transnational phenomenon that spoke in reactive ways to the political organizing and mobilities of people of color.[7]

Critical race theorists take these ideas further to establish how whiteness is not merely a popular category of personal or global identity but a social entitlement that has provided access to material and political resources. In Black Reconstruction, W. E. B. Du Bois argued that whiteness presented Euro-descent laborers at the time with a kind of "wage" or social capital that compensated for their meager earnings and hard toil, and thus was a class category as much as a racial one that forestalled labor organizing across racial lines.[8] Historian David Roediger drew directly from this idea in his foundational book Wages of Whiteness to demonstrate how whiteness was a claim that appealed to Irish workers for the ways that it could distinguish them from free Black workers and elevate their own low social status and stigmatization. Racial categories are always formed in opposition to other racialized practices in a historically and culturally shaped racial hierarchy, an idea crucial to our work, but also whiteness in particular has what Du Bois terms proprietary dimensions. This is clear in Southern miscegenation laws, for instance, yet it is less common to view coded public articulations of whiteness as having their own proprietary qualities.[9] Building on these multistranded insights into whiteness, regional iconography is not merely a spatial representation but a way of tying white political-economic and imperial claims to land into a powerful and persistent knot with white fears and fantasies about the racialized body politic.

A key feature of critical studies of whiteness is the presumption that racial distinctions reproduce themselves culturally in many different, non-obvious ways that reach far beyond individual, racialized bodies.[10] Whiteness is a compulsory yet impossible ideal; it can but does not only refer to actual people and their skin color, but also to affective and ideological pressures on all people within white supremacist social formations to act in accordance with shared but ever-shifting assumptions about being white.[11] This is critical because regional tropes promote whiteness even though they only infrequently feature white bodies. Whiteness is as much about that which is devalued, silenced, or ignored in common portraits of the Midwest, or the "historical anti-logic" of racial capital and imperial formations.[12] Carefully untying and unraveling these knots in order to parse the inconspicuous and obscured dimensions of white supremacy in regional tropes—in relation to seemingly more visible forms of racial difference—is a key feature of our analysis. Here too, critical race studies have developed specific approaches to these omissions.

Whiteness can be imagined as similar to dominant culture: a deeply influential, historically and culturally specific set of embodied values, persuasions, inequalities, identifications, associations, and place-making activities and practices. This means that whiteness is not borne out simply through individual actions, as in common notions of racism that equate it with individual prejudice.[13] Rather, it is a structural force that many individuals participate in without ever fully being aware of it. Key to the reproduction of whiteness is its public circulation in camouflaged ways that make white practices and claims appear dominant without white people seeming to openly and explicitly grant them much value or importance. Thus our main focus is on accessible, publicly circulating images of the Midwest, from popular films like the *Wizard of Oz* to contemporary news articles in the *New York Times*. In her recent book on the US white power movement, historian Kathleen Belew notes, "White power should be recognized as something larger than the Klan, encompassing a wider range of ideologies and operating simultaneously in the public and underground."[14] Looking at whiteness requires also attending to its connections with specific, varying forms of nationalism, class, ableism, sexuality, and gender. It is not surprising that the Midwest is complexly tied to the resurgence on the national stage of forms of white working-class masculinity today, because it has often been used as a screen onto which forms of whiteness, labor, and masculinity have been projected. Some people can find these qualities of the Midwest generative, in other words; they can selectively tune into and out of them at different times like airborne radio waves in order to find a station, a signal that moves them.[15]

In the post-2016 era, white racism has seemingly become more publicly apparent to whites themselves, notably in the Charlottesville, Virginia, alt-right white nationalist rally, the continuing murder of Black individuals by police, and increasingly quotidian acts of hate and violence against immigrants, Muslims, Jews, LGBTQ individuals, and people of color. This is apparent in racist violence and racist talk, most obviously by members of the white power movement in the United States today, but not only them. As anthropologist Jane Hill writes, "Much of the everyday language of White racism has not gone underground. Instead, it circulates in the full light of day. Every slur, every stereotype in its repertoire receives frequent exposure and publicity."[16] These forms of racism are undeniable. At the same time, whiteness performs ideological work through hidden, covert forms of racialization. Such "racism without race" is a cultural process that is part of a gradual movement in the post–civil rights era toward racial formations that operate in subterranean, subtle ways.[17] Whiteness is also remade through a continually shifting terrain of possibilities for the expression of racial identity. In the post-2016 era, there are active attempts to claim acceptable forms of middle-class whiteness, a cultural process that consists of distinguishing racist from antiracist or decolonial styles, practices, and discourses of whiteness.

There is also a perceptible cultural process afoot that distinguishes plain whiteness—often associated with the Midwest—from ethnic whiteness, reinvigorating a complex set of distinctions in US history between ethnicity and race. As we discuss further in this chapter, tensions between being plainly white and being ethnically white, not fully white, or noticeably Jewish, Italian, Portuguese, or Polish have been part of the policing and expansion or contraction of whiteness at different times in US history. In the current moment, a number of cases have been widely discussed in the media whereby white people, such as Jessica Krug and Hilaria (Hilary) Baldwin, have sought to distance themselves from plain whiteness by falsely claiming ethnic and racial identities different from their own. Commentators have noted that this kind of appropriation—not just of an identity but of a history and of resources, in the case of Krug's fellowships and positions—is actually quite indicative of whiteness itself, a constant that can be seen across time.[18] But these troubling cases also tell us something about the continually moving target of whiteness and the cultural attraction and value attributed to being ethnically not quite fully white, as part of contemporary white progressive attempts to escape or distance themselves from plain whiteness (a sharp contrast from the early twentieth century, to be sure, as we will show). With the story of Jessica Krug in fall 2020, a columnist for *Newsday* summarized it in a similar way as did thousands of other online commentators: "An academic who teaches African history has confessed that she has misrepresented herself as a Bronx-bred Afro-Latina when she actually comes from a white Jewish family in the Midwest."[19] The Midwest does double duty here as a revealing site to be from and a place that confirms the plain or ethnic whiteness hiding all along behind Krug's façade.

Efforts to recuperate virtuous forms of whiteness—in contrast to morally corrupt or devalued whiteness, whether plain or not—can be traced to at least the US Civil War. The Midwest was central to the moral reclaiming of whiteness in the Reconstruction era, as regional tropes covertly valorized white independent labor as regional tropes covertly valorized white independent labor while devalorizing forms of labor that came to be associated with the South.[20] In chapters 3 and 4, we trace comparable uses of the Midwest today as a national screen on which to project and imagine distinctive styles of whiteness, with the region instead often the source of devalued, class-marked varieties in relation to more educated, morally virtuous, anti-racist whiteness. Both moves reproduce the cultural power and presence of whiteness on a vast, far-reaching cultural scale, even if they are given to slightly different ends. Focusing on the concerning rise of the white power movement, as Belew does, is important. But as anti-racist activists have long known, mundane white structural power and white sensibilities are slippery—just when you think you have them in your grasp, they flexibly shape-shift and recapitulate their grip on culturally dominant forms. Focusing only on examples of openly hateful bigotry also misses the role of seemingly benign representations in affectively *moving* the US white power movement into action in the first place. While tracing these many points of overlap exceeds our focus, a key part of our approach is carefully analyzing how widely circulated Midwest regional tropes can covertly signal a subtext of racialized meanings, which can then be taken up and acted upon by anyone, whether they belong to a racist organization or not.

III. TRADITIONAL AND MODERN: MIDWESTERN TROPES IN TENSION

In the United States, nationalist narratives about white settler economic and political interests have long deployed images of the Midwest—regardless of how those images represented or spoke to those select few who chose to self-identify as "Midwesterners." Though the Midwest region came to be nationally and globally recognized in the post–Civil War era, as we discuss in chapter 2, it attained its expanded geographic sense (including Kansas, Nebraska, Michigan, Illinois, Ohio, Wisconsin, North Dakota, South Dakota, Minnesota, Iowa, and Missouri) around 1902 and became a major place designation a decade later.[21] One can identify the formation of regionalist belief and investment in a distinct "Midwestern-ness" to the same period, especially in relation to radical transformations happening in many of the world's urban and industrial centers.[22] With the early twentieth-century emergence of a distinct regional identity, the Midwest itself became emblematic of industrialism, both as the prime location of assembly-line Fordist manufacturing and as its pastoral foil. And because of the shifting language of whiteness and class at the time, it came to absorb and be associated with a specific form of racial capitalism.[23] The racial dimensions of this form of capitalism may only become fully apparent to the white general public when defensively articulated in forms of populism, challenged in Civil Rights movements, or gradually eroded through the slow, painful process of deindustrialization. Thus, as we explore, the whiteness of the Midwest is deeply entwined with the building of industrial capitalism, its pastoral foil, and its decline through deindustrialization, not only as an economic system but even more a social system with specific entitlements and forms of white opportunity and social mobility.

In the early twentieth century, the Midwest region was considered a paragon of modernity—due to Henry Ford's 1908–1913 promotion of automated manufacturing and factory labor—even as it evinced a non-modern or traditional sensibility tied to agrarianism. However, even in the mid- to late nineteenth century, scholars suggest Midwestern pastoralism was an invented tradition because farming was by that time already complexly industrialized, producing in effect "Fordism before Ford."[24] Small Midwestern farms were woven quickly from the 1850s to the 1870s into an agro-industrial network of suppliers, distributors, and shifting technologies; within a few decades, many farms' yield produced a surplus, especially of grain, which found a market in the Northeast and in Britain. National advertising and sales networks sustained sizeable internal and external markets, which encompassed grains, meatpacking, beer, distilled liquors, furniture, leather products, paper from wood pulp, agricultural implements, and even mail-order,

FIGURE 1. Iowa Barb Wire Company in 1885, Wikimedia Commons.

FIGURE 2. An aluminum factory where women work alongside men to produce war materials, 1942, Cincinnati, Wikimedia Commons.

wood-frame, Craftsman-style homes. The Midwest is filled with cities of less than one hundred thousand, like Battle Creek, Kokomo, and Springfield, Ohio. These medium-sized cities were central to industrialization and the scaling-up of a constellation of production and export processes, but they are largely written out of stereotypical portraits of the region.[25]

Let's take a closer look at the contradictions and inconsistencies of the agrarian mythology, considered more deeply in chapter 2, to better appreciate what ideological role it played in shoring up white claims that, much like today, occurred at a time of rising economic and political inequality.

The global, modern, and scientific, rather than necessarily insular and traditional, dimensions of early twentieth-century Midwestern farming are visible when it comes to poetry, film, and fantasy. It is also visible in more banal forms through the region's most emblematic crop: corn. Corn's industrialism further challenges the myth of the pastoral, traditional Midwest. Considerable work was invested in turning corn into a marketable commodity, work that destabilized other food and grain markets and had global ripple effects. Corn was never only grown for human consumption but created animal feed for livestock, going on to underpin the cattle, pig, and chicken industries. Not only ethanol, cornstarch, ascorbic acid, maltodextrin, corn flakes, popcorn, and corn syrup but other new corn products and techno-scientific derivatives were continually innovated to sustain and expand markets.[26] In turn, over the mid-twentieth century, commercial fertilizers, technologies, soil additives, herbicides, processing instruments, genetic modification and later corporate seed patenting arose as related industries. And these interventions indelibly changed human, animal, and plant biology as they experimented with ratcheting up production, making many American farms more "factory" than garden.[27] As with the agricultural production processes described above, the pastoral traditionalism that characterized the Midwest was a fiction that concealed all the nature-culture hybrids and market intensification ventures that made mono-cropping possible.

Moreover, in line with popular notions of the heartland Midwest as America's breadbasket, corn was in many ways a national and not merely a regional product from the late nineteenth and early twentieth centuries, actively supported by the federal government. During World War I, for example, the Wilson administration encouraged people to save wheat grain to send overseas, as in its "Wheatless Wednesdays" campaign, which had the effect of increasing corn consumption.[28] At the height of the Great

Depression, price supports that continue today were introduced to aid struggling corn farmers. By the late twentieth century, corn was part of controversial US foreign aid programs and global market-creation projects that made the United States the world's largest exporter of corn and sent cheap subsidized US grains to the USSR, China, Japan, and many other nations. In short, though corn is often symbolically associated with Midwestern pastoralism and provincialism, its role as a national product, focus of extensive science and engineering, and global export exhibits the complex integration of Midwestern agriculture into national and global markets more broadly.

Even though Midwestern farming was entangled with global markets from the start, widely circulated regional *imagery* has long publicized the view of a pastoral heartland by focusing heavily on the visual features of mono-cropping and insular, bucolic landscapes. One need not look far to find these associations today. "There's nothing like the heartland of America," writes freelance writer Marina Nazario in a 2019 blog post for a travel website, titled "You Know You're from the Midwest If . . ." Unsurprisingly, the image selected for the piece is a photo of mono-cropped, flat farmland. When paintings, films, commercials, news reporting and television shows repeatedly depict endless, uniform rows of wheat, corn, or some other mono-cropped commodity, they help conceal the actual economic diversity of the region. In 1850, for instance, only 53 percent of the white population in settlement boom-time Wisconsin described themselves as farmers. And even those who answered the survey in this way were not merely describing what they did for a living when asked, "Are you a farmer?" This job description was also an aspirational category tied to landholding, not always an economically viable livelihood.[29] Farming was often a part-time activity supplemented in the 1850s and later on with mining, forestry, and the work of building other farms, railways, and roads. Mercantile trade, finance, and manufacturing in the form of resource processing like grain milling and skilled trades like blacksmithing were part of the division of labor in the Midwest from the early 1800s.[30] As geographers Brian Page and Richard Walker opine, "No historian of the Industrial Revolution in Britain imagines that it involved trade, information, and division of labor alone; every account of British industrialization (or that of New England) emphasizes the development of machinery, the factory, new metallurgy, the steam engine, new labor skills, and management. Why is it that in discussions of the Midwest all this appears to be forgotten?"[31] What Page and Walker point out is that one characteristic occasionally associated with

FIGURE 3. *Flying over the Midwest*, Benjamin Reed, 2011, Wikimedia Commons.

the Midwest—industrial manufacturing—can be completely left out of the picture whenever one chooses, performing a sleight of hand where instead the region is represented as traditional, agricultural, bucolic, and old-fashioned. They go on to argue that the burgeoning steel industry came to deeply shape the economies of northeast Ohio, northern Indiana, and Illinois. Finally, the northern sections of states such as Wisconsin, Minnesota, and Michigan have principally featured mining, lumber, and manufacturing industries since the nineteenth century rather than agriculture, which was more common in the southern portions of those states.[32]

All of this points to an important insight: By the early twentieth century, pastoral agrarianism was an ideological construct with national and global significance, rather than an image that accurately reflected economic conditions in the Midwest region. To be clear, the Midwest region of course features bucolic landscapes of corn and wheat fields in some places, and more than a small number of Midwestern rural areas have relied on farming as their main livelihood. That alone does not account for the longevity and homogeneity, one might even term it the *cultural mono-cropping,* of pastoral heartland tropes. That is, taking into account all of their omissions and inconsistencies, an important question becomes: Why has the homogenous image persisted and gained heightened significance at certain times in the face of substantial, widely available evidence that challenges or complicates it? Answering this question requires that we put the iconic white Midwestern farmer into the emerging global and national formulations of white rural agency and property holding described by Du Bois. The early twentieth century white rural citizen was imagined to have worked hard for everything *he* had, and to labor and toil in relative obscurity but without substantial complaint. This virtuous worker, literally making things from the ground up, was the white moral center of an increasingly divisive set of arguments about belonging, deservingness, and nativism in the 1920s.

The need for new and moving conceptions of virtuous whiteness were a product of more than economic precarity and anti-colonial resistance. They also had to do with the history of intra-racial divides leading up to the 1920s. As cultural studies scholar Lee Bebout notes, "Whiteness is multiply constituted, often contradictory, and reliant on its various Others."[33] Sharpening racial distinctions between whiteness and color informed these articulations of white rural agency, just as the Immigration Act of 1924 tightened the link between citizenship, xenophobia, and whiteness in the United States. Prior to that time, European immigrants had been targeted as foreign and unfit for American citizenship by bourgeois white nativists. The Massachusetts-based Immigration Restriction League, for instance, characterized Europeans from Italy, Poland, and Hungary as uneducated and "removed from us in race and blood," successfully lobbying to pass the Immigration Restriction Act of 1896 on that basis.[34] Changing taxonomies of whiteness in the early twentieth century—formed diametrically against free Black labor and workers of color—gradually incorporated Irish, Jews, Italians, and other ethnic Europeans, though to different degrees. Yet the color line was always more fixed and impermeable for racialized groups like African Americans. The one-drop rule designated anyone with a Black biological parent to be Black and not white in both de facto and de jure forms, such as through anti-miscegenation laws that persisted in Louisiana until the 1970s. Moreover, though Mexican Americans were classified as legally white in the mid-nineteenth century, they were frequently excluded from benefits of citizenship, such as jury duty, leading to a status of "social nonwhiteness" and perpetual foreignness in spite of the legal category.[35] Though the "melting pot" is now often associated with a positive assimilationist view of Americanness (see chapter 3), the term comes from a 1908 play by that name that largely took whiteness as a prerequisite for assimilation, naming

Dutch, Greeks, Jews, Poles, Norwegians, Welsh, and Armenians as indisputably American but tacitly excluding Puerto Ricans, Chinese, Japanese, and African Americans from that vision.[36]

Though this enduring color line is often imagined to be exclusively American, Du Bois knew the white/nonwhite binary was a colonial invention meant to facilitate governance.[37] It bears repeating that the notion of the rural white landholder gained fuller expression in Anglo colonial contexts in reaction to the political organizing of populations of color around the globe. Among the more influential books at the turn of the twentieth century, read by Theodore Roosevelt and British, American, and Australian literati, was *National Life and Character: A Forecast* (1893) by Charles Pearson. Though the book set out to document political rebellion and self-rule among populations of color, including through the Haitian Revolution, it was read by some whites as an alarming text that indicated that people of color would one day exceed and rule white people, galvanizing a white/nonwhite binary. Some were fearful that, according to one prevailing argument, civilized life would make white people feeble or weak and, capitalizing on scientific racism, that white birth rates needed to be kept high. This text and other circulating notions of the white man's burden may have caused Roosevelt himself, who expressed concern about white vigor, to take "an imperial turn" in the 1890s, which fueled US imperial expansion into Hawaii, Cuba, Puerto Rico, Haiti, and the Philippines.[38]

Ideas of whiteness were constantly in flux globally. This is partly because they were never random or idiosyncratic, but formed in relation to other racialized positions and places, well beyond the United States as Du Bois argued. It is important to remember that the United States did not simply act as an imperial power, expanding its territorial claims outside and within its perceived boundaries, it also reacted to movements of Black and indigenous people of color who were seeking emancipation throughout the colonized world.[39] Many of these anti-colonial efforts were globally dispersed and enclosed in specific sites of struggle, but some like the pan-African movement of Garveyism—based on the Black nationalist ideas of Marcus Garvey—recognized the scale of white political and economic supremacy across distinct world sites.[40] Additionally, other places and times are caught up in and help give reality to a global white supremacy, both in terms of the colonial past and its enduring influence. As anthropologist Jemima Pierre explains in her ethnography of Accra, Ghana, global white supremacy is evident in the attraction and force of compulsory whiteness in the lives of West Africans today: "The desire for, and the various attempts to attain, real Whiteness is virtually universal. Within the context of global White supremacy, Whiteness/lightness—in terms of its symbolism, corporeal representation, and material benefits—is desired by most, including those who already have membership within racial Whiteness."[41] The white iconic male Midwestern farmer-worker and other Midwestern figures must be placed within, and seen as influencing, this mutable racial taxonomy of white/color that was formed in ongoing dialogue with global projects of empire and colonization. In relation to these formations, early twentieth-century Midwestern figures bespoke broader global and historical divides between modern and traditional, urban and rural, which could both avoid explicitly racializing the scope of any conflict (when necessary) and yet also place these conflicts onto a grander world historical stage of (white) power and progress.

The emergence of the heartland idea also coincided with violent rebellions within the territories claimed by the United States. The so-called "closure of the frontier" is now discussed as if it were a foregone conclusion (see chapter 3), but the very real presence of anti-colonial resistance was enough of a threat that rebellions at Wounded Knee (1890) in South Dakota and Bud Dajo (1906) in the Philippines were put down with excessively brutal violence. Not long after, in 1921, prosperous Black neighborhoods were bombed from above with incendiaries from private planes in Tulsa, Oklahoma; this was done in response to resistance on the part of members of the Black community, who dared to stand in the way of a white lynch mob. There are, moreover, many more forms of activist resistance and white supremacist counterattacks that have not been fully documented or that have been distorted in the historical record. Historian Herbert Aptheker points to these problems with fully understanding the scope of Black and indigenous resistance in his pathbreaking documentation of slave revolts in the United States: "It is highly probable that all plots, and quite possibly even all actual outbreaks, that did occur, and that are, somewhere, on record, have not been uncovered. And the subject is of such a nature that it appears almost certain that some, perhaps many, occurred and were never recorded."[42]

Thinking in terms of the dominant narratives of the Midwest, however, one has to wonder: Why would people be moved to speak and spread ideas of the Midwest as a national heartland, at these points in history? One answer to this question would be that public conceptions of white virtue represented forms of life-generating capacity, in marked contrast to which stood the unruly bodies of nonwhites at home and abroad.[43] At the same time, whiteness was not then and is not now a stable identity made more stable through the oppression and suffering of others. Put another way, whiteness was continually shifting in dialogue with efforts to claim or maintain access to forms of economic and political resources, not simply in an explicit, clearly defined contest with other racial identities. Changes in what counted as white virtue were necessary in part because of other systemically reproduced forms of inequality related to increasingly unstable and global capital flows and value fluctuations. As in other parts of the world, distinctly "rural" political agency took different forms. In the Midwest, it manifested in the success of populist movements, from the Prohibition movement to anti-government, anti-Semitic, anti-gold, and anti-war conspiracy theories.[44] Both renewed regionalism and the populist movements of the late nineteenth and early twentieth centuries were in many ways outcomes of the contradictions of wealth inequalities and the failed promise of progress. "The Midwest" was not only a literal location for some populist members and struggles, but an important idea that developed around the same time to offer ways to think through and benefit from these tensions, much like the well-worn political slogans of our day.[45]

Since that time, ideas of Midwestness have been tied, over and over again, to certain American ideas of failure and success that hint at race without explicitly declaring it. And Midwestern economies have paradoxically evoked time and again the twin values of the traditional and the modern, of insular, seemingly foundational small-town mores associated with farming and of cutting-edge, more globally linked manufacturing work. What ties the traditional and modern together is a narrative of linear progress. Working with these ideas of progress has been absolutely central to global empire building and colonialism, to claims of white virtue in bringing forms of civilization to the colonized. Consequently, it is possible to label people, practices, and places as "backward" in ways that make veiled or indirect suggestions about the connections between race and class. Keeping whiteness murkily clouded in other concepts is an ideal discursive move, arguably, if familiar and direct appeals to white virtue are imperiled. Thus the Midwestern trope became a popular way of exploring and exploding this tension of modernity/tradition, and the white/nonwhite divisions with which it is loosely linked globally, without ever finally overcoming them. This paradoxical tension can make it challenging to think about the many facets of "the Midwest" together.

IV. "SHEAR THE ORNAMENT OFF": PLAIN SPEECH AND WHITE VOICES

All racialized populations suffer from the possessive investment in whiteness in some ways, but the historical and social circumstances confronting each group differ. Consequently, alliances and antagonisms, conflicts and coalitions, characterize the complex dynamics of white supremacy within and across group lines.

—George Lipsitz 2018[1998]: 67

As we have said, whiteness is never a stable subject position, but a political and relational set of occasionally contradictory meanings. In this way, whiteness is much like the Midwest. By calling whiteness unstable, we mean both that it has changed historically, as mentioned in the previous section, and that in actual, everyday interactions it can emerge and change in relation to other racialized positions. While whiteness can seem to float around or apart from direct preferential claims to property or work, it benefits from this slipperiness and is inextricably tied to struggles over economic resources. White speech offers a clear example. How we talk is another way that race gets socially reinforced, even though it can seem at first glance unrelated to patterned inequalities of money, property and so forth. Yet looking more closely at white discourse reveals a complex cultural process of distinguishing among styles of white speech marked by class, gender, and region that are more or less noticeable as distinctive in every given instance. In this last section, we look closely at circulating images of Midwestern speech and study how they demonstrate these complex dynamics of whiteness in action, variously serving as a basis for critiquing the ties of whiteness and the Midwest or reifying valued, classed forms of whiteness through singling out less polished, sophisticated, or seemingly "correct" white varieties. In line with the quote from Lipsitz above, this is about how whiteness relies on intraracial distinctions among differently valued kinds of whiteness as much as it can sometimes shape-shift to envelop these into an all-encompassing, homogeneous racial whole, pitted against persons, spaces, and qualities identified socially as Black, indigenous, and of color.

Linguistically speaking, one commonly repeated fact about the Midwest is that for a time it provided the country with its baseline accent. Midwestern speech patterns are common in contemporary news media and mimicked by presidential hopefuls and popular pundits—Midwestern speech is the accent of no accent, to paraphrase Donna Haraway. Yet when we look deeper, we can see that maintaining the notion of Midwestern speech as a baseline, inconspicuous or "unmarked" standard requires considerable work. It means that other speech varieties have to be continually made to appear nonstandard or not quite standard—to be noticeable as especially regional, coarse, highfalutin, stylized, or quirky in some way—in order to conjure the imaginary of the standard itself. Shortly after Britt arrived in Minneapolis–St. Paul in 2005 to begin ethnographic research there, a friend from St. Paul jokingly loaned her cassette tapes from the "How to Talk Minnesotan" humor series. The tapes codify as prototypically Minnesotan the rhythm, catch phrases, and tonal curves of Swedish- and Norwegian-accented white speech in English (e.g., "You betcha"), much as in the film *Fargo*. They assume white Minnesotan speech as generically Minnesotan and, through their humorous sample phrases, they tend to depict white Minnesotans as unworldly, naive, overly polite, and emotionally reticent. By engaging in a form of self-parody, the humor tapes manifest and challenge broader stereotypic portraits of white Midwesterners. Yet they also demonstrate that even white regional Midwestern speech—long thought to be homogeneous or a uniform national baseline—has considerable variety. And their variety actually helps uphold the idea of an existing Midwestern plain speech that acts as an unmarked white standard. Speech forms with noticeable white ethnic origins, as with the Scandinavian-language influence in the Upper Midwest, can serve as an apparent white style that does not quite achieve the plainness aspired to in supposedly unmarked white forms. Think of it this way: by having more than one way of sounding "Midwestern" (including some varieties that are openly but gently mocked), it is actually easier to identify the speech that is not quite correct, all while keeping un-mocked, unnoticeable versions of Midwestern speech in place as ideals for things like newscasting.

Indeed, a variety of writers have expounded specific voices and styles as distinctly Midwestern and such voices have often been coded white or associated with white ethnic identities. Separate from the way individual authors' work critiqued or represented life in Midwestern communities, this dimension of Midwestern writing could inadvertently uphold a sense of the Midwest as a white pastoral heartland as it circulated nationally. Sinclair Lewis's novel *Main Street*, for instance, is known for capturing in written form the plainness of small-town, white Midwestern speech.[46] A more recent example is Garrison Keillor's humorous and sometimes subversive Scandinavian American view of rural Minnesotan life in *A Prairie Home Companion*. As Nebraskan author Wright Morris revealed of his own writing style, "The characteristics of this region have conditioned what I see, what I look for, and what I find in the world to write about. So I believe in shearing off, in working and traveling light. I like a minimum of words arranged for a maximum effect. . . . As the writer of the South inclines toward the baroque, and strives for the symbolic ornamental cluster, the writer on the plains is powerfully inclined to shear the ornament off."[47]

Literary work that has taken the Midwest as its object thus echoed in fiction some of the features and values of early twentieth-century Regionalist painters (discussed further in chapter 2), specifically their dedication to realism, lack of ornament, masculinity, and emphasis on landscape.[48] These features have attempted to produce Midwestern style as a virtually unmarked variant, free of noticeable flourishes. The virtue of simplicity is of course a well-established theme in Western philosophy and political theory as well as Protestant Christianity. Thomas Jefferson, for example, took inspiration from Greek philosopher Epicurus who advised that "simple and plain living is conducive to health," an idea that influenced Jefferson's eighteenth-century romanticization of the self-sufficient American settler-farmer (as we discuss in the next chapter).[49] Yet what has not been discussed as much is how this commitment to plainness and simplicity became attached not only to the Midwest but also to whiteness.[50] The notion of restrained plain speech—associated with some though certainly not all Midwestern dialects—has played a substantial historical role in reinforcing other linked claims of race, gender, and class that similarly seek to fly below the radar, particularly whiteness. These qualities of plain ordinariness are not inherent in the Midwest, but they have been actively made over a century to seem naturally given to the region, its landscapes, and its inhabitants.[51] And they have had alternately positive and negative associations, sometimes used to affirm white virtue and other times to signal the absence of sophistication and moral propriety.

This insight can be applied to early twentieth-century literary work on the Midwest. If we revisit Lewis's famous *Main Street*, for instance, it is possible to read the novel as a satirical commentary on higher-status and more socially stigmatized, lower-class practices of whiteness. *Main Street's* geographic center of Gopher Prairie was based loosely on Lewis's own hometown of Sauk Centre, Minnesota, and portrayed its narrow mores, tradition-bound intractability, and drab physical environment—upturning the romantic pastoral tradition—through the eyes of the white middle-class protagonist Carol Kennicott. Yet the novel's narration also betrays a virulent classism that disparages the uncouth, ignorant, and unsophisticated ways of the white Midwesterners with whom Carol interacts. Carol imagines herself, by contrast, as worldly, not immersed in small-town politics, well read, and educated. Strikingly, the novel takes as one indicator of Gopher Prairie residents' backwardness their lack of adeptness with what we might now term white cultural appropriation. In one scene, white residents of Gopher Prairie, at Carol's invitation, don Chinese costumes and eat what the narrator refers to as a Chinese meal. The residents' lack of knowledge of what Carol understands as Chinese ways is a subject of Carol's mockery and scorn and, by contrast, seeks to demonstrate Carol's cosmopolitanism. This scene and others advance through Carol's narration a white gaze and class politics of cultural appropriation, taking them to be desirable and unproblematically foundational to a white middle-class sensibility. In this framework, the novel's poor or uneducated whites do not meet Carol's classed standard of whiteness and worldly sophistication. Yet the white residents retain some pride in their locality; they are not "putting on airs," as Carol does. Thus the novel distinguishes among these classed forms of whiteness, showing their reliance on distinct practices and sensibilities, and calls into question the relationship of white virtue and middle-classness.

Other writers in Lewis's time even more openly mobilized white Midwest settings in order to articulate forms and practices of whiteness and class. In *The Ways of White Folks*, Langston Hughes troubles the behaviors of white people of a variety of distinct statuses and class positions through the eyes of Black protagonists.[52] Several of the book's short stories take place in the Midwest. "Cora Unashamed" tells the experiences of Cora Jenkins, a forty-year-old Black maid who works for the white middle-class Studevant family in rural Melton, Iowa. Jenkins is from the only Black family in Melton, and while she is treated terribly by the Studevant family, she imagines in the book's narration that her treatment could be worse in a lower-status white home. Hughes's writing periodically evokes a white logic, positioning, and racist language toward Black residents like Jenkins in order to draw attention to it and estrange it to the reader. This move has the effect of also suggesting at times that Jenkins's own experience is so shaped by such violent and derogatory views of Melton's few Black residents that her self-conceptualization sometimes blurs with them. Hughes's story paints the Studevants as a morally corrupt middle-to-upper-class white Protestant family who would rather kill their own daughter (through a risky back-room abortion) after she gets pregnant by a working-class Greek American young man than suffer the blow to their social status delivered by her pregnancy out of wedlock. Cora, who had a baby that died of whooping cough, is outraged by the disregard for life shown by the Studevant women toward their own children, and she publicly shames them at their daughter's funeral. Whiteness and class are mobilized by Hughes here in a compelling and evocative morality tale. White elites' own humanity is called into question through their eugenicist logic and dire focus on the purity of white racial stock. Hughes shows that the Studevants are willing to kill their own kin rather than produce what they perceive as a degraded form of whiteness, weaving together attention in the story to powerful intra-racial distinctions among kinds of whiteness as much as white-Black relations in the Midwest.

As a result of the region's iconic role in founding US settlement myths, artistic work about the Midwest like the fiction of Lewis and Hughes has often evoked or grappled with whiteness, whether inward-looking, eugenicist, closed-off, seemingly cosmopolitan, or politically mobilized. Our point is that, even though they rarely analyzed the whiteness of the Midwest as part of a widespread imperial and global project, cultural commentaries on the Midwest, ranging from the region's most iconic early twentieth-century novels to banal contemporary gag gifts, have often drawn attention to the plainness, ordinariness, or unmarkedness of Midwestern people and their speech and sensibilities, sometimes taking these as synonymous with or part of the cultural life of whiteness and sometimes not. Though they only rarely made explicit mention of whiteness, well-known Midwestern artistic and literary work can be evaluated as relying on the assumed tableau of whiteness associated with the region and its inhabitants in order to demarcate varieties of classed, gendered, and regionalized white styles, making in the process various kinds of whiteness either more desirable and virtuous or less so.

Authors like Langston Hughes used the whiteness and insularity of Midwestern towns in a national imaginary in order to highlight white practices and positions, especially in relation to Black Midwesterners, and critique white eugenicist logics hiding in plain sight. Yet, even in cases where some white variants appear more culturally visible or marked, as in Upper Midwest *Fargo*-style white dialects, we maintain they do not fundamentally challenge the dominance of whiteness linked to, and reproduced through, images of the region. By making some speech variants appear humorously hyper-white, for example, attention is drawn away from the more ubiquitous spaces, associations and practices through which whiteness gets made and remade as a form of structural power. Thus, by "shearing the ornament off," expressions of Midwestness fly below the radar and appear as plain, real, and foundational as the land upon which the nation is built.

V. CONCLUSION

How is our glorious country plowed?
Not by iron plows
our land is plowed by tanks and feet,
feet
marching.

—from P. J. Harvey, "The Glorious Land,"
on the album *Let England Shake* (2011)

The Midwest has served as both the seeming ideal version of white virtue and the very opposite in disparate spaces and times. These ranged from the classed satire of Lewis's *Main Street*, where poor, rural Midwestern whites exude negative parochialism, to the Midwest as one among many veiled sources of Anglo white virtue increasingly harnessed to combat early twentieth-century anti-colonial resistance movements. That the global color line was replicated through internal, protected national "heartlands" should not be surprising; yet it is hard to imagine the Midwest—this most insular and non-global of regions—as a center of globalizing forms of white supremacy. It is precisely this difficulty in thinking all the Midwest's contradictions together, however—its tradition-bound intractability, modern manufacturing, backwardness, farming lifestyles, and cities—that makes it a productive screen and site for the ongoing, dynamic work of white supremacy. As we have shown, white virtue has emerged in dialogue with the Midwest in different forms at different times, sometimes meaning white life-generating capacity, deservingness, simplicity, and straightforwardness. And these "virtues" could find expression through varying cultural activities, such as speech styles, labor practices, family sizes, and even landscapes.

We suggest that white virtue actually thrives through its oscillating poles of expression. When Midwestern practices of whiteness are cast as morally corrupt or backward, such as with Lewis's book, it may be tempting to label them simply as a form of classism. In our current lives working at a separate East Coast college and university, it is common to hear politically left, middle-class white colleagues bemoan "middle America" and shake their heads in exasperation at the political choices of white people in the center of the country. When Britt told one new colleague that she grew up in the Midwest, the individual—who also grew up in the Midwest, it should be noted—replied, with a tone of tongue-in-cheek sympathy: "I'm sorry." Classism and class-based political positions shape how and why white middle-class and upper-class people of many different backgrounds and regional locations may distinguish themselves from white people (referring to white working-class people) in the Midwest. But we would suggest that what we have called white virtue is actually reproduced *through* the white people, practices, and places that seem *not* to have it as much as those who do. Contests of white virtue at different times have relied on the Midwest, including in the current moment, to signal degrees of white goodness or badness, as a screen of shifting values. In the process, the navigational coordinates of whiteness are plotted, and positions can be realized through the tacit, often contradictory stories of whiteness imagined through the region. And this work collectively supports white supremacy by reproducing the presence and political and economic interests of distinct forms of whiteness and class.

The Midwest is a stage or screen onto which ideas of nation and race are projected and become entwined with imperial and racial projects at a global scale. Whiteness can have a similarly imperceptible or unmarked dimension to it. It is partly for this reason, historically, that one could argue Americanness, Midwestness, and whiteness seem to fit so well together as concepts. As we have argued, white virtue gets attached to seemingly neutral or descriptive aesthetic values, particularly plainness and straightforwardness. To some, it may appear as if these values merely exist, and there's nothing more to say about them. Yet they serve as free-floating vessels, picked up and set aside as needed in the deep political work of racialization. Furthermore, these "virtues" are inextricably tied to and powered by the real stakes of access to well-paying jobs, property, houses in "good neighborhoods," family inheritances, and so on. Emerging across speech styles, landscapes, feelings, financial dealings, and bodily dress, the patterned qualities of Midwestern ordinariness point clearly to their racial significance, their unspoken but obvious connection to white virtue. In this way, the often commented-upon plain, straight lines of row upon row of corn, the flat landscapes of "flyover country," are mobile images that can, though do not always, reinforce covert racial aesthetics of simplicity, plainness, and ordinariness. Their celebration and denigration, their boring and banal qualities, and the fact that they seem to be about things and not so much people, all work to reproduce race as an ongoing practice only partly tied to bodies. Thus, widely circulated images and tropes of Midwest landscapes, among other cultural activities like speech, participate in a kind of cultural mono-cropping, effusing a base-line of white styles and sensibilities that can appear virtuous or help produce forms of white virtue through contrast.

The Midwest was the first truly "foreign" place my wife or I had ever lived. Even so, there were many similarities to the Northeast with a common origin in settler colonialism. First, there were the names. I had grown up in Wayne County, New York, in a rural hamlet, a highway drive away from Monroe County and the city of Rochester. In our first years in Michigan, my wife and I lived in Ypsilanti, a short highway drive from Wayne County and the city of Detroit, bordering Monroe County, on the one side, and Rochester Hills, on the other. The familiar names of long-dead white settlers greeted us even as they presaged the colonial usurpation of the lands we had moved between: Anthony Wayne, whose defeat of the Western Confederacy alliance opened up the Old Northwest beyond Ohio; Nathaniel Rochester, whose land speculation activities boomed with the growth of the Midwest; and James Monroe, who would oversee the growth of the Old Northwest territory as president. The results of two centuries of settler colonialism followed us and dictated the path we had taken.

Ann Arbor was mostly white, as had been the communities where I grew up in western New York. The only Black kid in my grade at school would occasionally playfully call attention to this fact. No one was Jewish where I grew up (though my parents had us celebrate Hanukkah now and then, ostensibly so we'd grow up "multicultural"), no one was Latinx, some claimed distant Native American ancestry. In Livonia, a suburb of Detroit where my wife and I later moved, the near complete geographic segregation of white from Black took the form of the notorious "8 Mile." Michigan friends we made would occasionally look at us strangely or openly call us out for going to "the wrong" (meaning Black) grocery store or gas station. The Midwest, it turned out, was all too familiar when it came to the legacy of segregationist racial politics of all kinds. And even where it was initially perceived as different, in terms of geography and character, I quickly found it relatively indistinguishable from the also sort-of-westerly and just-as-white part of the East Coast where I was raised.

—Reno

My dad taught philosophy at the local community college in Muskegon, Michigan, a town of one hundred thousand, beginning in the late 1960s and my mom worked a clerical job at the college bookstore. When my parents came to the area for my dad's job in 1967, they initially lived for ten years in an apartment in the city of Muskegon, which was racially mixed. However, unbeknownst to them, they took part in a smaller-scale, Muskegon version of white flight when they moved in 1977. Their move to Norton Shores and that of other white people like them—with extensive support from the redlining policies of the banking and real estate industries—racially segregated distinct city neighborhoods: Muskegon became less white and more Black, the city of Muskegon Heights or "the Heights" became known as the city's primarily Black neighborhood (with over 78% of the population African American by 2010), and Norton Shores, North Muskegon, and other areas whitened, concentrating economic and political resources along with higher property values.

Muskegon itself was also implicated in a wider set of racial associations that distinguished it from neighboring coastal towns. When I was growing up, people sometimes wondered why Muskegon kept failing at its postindustrial economic reinvention, especially in relation to tourist-oriented, more solidly middle-class Grand Haven to the south. Tracing how this view of the city is linked to race and class has taken me longer to figure out. Of the larger Michigan towns on Lake Michigan, Muskegon participated the most in the Great Migration, actively recruiting Black workers from the South in the 1920s to the city's foundries and mills. Compared to Grand Haven's 95 percent white and 0.7 percent African American population, the city of Muskegon in 2010 was 57 percent white and 35 percent African American. The immense role that whiteness had in consolidating political and economic wealth, as well as the awareness of this difference, shaped how people obliquely talked about race through place without seeming to talk about race at all.

—Halvorson

CHAPTER 2

Heartland Histories

Sometimes living in that big White House in Washington can leave you feeling
a little fenced-in and isolated. But there is a tonic: visit a state where tall wheat
and prairie grasses reach through a wide open sky; be with people who are keeping
our frontier spirit alive—people who work the soil have time to dream beyond
the farthest stars. Here in the heartland of America lives the hope of the world.

—Ronald Reagan visiting Kansas in 1982 (Cited in Shortridge 1989: 141)

I. INTRODUCTION

Ronald Reagan's soaring 1982 rhetoric about the Midwest exhibits over a
century's worth of cultural work that solidified such qualities of the Midwest trope in a national imaginary. What is less obvious, perhaps, is how
speeches like this use regional talk to link the nation with race, on the one
hand, and empire, on the other. On the surface, Reagan, for instance, more
clearly linked national projects with race during his presidential campaign
when he lauded "states' rights," which directly echoed the coded language of
pro-segregation white southern politicians, just a few miles from the infamous "Mississippi burning" murders. Or consider how Reagan connected
national projects with empire in his characterization of the Soviet Union
as an "evil empire" to the National Association of Evangelicals in Florida
in 1983, a framing that helped ratchet up bellicosity and military spending
during the Cold War. Compared with these examples, the discussion of
the Midwestern "wide open sky" would seem rather banal. We argue, however, that this is exactly the appeal of regionalism, as a cultural logic. The
heartland trope effectively links all three—race, nation, and empire—even
though this work is barely noticeable.

Cultural representations of Midwestern land, plants, and farming have been important as crucial tableaus through which struggles over American belonging and imperial statecraft have been reproduced. Visions of verdant productive landscapes and "wide open skies" accompanied notions that land that belonged or once belonged to indigenous people was open for white settlement. Settler colonialism imagined it was both making these lands better and enjoying what nature or God provided. We thus look selectively at the qualities and exclusions of US national white pastoral mythology as it has been tied to the Midwest region. The notion of the Midwest as a pastoral heartland, principally featuring agriculture and hardworking white farmers, has been actively made through twentieth-century painting, film, news media, and literature. Specific political and cultural conditions and omissions contributed to the historical making of the white pastoral mythology of the Midwest that Reagan so effortlessly evoked in 1982.[1]

The cultural practices behind regionalisms are often imperceptible, and this quality can help further white supremacy, nationalism, and empire.[2] Regional representations have an ongoing cultural life that is dynamic and changes over time, with some dominant cultural identities and qualities made to seem naturally connected to regional territories and their inhabitants. Thus, the chapter takes the reader through a selective analysis of how the white pastoral mythology became anchored in Midwestern landscapes and why it took on special significance at particular political moments. These moments include the Depression-era 1930s and Regionalist painting; settler land seizures and native dispossession in the 1840s–1860s; and the growth of Midwestern industrial production in the early 1910s through the 1920s, along with a rising global wave of white supremacy. While the precise forms of Midwestern iconography have dynamically shifted across these different times, cross-cutting themes are apparent in Midwest regional tropes.[3] Prodigious regional imagery of green farm fields, abundant vegetables and industrious cultivation efforts have strengthened a set of cultural associations with national and global significance concerning the deservedness and virtue of white settlement and white property holding. Yet, in each historical moment, this exclusionary cultural imagery distorts the actual diversity and complexity of people and places in the Midwest.

II. MIDWESTERN GOTHIC: EARLY TWENTIETH CENTURY REGIONALIST PAINTING

Final Jeopardy Category: American Artists
Clue: This artist from Iowa once said, "All the really good ideas I've ever had came to me while I was milking a cow."
Coming out of the final jeopardy time limit, Alex Trebek remarks: "Obviously we're dealing with the Midwest."
Answer: Who was Grant Wood?

—*Jeopardy!* Episode 7601, aired October 2, 2017

An overview of dominant depictions of the pastoral Midwest has perhaps no better starting place than the famous Grant Wood painting *American Gothic* (1930), featuring a stoic Iowa farm couple, the man holding a pitchfork and looking intensely toward the viewer while the woman gazes plaintively off to the side. To begin with, this piece features the industrious and spartan white farmers commonly thought to populate the region. But already there are unacknowledged contradictions at play in such seemingly neutral representations. The satirical qualities of paintings like *American Gothic* were sometimes missed, at least by white viewers, though some Iowans found Wood's work insulting when it was released in 1930.[4] Wood's painting was part of a wave of image making about the Midwest in the 1930s, much of which we have inherited and continue to reference as important cultural touchstones today. Such paintings of the Midwest are useful to analyze because they were not relegated merely to elite art galleries but nationally circulated in publications like *Life* and *Time*, which were committed in the Depression-era 1930s to a conservative, hopeful, and recuperative view of national values.[5]

The iconography of the Midwest never merely existed but needed to be actively made and remade through a variety of media. One medium for the visualization of the Midwest region was publicly circulated art.[6] In the 1930s, following the stock market crash of 1929, the painter Thomas Hart Benton and art critic Thomas Craven engaged in an increasingly critical attack on the New York modern art scene, centered around the 291 Gallery run by Alfred Stieglitz and with ties to foreign, Parisian-based artists like Picasso. Their alternative art movement, which promoted the work of Benton, John Steuart Curry, Grant Wood, and others, came to be known as Regionalism and played a prominent role in constructing lasting images of the Midwest. Distinguishing themselves from the abstraction of the modernists, these artists favored representational art that, in their estimation, offered realist portrayals of themes of cultural significance, associating modernism, by contrast, with foreign influence, out-of-touch cosmopolitan art for art's sake, and self-indulgence. Ironically, the regionalist style was quite international and was already a stable component of nationalist art scenes in many European countries: German painter Fritz Mackensen, for instance, found national character in northern German villages and Ignacio Zuloaga depicted the Castilian countryside as quintessentially Spanish.[7]

Many of the American regionalists' most famous paintings, such as Curry's *Tornado over Kansas* (1929) and Wood's *American Gothic* (1930), featured pastoral landscapes and agrarian lifestyles that became iconic of the Midwest. Their paintings often emphasized an aesthetic vista of verdant and visually homogeneous farm fields for as far as the eye could see, as in Wood's *Fall Plowing* (1931) and Curry's *Kansas Cornfield* (1933). Such paintings were even picked up by Hollywood set designers who, in the case of Curry's *Tornado over Kansas* (1929), went on to produce iconic feature films like *The Wizard of Oz* (1939) that built directly on its imagery (see chapter 4). These various media solidified in the national imagination certain common tropes of the Midwest, especially that of a uniform Midwestern agrarian landscape populated largely by morally strict, unsophisticated, and hardworking white farmers.

What is particularly striking about the Regionalists' work is the extent to which it created a Midwest that did not exist at the time and arguably never has. The paintings of Curry, Wood, and Benton were done at the height of the Great Depression but their famous, most frequently circulated works ignored the environmental devastation of the Dust Bowl, the bank foreclosure on and seizure of many Midwestern farms, Midwesterners' class differences, and racial inequality (subjects more directly addressed by artists such as Dorothea Lange and Ben Shahn).[8] There are of course exceptions. For example, Curry produced work on racial violence, including the lesser-known *Manhunt* (1931), which critically portrayed the lynching of African Americans, and a controversial painting for the Kansas statehouse that depicted the 1859 hanging of abolitionist John Brown. Yet even in cases of Regionalist artists like Curry, who was a member of the anti-racist Urban League, national magazine articles often left out mention of their social criticism and characterized them in deeply nationalist tones.

FIGURE 4. *Fall Plowing* by Grant Wood, 1931, Wikimedia Commons.

Regionalism thus became indicative in the 1930s and early 1940s of both positive nationalist sentiment and of the dangers of fascism.[9] Regionalist painting came to be seen as emblematic of an especially American style of art and representing an American ethos and American values, which consolidated the Midwest as a national heartland. It visually publicized the idea that, in the later, 1949 words of novelist George Orwell, the American Midwest was an "inviolate" protected space, a beating heart of nationalist values.[10] Not everyone, however, saw this emphasis on region and national morality in a positive light. Some critics perceived in the Regionalist movement an overdrawn distinction between intellectual elites and populist issues and a bombastic nationalist rhetoric that drew comparisons to the regimes at the time in Germany, Spain, Italy, and Russia.[11] They were not wrong to do so. Some Regionalists like Benton openly projected a variety of misconstrued values onto Modernists and even expressed racist and homophobic views toward Jews like the photographer Alfred Stieglitz, going so far as to characterize Regionalism as a more masculine, less effete style of art. As Balken (2009) points out, though, both movements were committed to developing a distinctly American style and exchanged visual influences, even though inflammatory rhetoric obscured those interconnections.

Regionalist painting contributed directly to the notion of the Midwest as a pastoral heartland populated by hardworking white farmers. It facilitated an imagery of nationalism that drew on the Midwest as a location of white pastoralism, using several distinct erasures. The Regionalist critique of Modern art catalyzed the association of the Midwest with a series of opposing value hierarchies, as Regionalist painting came to be seen as traditional, linked to the past, realist, truthful or without ornate embellishment, American, heterosexual, masculine, able-bodied, and white. By contrast, Regionalists like Benton painted Modernists as cosmopolitan, over-influenced by foreign styles, more effete, intellectual, elite, navel-gazing, and less white or not white, particularly in the case of pre–World War II Jewish artists.[12]

Try to keep this influential imagery of regionalist painting in mind while we move back in time to the settlement of the Midwest. In many ways, the Midwest is best thought of not as a place, but as a blank canvas onto which writers, critics, artists, and their far-reaching national audiences struggled over images of Americans and American life. In turn, these portrayals contributed to a limited, rather homogeneous representation of the Midwest. Such images, as we argue, built on earlier, selective portraits of the region that emerged piecemeal from newspapers, art, photography, maps, and fiction and made the Midwest a cultural space of white landholding, naturalizing white settler property claims. Though Regionalist painting waned in the 1940s as a new internationalism came in vogue following World War II, such narratives have endured into the contemporary moment, not only through an array of visual media like film and art but also through fiction and magazine and newspaper articles.

III. "THE MOST PRECIOUS PART OF A STATE":
THE MIDDLE WEST AND SETTLER COLONIALISM
IN THE UNITED STATES AND ABROAD

With the more contemporary iteration of the Midwestern trope outlined, let's examine the deeper historical context for Midwest agrarian imagery, especially as it is connected to settler colonialism. In the United States, the rural was both a cultural ideal and object of governance that can be traced to the early days of the Republic, long before the sweeping changes accompanying industrial capitalism that regionalists were ostensibly reacting to in the 1930s. This is most obvious in Jeffersonian pastoral ideals that drove early westward expansion, codified in the Northwest Ordinance of 1787.[13] Jefferson advocated for a republic built on a patchwork of small-scale farms, with the subsistence farmer as a moral ideal and source of civic virtue. The whiteness of this imagined ideal subject was not merely assumed, but inscribed in law and social structure. As legal scholar Cheryl Harris writes, "White identity and whiteness were sources of privilege and protection; their absence meant being the object of property."[14] In the Midwest, the whiteness of property would become ideologically (if not materially) untethered to literal slaveholding, allowing for a distinct form of dispossession and domination. As we will show, whites were property bearers, and property ownership simultaneously consolidated whiteness itself. In other words, the Midwest settlement process, especially as it is memorialized in public art, cemented specific associations of whiteness with virtuous, small-scale property ownership.

Just before the establishment of the Northwest Ordinance, Jefferson wrote in 1785 that the government should ensure "by every possible means that as few as possible shall be without a little portion of land [because] small landholders are the most precious part of a state."[15] Over the course of the ensuing century, the abstract values associated with the rural landholder became anchored in the lived experiences of people within a specific region: the Midwest. But they also became portable through imperial operations with a far more global reach.

A. Midwestern Land Policy: Possession through Dispossession

Colonization of the midwestern United States indelibly transformed the landscape, carving the undulating fields now associated with the region. In 1831, while traveling from Detroit to Saginaw, Alexis de Tocqueville wrote that old-growth trees furnished "an immense and indestructible edifice under whose vaults eternal darkness reigns."[16] Within a few decades, white settlers were engaged in a vast project of chopping, felling, and sometimes burning the hardwood forest to clear fields for farming. The Midwest region was spatially divided according to a standardized rectangular system that largely ignored variations in the landscape—such as swells, salt springs, water courses, and mountains—in favor of a uniform geometry that would, in the eyes of its proponents, rationally and scientifically expedite the dispersal of land.[17] This spatial reorganization produced the checkerboard landscape now associated with the region, an image reinforced through plat maps and county atlases that many settlers used to identify their plots. Following the surveying of individual parcels, the Preemption Act of 1841 paved the way for the large-scale reassignment of land to white settlers by enabling heads of families, widows, and single men over age twenty-one who were citizens or in the process of becoming one to purchase up to 160 acres for $1.25 per acre. In the later and more well-known 1862 Homestead Act, each immigrant or native-born (non-indigenous) American was entitled to freely acquire 160 acres of land, so long as they were willing to invest five years in cultivating it. It is estimated that the United States. took control of more than two billion acres of land between 1776 and 1900.[18]

We focus in this section on land reassignment and native dispossession because the Midwest was invented as a spatial designation during this time, gradually sloughing off the earlier moniker of the "Old Northwest" after the Civil War.[19] Because of the scale of land seizure from native communities and the violence associated with it, the Midwest came to be associated deeply with white landholding and especially with forms of productive industry that, in the eyes of US policy makers, confirmed and staked white property claims, in deliberate contrast with native communities. As mentioned earlier, whiteness acquires meaning through its varying relationships with other racialized groups, or through a host of different tactics, and you can see this in attempts to erase indigenous communities from the Midwestern landscape. At this early time in the Midwest's history as a region, the meanings of whiteness were in flux but, by the Reconstruction, took on a more defined set of associations with respect to independent work and ownership of land. These associations of whiteness with property were actively yet covertly formed in contrast with circulating late nineteenth-century, national depictions of labor done by free Black people and other immigrant and nonimmigrant workers of color, such as Chinese and Japanese laborers.[20] For example, in 1905, the San Francisco Chronicle issued a series of vitriolic articles that suggested Japanese contract laborers, who had increased in number to ten thousand in California by 1890, were, among other problems, "undesirable settlers" due to their disposition and "transients who did not buy land" and would drive down wages for white workers.[21] The Midwest settler project—and its nationally influential imagery—must be explored with an eye to not only this national discourse on immigration but also the wider global context of colonial land grabs, occurring at roughly the same time in parts of Africa, Asia, the Middle East, Australia, and New Zealand.

Land reassignment was premised on a concept of private property holding that dispossessed Native Americans as legitimate property bearers. The land policy in the United States and other settler colonies like Australia and Canada was shaped by the work of English political philosopher John Locke, who argued that a property claim required one to show visible signs of improvement upon the landscape or cultivation.[22] This meant that Native American groups who foraged the landscape or did not practice farming in a way recognized by Euro-Americans were decreed to not have a legitimate property stake in their ancestral lands because they had not "improved" or cultivated them. Much writing around the time of the 1787 Northwest Ordinance portrayed Native American groups as wandering hunter-gatherers, in an effort to claim that they met the conditions that would support white settlement.[23] Locke, who had a vested stake in American lands through his seventeenth-century service to the English proprietors of the original Carolina colony and as a financial investor in the English slave trade, promoted the notion of an uncultivated American land going to "waste."[24] This discourse was echoed in much nineteenth-century American federal land policy. Chief Justice John Marshall, for example, described Indian territories in 1810 as "vacant lands within the United States" and the later 1841 Preemption Act stated dispassionately that parcels were now available because "Indian title has been . . . extinguished."[25] Thomas Jefferson thought that the best way to include Native Americans in the land policy he had proposed in the 1787 Northwest Ordinance was, in fact, to make them farmers.[26]

Think back to Regionalist painting of the 1930s. It presented in visual form a white bourgeois summary of a century's worth of policy making toward Midwestern indigenous communities, in which their literal and symbolic erasure from the land was central to transferring parcels to white farmers. Jefferson's land policy relied on a vast series of approximately 370 treaties and concessions in which Native Americans were forced to sign over or lost their land to the government under duress, warfare, illness, starvation, and other violent circumstances, all in an effort to move land into private ownership.[27] The Miami chief Little Turtle fought an American army attempting a foothold in the Midwest between 1790 and 1795 and, due to the starvation induced by five years' warfare, signed a land treaty in 1795 for some of their lands.[28] In 1804, Gen. William Henry Harrison deceived

FIGURE 5. Ojibwe people logging, 1919, Red Lake, Minnesota, black-and-white postcard, Wikimedia Commons.

four Sauk men into signing a document they could not read that ceded one-third of present-day Illinois and parts of Wisconsin and Missouri to the US government, later resulting in the Black Hawk War of 1832, which disputed the 1804 treaty.[29] Even though Ojibwe negotiated use rights of their ancestral lands in a series of nineteenth-century federal treaties, they were often harassed by local officials like game wardens and white landowners when attempting to enact their rights to hunt, fish, and forage on those territories in Minnesota and Wisconsin.[30]

Red Lake Ojibwe scholar Brenda Child (1998, 2012) has written extensively about the work of sustaining Ojibwe community amid colonization of native lands in the Midwest. A raft of progressively more restrictive federal legislation was instituted through the late nineteenth and early twentieth centuries that threatened Ojibwe territorial and cultural sovereignty. The Dawes Act of 1887 pushed for individual rather than collective property ownership on reservations, disrupting native land tenure systems. In the United States, as well as Canada and Australia, the residential school system, beginning in 1879 with the Carlisle School, tore Ojibwe children from their homes and families, and banned students from speaking native languages and practicing native customs. Additionally, the Curtis Act of

1898 authorized the Dawes Commission to move ahead with dividing up native lands without native consent. Altogether, this resulted in situations where native communities were "offered" by the state reservations much reduced and altered in size from their original territories. While 138 million acres of land were in tribal holdings in 1887, Native Americans possessed only 48 million acres nationwide by the time the allotment period ended in 1934.[31]

In the United States, nonnative children grow up aware on some level of physical violence carried out by settlers against indigenous people, but few learn of the violence that led to the loss of land, livelihood, and language. In the Midwest, this violence included ignoring the fact that many Native American groups had long been experienced farmers. The Potawatomi and Winnebago grew corn, squash, and beans around the southern shores of Lake Michigan. Cahokia was a city-state that existed from 1050 to 1350 CE across the Mississippi River from what is now the city of St. Louis. It was found archaeologically to have surplus corn stores prior to European occupation. In his 1833 autobiography, Black Hawk also describes Sauk in Illinois and Wisconsin enjoying an abundant corn harvest.[32] Moreover, Siouan groups in present-day Iowa, Missouri, and Kansas hunted animals while cultivating crops in a seasonal round. Thus, the notion of an uncultivated Midwestern tabula rasa was a fiction that served settlers' private property holding. Were it not for this historical erasure, invocations of Midwestern farming today would just as readily call to mind Sauk, Potawatomi, or Cahokia cultivation. Of course, the very term *Midwestern* already implies the violent usurpation of indigenous-held lands, without which this might still be glossed as Indian Country.

B. *The Unbearable Whiteness of Being: Private Property and Civic Participation*

Narratives and imagery of white cultivation linked to the Midwest region are not neutral representations in this context, but in fact central dimensions of property claims that shaped US settler colonialism and colonial projects elsewhere. Indeed, the continuing influence of such images means that the settler colonial project has not concluded but relies on an unfolding set of explicit and implicit structuring logics that maintain white economic and political control.[33] Property claims are cultural and historical phenomena that differently conceptualize property holding and that cement relationships among individuals and groups of people vis-à-vis the accumulation, dispersal, and restriction of access to resources.[34] What this means is that prevailing cultural systems of property do not only confer access to resources. They also tap into and fortify preexisting social narratives about how deserving and capable various groups are of safeguarding valued resources like money and land. Put differently, stories about who owns what are simultaneously about who should.

Let's return to Locke. His influential writing, which shaped Anglo imperial land policy all over the globe, was part of a wider set of conversations by European philosophers that debated what made the human subject capable of owning or having possessions (including possessing fellow humans). Historian Paul Johnson (2011) has traced the perhaps unexpected but consequential relationship between the seventeenth-century emergence of imperial property models like that of Locke, which directly informed the settlement of the Midwest, and circulating accounts at the same time by Europeans about spirit possession among African and Afro-descendant people. These European portraits of African spirituality convinced some prominent philosophers like Hobbes, Hume, Kant, and Locke (and other widely read writers) that Africans who participated in spirit possession didn't exhibit the same kind of self-authorship of their actions as Europeans did, or displayed an anti-modern absence of free will. The pernicious conclusion these Europeans drew and went on to promote through their writing was that Africans did not demonstrate the same capacities as Europeans toward private property, an idea that of course influenced both slavery and the later course of colonial land grabs.[35] Before spirit possession came to be seen as a separate cultural issue from possessing material things, European perceptions of African religious experience played a crucial role in exclusively defining and racializing the civil, property-holding subject of the modern nation.[36] At the center was the racialized, Eurocentric idea that certain kinds of self-possession had to be displayed culturally in order for people to be able to properly possess material resources like land and other valued goods.

So, prevailing cultural theories of property are theories of race, and vice versa, in that they involve concepts of differently racialized civil subjects and their capacity for and evidence of property ownership and citizenship.[37] Theories of property bore a direct connection not only to indigenous dispossession in the United States, as we have seen, but also to nineteenth-century colonial land grabs elsewhere. European imperial land seizures were built

FIGURE 6. Nicodemus, Kansas, the earliest and most prosperous Midwestern Black settlement, circa 1877, Historical American Buildings Survey, Wikimedia Commons.

through a historically shaped, racialized property-holding continuum. At one end was the racialized European image of Black slavery, where the subject is possessed, while at the other was the white bourgeois Euro-American male property bearer who was thought to positively and rationally exhibit ownership of oneself and one's actions. These two poles in the imperial Euro-American imagination of property relations created an in-between space in which most colonized people fell; from the perspective of European imperial powers, colonial subjects were capable of being private-property holders but needed to acquire the "civilizing" qualities of relating to property and other valued goods in a way that supported Western capitalist expansion. You can see this in Thomas Jefferson's call that Native Americans needed to be turned into productive farmers (despite the fact that some clearly had been).

White supremacy gets reinforced, we suggest, through prevalent images of dignified, decent property-bearing individuals that seem on the surface to not have anything to do with race. White claims of possession—not only of indigenous dispossession—need to likewise be examined as ongoing cultural efforts to both secure resources and to justify disproportionate white access by evoking the deservingness of private property ownership.[38] Now let's go back to reconsider the Regionalist painters' pastoral iconography. This prototypic Midwestern imagery does many things culturally, signaling nationalist values of independence, hard work, masculinity, and freedom. Yet it is also about establishing white self-authorship of actions on the landscape and producing the traces of white responsibility and reason through cultivation. This comes into relief when we attempt to imagine well-established American images of Black, Latinx, Jewish, or Chinese American farmers, for example.[39] Midwestern pastoral landscapes and images of agricultural abundance may seem highly prosaic, even boring. However, they culturally endorse Locke's definition of the civil subject as "the proprietor of his own person."[40] Enshrined in settlement land policy, this individual demonstrated responsibility for oneself and one's possessions and the very capacity for what was dominantly considered rational, private property bearing. This property model was central to Jeffersonian conceptions of American democracy, and its main features and spoils were racialized white.

C. Globalizing the Midwest Settler Model

A close analysis points to many omissions and experiences that call into question triumphalist narratives of white colonization in the Midwest. Yet, just as Midwesterners were influenced by the wider context of colonial land seizure, the Midwest was ideologically represented as a successful example of land policy and settlement that could be applied elsewhere.[41] In this process the Midwest would continue to elicit various stages and values of cultural progress itself, from traditional/modern and rustic/refined to wild/cultivated, precisely as the region and its inhabitants had been depicted in earlier settlement America in relation to the establishment East.[42] The Midwest came to serve as a policy model, a cultural symbol and an economic resource within various global projects linked with white supremacy. Global networks were critical to building ties among geographically dispersed colonial and capitalist projects. Yet in each case, the global dimensions of such projects were enacted differently depending on the actors involved and the cultural meanings they marshaled to these ends. This means that the powerful do not rule the world so much as they imagine one that suits their interests.

Within the other settler colonies of the British Empire, including New Zealand, Australia, Canada, and South Africa's Cape Colony, common tactics and policies were applied to spur capitalist development as had occurred by the 1870s in the Midwest. Though settler colonial approaches differed, what was confidently called the "progress industry" featured vast outputs of government funds to build transportation, such as canals and rails, and the establishment of banks that could support speculative land markets, which drove up prices and increased the prospect of wealth generation.[43] War was, as historian James describes it, "big business" in settler colonialism, and building an American empire within the Midwest strengthened military reserves that would later play a role in imperial expansion beyond state territories.[44] Furthermore, across Canada, New Zealand, Australia, and the United States, the white settler population was, in a sense, selected, as individual state governments sent thousands of scouts beginning in the 1840s to European countries to attract migrants.[45]

White land holdings were at the center of these world events, even though they are often analyzed separately. And settler colonialism in the United States and elsewhere is connected with other colonization projects through the common basis in white supremacy. Here, it is instructive to follow Frances Lee Ansley's definition of white supremacy: "A political, economic, and cultural system in which whites overwhelmingly control power and material resources, conscious and unconscious ideas of white superiority and entitlement are widespread, and relations of white dominance and non-white subordination are daily reenacted across a broad array of institutions and social settings."[46] Settler colonialism in the United States was linked to other national projects that were mutually implicated in the global spread of white supremacy. Circulating discourses of self-government (where political entitlement and economic title meet) were one common thread that cross-cut settler and colonial contexts. Linking the individual body and the body politic, colonial power rested on the notion of white self-responsibility and self-government, in contrast to colonized people's presumed incapacity for either ownership or self-governing. As we discussed earlier, building on a long, influential set of conversations in Western political philosophy, self-determination was not viewed as solely internal to the self but as a result of one's socially read actions and their consequences. These prevailing logics tightly wound together and racialized political representation, property holding, capitalist exchange, and rational citizenship. Such logics were key for alleging the supposed lack of these qualities in indigenous, Afro-descent individuals, and colonized people but, as we maintain, they were also necessary to confirm that white settlers and colonists exemplified such qualities. Thus the relationship of self-authorization and whiteness could be expressed through many different logics, art forms, and legal frameworks, some of which formed a far-flung, influential network of colonial exchanges.

The Midwest was, in fact, positioned in the midst of a largely unseen but geographically vast series of white Anglo policies concerning the racial composition, political authority and resource allocation of settler colonies. By the 1890s, several top Australian politicians, for instance, were actively imagining the continent as a "white man's country," pitting their racialist vision against the Reconstructionist United States.[47] While admiring the American state, Australian attorney general Alfred Deakin worried the US experiment in multiracial democracy was a tragic failure, implying racial problems characterized not only the South but also the North or Midwest through the then-unfolding Great Migration. Besides declaring the white racial identity of the Australian state, politicians set out to enact a series of legal measures that would ensure dominantly white racial composition, political representation, and economic control. Historians Marilyn Lake and Henry Reynolds (2008) show that, to do this, they strikingly looked back—through British imperial laws in Natal, South Africa—to the policies of the United States, thus completing a circle of mutually-informing exchanges that undergirded the globality of white supremacy.

What they alighted upon was the covert use of literacy and education tests as a means to stop undesirable immigrants from acquiring the rights of citizenship, especially that of voting and political representation. This was a thinly veiled, nativist white attack on African Americans, immigrants of color, and ethnic Europeans thought to be not quite white in the United States and, specifically in Natal, on Indian indentured laborers who migrated to South Africa in the mid-nineteenth century for agricultural work. Australians had followed the institution of a literacy test by the British in Natal Colony, which stipulated that all individuals applying for voting rights had to write their application in a European language. British colonists in South Africa had, in turn, discovered the test when it was first used to disenfranchise Black voters in Mississippi in 1890. Literacy tests had earlier been used in Connecticut and Massachusetts to restrict the political integration of ethnic Europeans thought by nativist whites to be not fully white. Like the covertly racialized white images of property stewardship that we have discussed, literacy could seem like a racially neutral standard for franchise rights even as it was weaponized to enact racial exclusions in political and economic resources. And a key red thread through these policies was the notion that full citizenship hinged on the "capacity for self-government"; proponents of literacy tests used this to suggest that failed literacy tests meant an inability for self-determination, a paternalist concept that could apply to a range of political and economic matters, as Locke had argued centuries before.[48]

Let's return to the Midwest. This wider context of Anglo colonial racial exclusion policies shaped dominant regional tropes of virtuous white land-holding and political participation. At the same time, they also complexly fed and drew from racialized structural inequalities within distinct Mid-western communities. Historian Darrel Bigham's meticulously documented *We Ask Only a Fair Trial* (1987) shows how these interlocking de jure and de facto forms of white supremacy worked to marginalize Black residents of Evansville, Indiana. In 1850, some 75 percent of the Black population in Evansville was illiterate, many of whom had migrated from the nearby South before the Civil War, whether fugitives or freed Black individuals.[49] Prominent whites imagined this characteristic to be indicative of an inher-ent racial trait and depicted Black Evansvillians as troublemaking, idle, and shiftless, ignoring the role of white racism in preventing Black access to pub-lic education. Eventually, Black schools were established with Black teach-ers, supported financially by white and Black philanthropists until the state began funding Black schools in 1868. Still, Black schools were underfunded, with per capita expenditures per student at $24 for whites and $13 for Black residents in 1898–99.[50] Evansville's Black population featured social and economic diversity in occupation and education levels, counting among its residents by the turn of the twentieth century an insurance agent, drug-gist, street cleaners, truck drivers, garbage workers, teachers, doctors, attor-neys, entrepreneurs, barbers, and a mortician. Yet, as Bigham persuasively shows, Black Midwesterners' opportunities and experiences in Evansville were directly conditioned by more globally influential, dynamic notions of self-sufficient good citizenship and their white racial subtexts and juridical backing.[51] And all this occurred a half century before the suburban white flight and residential segregation of the World War II period further racial-ized inequalities in the accumulation of wealth.

Scholar Sujey Vega's ethnography *Latino Heartland* also shows that the mythology of the self-sufficient white Midwestern farmer has long been propped up not only by government subsidies of grains and wheat, but also by a pattern of forgetting the central role of immigrant and nonimmigrant laborers of color in the settlement of the Midwest. In fact, by carefully studying local historical records, Vega shows how the claim in 2006 that Latino workers were "new" to Lafayette, Indiana, bears an eerie historical parallel to the same claim that was made in the 1950s and even earlier, such as in referring to Mexican employment in northern Indiana's steel mills in the 1910s. Latino migrants to Lafayette in the 1950s were Mexican families from Jalisco and Zacatecas, Puerto Ricans, and El Salvadorians. Historical erasures of Midwestern settlement, themselves a deeply entrenched American practice, fed directly into the hate-filled rhetoric and violence of the KKK's rise in central Indiana in the 1920s. And, while perhaps in a less extremist and more mundane form, they continue to be reinforced in the present day. Describing an activity enacted across virtually all counties in the United States, Vega notes how central Indiana fourth-grade school children take annual trips to sites memorializing Fort Ouiatenon and the Battle of Tippecanoe where harmonious images of white-Native collaboration mix with derogatory portraits of Native debauchery and the industriousness of white pioneers. Referring back to the history of Mexican settlement in the Midwest, Vega captures the stark way the white pioneer farmer-myth keeps reenacting "borders" to American belonging that unfairly make European-descent people seem more "American." As she puts it, "Some of the original Mexican families in Indiana actually had longer claims of Hoosier residency than many of those with European ancestry."[52]

So, the regional image of the virtuous white Midwest settler-farmer was a figure influenced by and speaking to the wider context of Anglo colonial racial policies, as well as one that reinforced white claims to belonging, property, and land. The global dimensions of the US settler model can be examined from yet another angle, as a transnational or hemispheric symbol marshaled in US interventions in the "Americas." In this way, the symbolic meanings of independent white labor, so long associated with Midwestern settlement, rely on places and people that seem to not have achieved such progress. White US travelers depicted Mexican men as being in need of modernized labor and US intervention during the late nineteenth-century presidency of Porfirio Díaz (1876–1911), reinforcing dominant tropes of the Mexican Other. As Lee Bebout writes, "during this time Mexican men were rendered . . . as potentially hardworking laborers who merely lacked a

Protestant work ethic and modern technologies. Such depictions evoked the potential of US investment when coupled with Anglo-American or mestizo colonial guidance."[53] This is one way that white supremacy worked through many different channels, with one of them being notions of industry and progress; in the process, whiteness came into being and relied on a host of specific circulating cultural images of difference that, on the surface, seemed to have nothing to do with whiteness. By the late nineteenth century, the United States was less interested in the frontier expansion of land borders on the continent and more interested in empire-building through the "territorial expansion of markets."[54] Thus Midwestern articulations of white industry and progress had a global dimension in that they facilitated, and went hand-in-hand with, US commercial enterprises that sought to bring economic development elsewhere. The frontier moved symbolically to those imagined elsewheres, seemingly distant, but woven deeply into the symbolic core of white American nationalism.

The globalizing influence of the Midwest "settlement model" is therefore evident in how it eventually became part of US foreign policy elsewhere, such as in Latin America. Lorek (2013) describes how US-based experts in rural sociology, such as T. Lynn Smith, were part of American Cold War policy in Latin America, particularly agricultural modernization efforts. In the early to mid-1940s, Smith was sent to collaborate with Colombia's government, particularly Miguel López Pumarejo, director of the Agricultural Credit Bank, and agronomists like Ciro Molina Garces, to design a plan for reforming land holding and creating a farming middle-class in Colombia's agricultural Cauca Valley.[55] While the United States was actively interested in shoring up security around the Panama Canal Zone, Pumarejo expressed a desire for expertise in "colonización y parcelación."[56] With their efforts supported by the Rockefeller Foundation, a key organ of velvet-glove US imperialism during the Cold War, Smith and the other US participants directly "premised their plans on the example of the US Midwest . . . regurgitating Turnerian understandings of their national history and character."[57] The proposed plan, which was never actually implemented, had even suggested the Cauca Valley be divided into parcels on the model of the Northwest Ordinance. Such a scheme, using the Midwest as a model for democratic stability and capitalist development, was also exported by the Rockefeller Foundation to Mexico in the 1940s. The US team's ideological adherence to the agrarian model of the Midwest was so strong that their work "succeeded in places where Mexican farmers shared characteristics with their Midwestern neighbors to the north, and failed where they did not."[58]

With these examples, it becomes clear that the Midwest model also had clear economic importance in forming and shaping the flows of global capital. American financial capitalism cut its metaphorical teeth in western railroads and land grabs, which were critical to later colonial development in the Caribbean and Central America, the roots of which "were not in the West Indies, but in the U.S. Midwest," as historian Peter James Hudson points out. He traces the Midwest origins of the "imperial banking" of Samuel Jarvis:

> Before Jarvis grafted his organizations onto the project of US colonialism in the Caribbean archipelago, he profited from the history of white settler colonialism in the Missouri Valley. Two decades before Jarvis reached Santiago de Cuba, he began as a mortgage broker in frontier Kansas. . . . Jarvis-Conklin emerged as the preeminent institution serving as the intermediary for the capital "irrigating," to use the parlance of the time, the US West. It lent Atlantic capital, the savings of the middle classes of England and the eastern United States, to the white farmers, drovers, and ranchers settling the states and territories west of the Missouri River.[59]

Choices about where to invest and divest money are never a product of neutral decision-making or cold calculation, of course. What the example of the Midwest offered to bankers was an alibi for predatory and speculative lending. Wall Street bankers, including those affiliated with City Bank and Chase Bank, used the "success" of the Midwest model to extend debt-servicing and speculative market practices to the sugar planters and exporters of the Caribbean. As Populists would later point out, this was certainly more profitable to financial speculators than many Midwestern farmers, who did not want to sell to places in Latin and South America instead of Europe, let alone compete with them. Midwestern hog farmers, for instance, even sought out special Berkshire hogs to appeal to European tastes.[60] Nevertheless, the Midwest was caught up in the building of this web of "global finance," not only serving as a proving ground for its tactics but also in reinforcing a grid of associations that linked "domestic patterns of racial thinking" and white supremacy with "shareholder dividends."[61]

The imagery of settling, cultivating, developing, and improving the landscape of the Midwest thus served to naturalize Manifest Destiny, while it simultaneously furthered American empire and forms of colonization else-where through the expansion of land and financial policies. Even in cases of agrarian landscapes that feature no human figures, they inadvertently negotiate the relationship of whiteness and insularity by valorizing the nationalistic farming narratives so closely tied to the region. As a seemingly fixed, foundational, and realist dimension of experience, it is no wonder that landscapes are crucial to, yet have often been overlooked in, the cultural reproduction of race. By seeming to effuse certain qualities and not others, landscapes naturalize broader systems of national belonging and racial inequality. Progress narratives of Midwest settlement, which foreground the resilient, virtuous, and economical white farmer (in contrast with the supposedly dependent or unresourceful other), conceal all the failures, vio-lence, and various kinds of opposition that characterized white coloniza-tion. These range from the intergenerational trauma and dispossessions of Ojibwe groups described earlier to white Europeans' devastating lack of skills and knowledge about the ecological terrain of the Midwest, which in one case resulted in seventy Minnesotans freezing to death in 1873 as they succumbed to the harshness of settler life.[62]

Additionally, such narratives also characterize settlement as a project of white industry, covertly linking economic production with the social repro-duction of whiteness. Substantial evidence disputes this hegemonic narra-tive. For instance, early Minnesota, in contrast to the neighboring Dakotas, had a racially diverse population of African American, Native American, and mixed-race, primarily African American and Ojibwe, residents.[63] The Twin Cities' location along the Mississippi River was a channel for free Black individuals and fugitives fleeing points farther south. Minnesota's mixed-race population played a critical role between 1820 and 1870 in estab-lishing the state's roads and in developing the territory through their lin-guistic abilities and knowledge of the region.[64] We will consider additional exceptions to hegemonic depictions of the agrarian, white Midwest in the chapters to follow. Nonetheless, a mythos of the rural white Midwestern farmer began to take hold in the late nineteenth century and continued to gain significance because of how it wove together specific kinds of American nationalism, property claims and empire building, with global projects of white supremacy, as well as the way it spoke to forms of rapid political and economic change.

IV. CONCLUSION

My grandfather came out of Iceland
where he took orders from the Danes and starved.
After he died, I found his homestead paper
signed by Teddy Roosevelt,
the red wax was still clear and bright.
In the corner, a little drawing of a rising sun
And a farmer plowing his way toward it.
A quarter section, free and clear.
On his farm he found arrowheads
every time he turned the soil.
Free and clear. Out of Iceland.

—Excerpt from *The Dead Get By with Everything* (1991) by Bill Holm[65]

The common image of a pastoral, rural Midwest has served the white racialization of the region. This depiction gained cultural significance because individuals saw it as a genuine representation of Midwestern place-based identity and belonging. But not all places and not all people provide stable anchors for these regionalized identifications. Major US cities have largely been conceived as a block devoid of specific regional affiliation since the 1920s and 1930s, and dominant cultural notions of the Midwest frequently exclude urban and industrial zones and cities like Detroit and Chicago.[66]

Rural, pastoral characterizations of the white Midwest have thus been formed in opposition to what came to be called in the post–World War II era "urban America," a racialization of space that has often been associated instead with Blackness. Civil rights groups brought these issues to the fore by protesting so-called "urban renewal" campaigns and the building of the national highway system in the mid-twentieth century, both of which demolished Black housing and displaced Black neighborhoods while euphemistically claiming to "reclaim blighted areas."[67] St. Louis' Gateway Arch, itself a monument to the frontier expansion we have discussed in this chapter, was built in an area created by razing an African American neighborhood and, as historian Richard Rothstein points out, displacing its residents to outlying areas, including Ferguson.[68] At the same time, open, wilderness, and "natural" spaces have often been racialized white and morally virtuous in US history, and we can see how the trope of the pastoral, spatially vast, flyover Midwest participates in this racial space-making project, which excludes long-standing Black engagements with the natural environment.[69] These racial divisions of space were not at all inevitable or merely about people's individual thoughts and opinions but have long been culturally powered with the financial stakes of access to property and land and policed through a vast web of government policies and laws.

Depictions of the pastoral Midwest also serve whiteness in a second sense. Though regional images are most readily thought to map space, they also contain less obvious relationships to time.[70] As literary theorist Walter Mignolo argues, "'Time' is a fundamental concept in building the imaginary of the modern/colonial world and an instrument for both controlling knowledge and advancing a vision of society based on progress and development."[71] Midwest regional images enlist dominant racial narratives through these more hidden temporal qualities. In this case, the pastoral imagery of the Midwest symbolizes a settler farming livelihood from which most modern white Americans have since departed but which they may nonetheless continue to rely upon as a key symbolic ingredient of American nationalism. By building on national myths of settlement and ignoring inequalities in access to land and land ownership, Midwestern imagery presumes the whiteness of farming—frozen in a timeless, traditional present—and makes it primordial to the US state and its citizenry. This view of the Midwest can today be the source of white derision and parody or comparative self-fashioning and nostalgic longing.[72] However, in this temporal horizon, whites can be either behind or ahead, but the linearity of developmental time seems to exclude all others entirely.

Finally, representations of the Midwest have served to manifest desirable, often nostalgic images of white pastoralism. Since the Middle West was already tacitly coded white in settler narratives, the region became associated with a moral portrait of egalitarian, anti-slavery, and hard-working farmer whites, a portrait tied to the future and past of the nation. The Midwest was, perhaps unsurprisingly, portrayed as a more democratic and egalitarian counterpart to the South. Similarly, Midwesterners were believed to have demonstrated considerable loyalty to the Union by enlisting to fight in the Civil War at higher numbers than other northern states; Indiana, Illinois, Ohio, Iowa, Michigan, and Wisconsin all enrolled more soldiers than New York or anywhere else in the East.[73] That Abraham Lincoln was a product of the Midwest, having famously grown up in an Illinois log cabin, only served to reinforce this dimension of the national narrative. This imagining of the Midwest ignores that states that became part of the region—or are loosely considered part of it—were slaveholding states, like Missouri, or benefitted from the sprawling cotton trade built on slave labor. With the Midwest as an anti-slavery heartland of the nation, national narratives could recuperate a virtuous white citizenry that had always worked hard independently for what they had (or without slave labor) and begin a centuries-long process of associating more racist, less virtuous whites with the South and more cosmopolitan and thus more corrupt whites with the North.

Regional Mythmaking

Mythmaking about the Midwest is ongoing. This means that regional myths are not "in the past" or "over there"—there is still an urgent need to contend with them. Furthermore, stories coalesce around specific figures and objects, which become imbued with the weight and tone of history. Consider again a painting like Grant Wood's *American Gothic*, which is reprinted and restaged over and over, carrying with it certain (problematic and partial) assumptions about what it is to be Midwestern. Not only does *American Gothic* tell that story, but people can recreate and recontextualize it to call that story into question (by using unusual figures for instance, in place of the stoic white farm couple, or by changing the familiar pitchfork to a laptop or smartphone). This can provide a counterpoint to dominant stories about people and places or, put differently, retell those stories in ways that reveal their contested and unequal origins.

It is important to unpack familiar mythmaking about Midwestness, as it has shifted across distinct cultural sites and genres. These range from supposedly "deplorable" Trump supporters to poets turned "inward" and migrants to the Midwest allegedly resisting assimilation (chapter 3) to popular cultural characters like Superman, Dorothy Gale, and Freddy Krueger (chapter 4), to news reports on the role of Midwestern states in the 2016 presidential election (chapter 5). In all of these cases, recurring ideas of white virtue, and the tensions thereof, emerge in conjunction with ideas of the Midwest and tacit claims of white supremacy. This is true, we argue, even when what people think they are doing is calling out "Midwesterners" for alleged racism and insularity. Such is the power of the Midwestern trope that it can tell more than one story at a time. To see this, we argue, requires attention to how "self" and "other" are imaginatively restaged through a regional idiom.

It is also important to contest these tropes, that is, point out where they fail to represent the reality of people and places that fall within the Midwest. This means uncovering where assumptions about regions come from and how they are reproduced, by highlighting acts of storytelling in conjunction with alternative representations of Midwestern life and people. This both reveals and explains the cultural work that the Midwest trope performs while communicating its serious shortcomings, something long recognized by Midwesterners of many different backgrounds and experiences. Only by taking into account the invented Midwest, that taken-for-granted and imagined setting for so many stories, can we gain a better understanding of race and region in everyday life.

CHAPTER 3

Inside Out

The Global Production of Insular Whiteness

I. INTRODUCTION

In 2016, then presidential candidate Hillary Clinton referred to her rival's base as a "basket of deplorables," adding, "They're racist, sexist, homophobic, xenophobic—Islamophobic—you name it." The Trump campaign and Trump supporters seized upon this as an unfair accusation and even co-opted the "deplorables" label as a tag online and in election merchandise. Far from substantiating Clinton's claim, they argued that her speech revealed a pernicious mischaracterization of unmarked (white) America. As cultural critic Joshua Lam argues, "the way Trump supporters are viewed has become almost inseparable from representations of the Midwest. Clinton's two "baskets" of Trump supporters thus represent competing images of the United States—images that are often articulated through the Midwest as a metonym for the nation."[1] Both the "basket of deplorables" speech and its reception reveal regional and racial divides and their circulation through mass media (see chapter 5). In this chapter, we argue that these events, the projection and embrace of deplorability, of good and bad whiteness, are linked to insularity, a widespread value associated with the Midwestern trope.

Depictions of Midwestern insularity can be subtle. They can also normalize certain forms of prejudice against people who are different even as they ostensibly do the opposite. Consider the recurring and very popular "Stefon" segment that appeared on *Saturday Night Live*'s "Weekend Update" block from 2008 to 2013. Played by impressionist Bill Hader, the Stefon joke involved the queer, titular character describing the imagined counter-cultural weirdness of urban America. In each segment, the host would ask Stefon to suggest things that tourists could do in New York City. Instead, he would predictably introduce entirely fictional and increasingly bizarre venues filled with fantastical, abnormal, disabled, and ethnically marked others in absurd situations. From his first appearance on "Weekend Update," on April 24, 2010, the bit remains the same:

> *Seth Meyers:* Where can families go, if they're looking for a great time in New York City?
>
> *Stefon:* If you're looking for a good time, look no further. New York's hottest club is *Crease*. Club promoter Tranny Oakley has gone all out. And inside it's just everything: lights, psychos, furbies, screaming babies in Mozart wigs, sunburnt drifters with soap-sud beards.
>
> *Meyers:* I'm sorry, what?
>
> *Stefon:* You know it's that thing where a hobo becomes a rich man, so they take a big bubble bath.

In his very first appearance, Meyers makes very clear *who it is* that would not be open to Stefon's world. These suggestions are meant for "regular run of the mill people . . . maybe from the Midwest," Meyers explains, to which Stefon mutters, "Kansas," before providing yet another absurd example. For the Stefon joke to work, it is not enough for the character to be strange, in other words. There needs to be a witness to Stefon who is not judgmental (played here by Meyers, the "straight man" or audience stand-in in the act, in both senses) and an unseen, judgmental witness (for instance, from the Midwest or Kansas). The joke works not only because of Stefon's extreme recommendations, but also because they appear especially odd, in contrast with the presumed prejudices of an insular other. The projection of insularity involves "Midwestern," "run of the mill people," but also entails a divide between more cosmopolitan, less bigoted people and those who are perceived as insular by comparison.[2]

Insularity can be found in unexpected places, even in an *SNL* skit where a taken-for-granted, bigoted other is implicitly placed (as Midwestern) and a marked queer other is explicitly rendered impossible to accept, by contrast. Yet, the opposite geographic placement can be just as effective at highlighting differences at the intersection of sexual and spatial orientations. In a debate with French philosopher Sylviane Agacinski, for example, cultural theorist Judith Butler accuses her opponent of irrational fears about queer uses of biotechnology. While there are perhaps good reasons to be concerned about corporate-driven biotechnology, Butler adds that: "it seems a displacement, if not a hallucination, to identify the source of this social threat, if it is a threat, with lesbians who excavate sperm from dry ice on a cold winter day in Iowa when one of them is ovulating."[3]

Ostensibly Butler's comment is meant to lampoon Agacinski's fears about the Americanization of (specifically French) reproductive technologies abroad. How absurd, it would seem to suggest, that lesbians in Iowa of all places doing artificial insemination would be seen as any kind of threat. But would it work as effectively as a retort, were they from New York or California? It is unclear because the absurdity of the technological scenario is linked to a place, Iowa, which otherwise is given no comment. It could be that Iowa was chosen to make the scenario that much more bizarre because of its banality, that is, because one would not expect lesbians there; one would not expect biotechnology there; or one would not expect anything from there to be the source of a global social threat, especially not the threat of American sexual imperialism that has left Agacinski so vexed. Perhaps one or all of these account for Butler's choice of Iowa for a fictional and, it is suggested, impossible scenario to stand as an existential or political threat.

Something attracted Butler to write "Iowa." Something attracted Hader to say "Kansas." We do not claim that there is a deliberate choice made in either case or even a deeply held prejudice about the Midwest. What these instances share is a sense of the Midwest that is both widespread and yet only loosely stitched together through shared and barely examined assumptions about people *from there*. "From at least as early as Mark Twain's accounts of Tom Sawyer and Huckleberry Finn's exploits in the latter half of the nineteenth century to the daily trials of Leslie Knope in the twenty-first century," Adam Ochonicky writes, "the Midwest has been constructed as a space of simultaneous attraction and repulsion."[4] If the Midwest is presented as a region that attracts and repels, as Ochonicky suggests, that is partly because it is frequently depicted as insular—that is, as closed off and closed minded. Midwestness, in this sense, is simultaneously used to point to a regional space and a people that are routinely associated with prejudice and intolerance, on the one hand, and simplicity and provincialism, on the other.

Regional insularity, as connected to the imagined Heartland, meant and continues to mean different things, both to people living in the United States and around the world. In this chapter we do not take insularity to be a fact about anyone, but as a cultural and historical value, whether attributed to others or proudly self-ascribed (as happened with the "deplorables" label). Whether insularity is playfully lampooned as backward, cultivated as an aesthetic sensibility, held up or derided as a political identity, what concerns us is not whether this characteristic is actually representative of people in or from "the Midwest," or elsewhere, but the extent to which various social actors help reproduce insularity and the Midwest as interconnected tropes. More specifically, we document how these practices can give substance to ideologies of whiteness and, ultimately, to projects of white supremacy.

The attraction and repulsion of Midwestness is connected with the attraction and repulsion—the desirability—of whiteness, and ultimately to white pride and white power. This can be hard to recognize precisely because embracing insularity or labels of deplorableness are more vague than direct claims of racial superiority. And yet, this vagueness can help make whiteness appear desirable, because it makes these practices seem partly a choice of personal style or opinion rather than a structural issue of race.[5] The trope of insularity is in fact applied in a variety of ways, some of which might even appear contradictory. Consider the Stefon sketch again. *Stefon* is also insular, that is, unwilling to adjust his local sensibilities in order to include others who are inevitably resistant to his world. Indeed, the "Weekend Update" host repeatedly expresses disappointment at Stefon's lack of awareness of the insularity of ordinary (i.e., "Midwestern") America. In effect, the host makes it clear that Stefon may be unwilling to adjust to difference as well, the unimaginably ordinary other.[6]

In effect, claims of insularity can stabilize (or "essentialize") imagined separations between groups of people, making them seem natural, even when appearing to challenge attitudes of prejudice. Depictions of Midwest insularity can actually reassert the differences that so-called "deplorables" imagine, in other words, even while judging "them" as insular. When Hillary Clinton later recounted the deplorables incident, she wrote, "When white voters are encouraged to view the world through a racial lens and to be more conscious of their own racial identity, they act and vote more conservatively."[7] One reading of Clinton's later evaluation of this incident is that, once white people become more "conscious" of difference, they are bound to react with insular prejudice. Therefore, in one interpretation of Clinton's response, while "what happened" was unfortunate, the attitudes of Trump supporters are a predictable result of the reality of radical difference dividing them from others. By implication, one could assume that the burden is on those who appear *too different* to accommodate themselves to the desirability of whiteness (for the purposes of "electability," for instance), not to question that desirability in the first place.

If insularity is a marked condition of archetypical "Midwestern" characters—as Adam Ochonicky puts it, from Tom Sawyer to Leslie Knope from the popular and Indiana-based TV series *Parks and Recreation* (2009–2015)—it is precisely because insular whiteness elicits a wide assortment of reactions and serves various ends. Those who invest in a kind of insular localism as a central value may do so to their credit or to a fault, depending on how this is represented and interpreted in practice. As with other representations of region, moreover, Ochonicky explains that "the concept of the 'normal' Midwest is susceptible to being appropriated in support of extra-regional ideological and political agendas."[8] Specifically, he traces the trope of the insular Midwest to Frederick Jackson Turner's well-known "frontier thesis," according to which the settler colony was in danger of becoming culturally stagnant as a result of losing the challenge and adventure of years past. Insularity is thus coded as white, as a quality of settlers who had finally settled down and turned inward. As Kristin L. Hoganson puts it, "Locality began, in the heartland as elsewhere in the United States, as an ideology of conquest."[9] She continues: "Those who disdain the rural Midwest as a last holdout of locality misread its history. Since the beginning, the seeming locality of the Midwest has served colonialist politics, having originated in colonial denial."[10] Put another way, insularity claims are an actively asserted element of multicultural, settler societies that maintain white supremacy in a variety of obvious and non-obvious ways. Insofar as people and places imagined as insular are thought to be unwelcoming to outsiders and new ideas, it is as if geographic borders and cultural sensibilities were working in concert to produce a sense of isolation from the wider world beyond. Like being virtuous, hardworking, or capable of self-government, as discussed in previous chapters, being insular is therefore about how people compare themselves with one another. Rather than an isolated, objective fact about people, when insularity is identified, in oneself or in others, selfhood and otherness are restaged in suggestive ways.

II. INSULARITY AS RACIAL MACHINERY

The relationship between white supremacy and insularity is as old as the first American colonies. The trope of insularity was part of the ideological and material machinery of whiteness put in place in the Virginia colony. English insularity, according to critical theorist Steven Martinot, meant policing official and intimate interactions: "The quirk of the Virginia colony was that, in insisting on English insularity, it centered itself culturally on a purity concept that could be concretized only through the control of motherhood."[11] Imagining a nation and imagining a settlement are distinct cultural realities. At the same time, fostering connections between thousands of strangers presents some of the same problems as it would were they to number in the millions. From the initial colonization of the New World, English rulers used ideas of racial purity to erect social divides and, in effect, "insulate" racial groups from one another. To produce sameness between whites and difference from nonwhites was central to the racial capitalism that characterized both the Atlantic slave trade and English industrial capitalism. Given that there is nothing natural about these racial distinctions and the life experiences they afforded, putting such differences into practice required a lot of imaginative machinery, the point of which was to promote racial insularity as a foundational element of colonial society. This imaginative machinery reaffirmed "an insular English social identity as a form of social control" in order to govern both English colonial settlers and enslaved African people at a time of intense geographical and social flux.[12]

The planned insularity of the English colonies linked the purity of whiteness as an imagined *localized* essence in particular settlements to the categorical bordering of *geo-political* divides between English and African bodies. Ochonicky ties the dominant trope of a closed frontier with early twentieth-century literary accounts of the Midwest as culturally backward because the region was thought to be geographically isolated and isolated because it was backward. As insularity became associated with Jackson's frontier thesis, it was appropriated by Americanists decrying the loss of white purity through contact with people labeled nonwhite. That was imagined to be the case, as in the Virginia example, because close contact with indigenous people on the frontier helped, paradoxically, to reaffirm whiteness as a project of settler colonial domination and an erasure of difference. These systems of racialism, with rural whiteness at its center, were connected to the appropriation and representation of land. As war with native tribes began to conclude over the course of the nineteenth century, whiteness was increasingly defined through increased insularity and ever-finer distinctions between kinds of whiteness.

While the frontier was allegedly closing, two other events were occurring, one global and the other national. First, political and economic elites were attempting to sculpt a more muscular, imperial project out of existing settler colonialism. This co-occurred with the dramatic global migrations of the post–Civil War era. There was thus also growing awareness and anxiety around immigrants coming to America from Europe and Asia and the internal movements of the Great Migration. This twofold geopolitical moment is important to note because, as we will discuss below, the transition to avowed imperialism was clearly linked with white supremacist goals at the very same time that ideas about more or less desirable kinds of whiteness were being debated and converted into policy. Insularity, in this sense, is more accurately identified, as in the case of the Virginia colony, not as the diagnosis of a personal attitude (one of prejudice, for instance), but as the systemic imposition of *racial bordering*, in keeping with Frances Lee Ansley's definition of systemic white supremacy (see chapter 2). There are broader storytelling practices at work here that make use of these projections of insularity. Specifically, insularity claims are evident in both representations of the Midwest and projects of white supremacy over the past century; they are also linked to colonial interactions with indigenous communities going back several centuries.

III. MIDWESTERN POETICS: AESTHETICS OF INSULARITY

The seeming insularity of the heartland may tell us more about our angle of vision than the scope of the field.

—Kristin Hoganson (2019: 35)

A more positive meaning of insularity in relation to the Midwest can also be found. For instance, insularity is evident in national discussions sparked by the Populist political movement of the late nineteenth century. The Populist movement is frequently described as the most successful third party in American political history, involving what (at the time) was an unusual coalition between Midwestern and Southern states. While common political sensibilities are not unheard of in these regions, and have been a matter of discussion as recently as the 2016 election of Donald Trump (see chapter 5), what made the Populist movement distinct at the time was its shared opposition to non-agrarian commercial sectors, corporations, and the financial sector, which had come to dominate the American economy. Put differently, Populists did not simply arise from particular regions, but articulated "regional" (agrarian, non-urban) policy reforms, such as currency inflation. Importantly, the Populists were also characteristically modern or, as Charles Postel puts it, invested in visions of progress and modernization.[13] What defines the positive Populist project, therefore, is not an insular resistance to change, but an insular desire to change through local self-determination. In this more positive version of insularity, outsiders are not resisted only because they are different, but also because they seek to dominate local affairs.

Insular inwardness of this sort can have many different cultural manifestations, valued more and less positively. Insular inwardness can refer to seemingly more personal and existential projects of identity and to the specificity, uniqueness, and force of local history. On the one hand, a desire or compulsion for inward self-examination is historically coded, in the American settler-colonial state, as a social practice restricted to those privileged enough to do so, especially elite, able-bodied, and white cisgender men. As we discuss, characteristic in this regard are white, male poets, such as Robert Bly, who aspire toward inward-looking self-examination, while also disavowing the systems of privilege through which these projects are made possible. This cultivation of inwardness is, of course, far older as an aesthetic sensibility than the invention of the Midwest. In Protestant and especially Pietist history this construction of interiority is quite prominent, but the poetic interplay of the wilderness of the soul and unseen or unexplored frontier spaces has shaped more secular notions of interiority and intention as well.[14] Insular inwardness is always built on a nested series of oppositions from which it derives social and historical value, often in tacit and direct contrast to a series of others. This doesn't end with Midwestern poets like Bly. There are also lesser-known and more extreme examples, such as the early twentieth-century exchange between American and German Nazis, that show how exclusionary assumptions about insular inwardness can be scaled up and fused with explicit projects of white supremacy. Poetry is not equivalent to literal Nazi propaganda, to be clear, but this peculiar comparison does show the wider spectrum that white supremacy always consists of and is sustained by.

A. The Inward Path: From Midwestern to Masculine Mythopoetics in Robert Bly

I float on solitude as on water . . . there is a road . . .
I felt the road first in New York, in that great room
reading Rilke in the womanless loneliness.
How marvelous the great wings sweeping along the floor,
inwardness, inwardness, inwardness,
the inward path I still walk on.

—Robert Bly, "The Night Journey in the Cooking Pot" (1973: 59)

Despite growing skepticism about Midwestern pastoralism in art (see chapter 2), insularity—in the form of poetic inwardness, of self-inventory and self-analysis—took on growing importance among some mid-to-late twentieth century artists who took inspiration from German nineteenth-century literature, especially the poetry of figures like Rilke.[15] Among these, one of the most polemical has been the poet Robert Bly (b. 1926). Bly, who himself has translated Rilke's works, is not only interesting because he is from Minnesota per se (so are Prince and Bob Dylan). Being identified as the "Minnesota Transcendentalist" (in critic Joyce Peseroff's words) became part of Bly's brand as an award-winning poet.[16] On the one hand, the Midwest and Midwestern landscapes in particular have often been a poetic resource and subject for Bly. As poet Louis Simpson notes, "It is easier to call for spiritual life than to represent it in poems, and yet he was beginning, in certain poems about Minnesota, to give the sensation of his ideas."[17] On the other hand, Bly's observed Minnesotan-ness has often been remarked upon by others. "Instantly upon meeting him," poet David Ignatow writes, "I recognized an out-of-towner, a Midwesterner by his demeanor and accent." Ignatow goes on, calling upon the most familiar tropes of pastoral place and character: "I was amazed at his pleasure in city themes—this from a Midwesterner who I sensed was from wide open spaces, miles from urban life, a man who had probably grown up amid fields of corn, wheat, barley and rye, amid horses and wild flowing grasses that stretched toward the horizon for endless miles."[18] Ignatow's entirely imaginary description of Bly is common. Tellingly, it also involves a projection of insularity on the poet insofar as it is thought amazing that the Midwesterner enjoys "city themes" and is not repelled by them. But there are unexamined dimensions to these readings of Bly's work, including Bly's own. What they show is how ideas of white grievance are not only found at white power or alt-right protests and riots but find expression, perhaps surprisingly, within the inward-looking sensibilities of an award-winning "Midwestern" poet and his critics.

To understand Bly the myth, one only has to consider appraisals of his work by critics who repeatedly emphasize that it was created by a Midwesterner, about the Midwest, and somehow fundamentally Midwestern in its aesthetic. This last point is key because it demonstrates how the inwardness and themes that characterize Bly's poetic style are covertly steeped in the trope of virtuous and unmarked whiteness. Furthermore, this underlying association with the trope of Midwestness, identified over and over again by Bly's critics, also helps explain Bly's later, much remarked-upon turn toward a branch of the men's movement. That movement comes in many forms, typically organized by men and for "men's rights" and self-help. Bly's contribution is often characterized as more philosophical than political. Yet, while whiteness was covertly central to Bly's earlier work and critical appraisals of it, this quality became harder to miss when it was later mobilized to articulate the anxious privilege of the white, male subject.

First, it is clear that, for his critics, Bly's Midwestness is significant for their interpretation of his work. Bly's Midwestern origins made him stand out in a mythic way, as Simpson put it, "the only other person I knew of who had gone to St. Olaf's was the Great Gatsby."[19] The comparison is apt. Like the fictional Gatsby, the fictional Bly was a Midwesterner who had earned the attention of Eastern elites in large part because of the myth he created about himself through his words. Critically, this meant not simply referencing pastoral ideals, as landscape painters in the regional style had done (see chapter 2), but drawing on the pastoral outer world to cultivate inwardness as an aesthetic ideal.

We take inwardness, as a poetic style and subject, as a positive, even spiritual gloss on insularity. To be inward is to close oneself off from the outer world or to emphasize a deliberate process of self-reflection. However, the key, for Bly, is that this process is a rejection of a specific "outer world," particularly that associated with the urban and cosmopolitan East and its dominant poetic tradition. As critic Walter Kalaidjian describes Bly: "His career's founding moment turned on the decisive break with America's urban present, dramatized in Bly's retreat from New York City to the family farm in rural Minnesota. His early 'subjective' poetry not only takes this pastoral flight as its major theme but, more importantly, inscribes it as an immanent feature of its rhetorical forms and verbal style."[20] The flight from

New York also meant a flight from the world of modern poetry, as associated with T. S. Eliot, for instance. In ways that echo the tensions of the 1930s between Regionalist and Modernist painters, Bly's poetic inwardness hinges on a series of distinctions in which inwardness attaches ironically to one mythic, white, and insular Midwestern outer world and simultaneously signals Bly's flight from a cosmopolitan, racially diverse outer world (symbolized by New York).

Just as an inward journey begins with leaving something behind (the Eastern and urban), not just any "outward" site would adequately serve to cultivate Bly's "inward" turn, as it was so aptly described by critics. The Midwest is the necessary outer counterpart that encourages Bly's insular or closed-off inwardness. "The snowy fields of rural Minnesota may have been, as Bly obviously thought they were, a place to encounter the world anew. But it is impossible not to conclude that they were also, especially in the 1950s and '60s, a place to get away from the life created by monopoly capitalism. . . . Bly wanted none of that."[21]

As this quote from poet Roger Mitchell suggests, the specificity of Minnesota ("snowy fields") is often referred to by Bly and his critics. However, in another sense the Midwest was essential as a backdrop for Bly's inward movement because of its ideological "historylessness." An ideal outward space to facilitate an inward journey to the eternal and timeless, the Midwest is regarded by those critics as a geographical manifestation of tabula rasa, as it had been for the settler colonial imagination (see chapter 2). Mitchell furthers this assessment by also writing: "What is astonishing about the silence in the snowy fields is not that we see rural Minnesota but that we 'see' the eternal . . . Minnesota clings to these poems only as a faint scent."[22] Bly's first collection of poems, Silence in the Snowy Fields was therefore about the Midwestern landscape, but only insofar as it could lead one inward, since "the book is concerned with placing man in the universe, seeking a basis for moral judgement, and with the conflict between any person's need for human contact and the poet's special need for solitude and inwardness."[23] These values were often made explicit. As poet Richard Howard elaborates, "Here the landscape that had seemed so 'merely' natural becomes an inner event . . . and we celebrate a metamorphosis, site becoming self and spirit."[24] It is as if the Midwest is a nowhere that, for the self, leads everywhere.

At this point we should ask: what kind of self? For Bly and his critics and fellow poets, insularity is an ineffable tension at the heart of everyone, universally. Yet it is worth noting the conditions that allow it to be so. The power of inward poetry only appears as such when staged in a compelling way by a white male poet who "returns from the East" to observe his family's ancestral Midwestern farm. If the landscape is without history, or in some sense an incidental path toward inwardness, it is arguably the unmarked dimension of Bly—*as a white man in the Midwest*—that allows his perceptions of bodily sensations and Jungian unconscious images to manifest "in a Blakean way, the transforming and divine energies of the universe."[25]

And this privilege of perspective, a perspective from nowhere and of everywhere, is even apparent in Bly at his most ostensibly political: Bly's collection *The Light around the Body*, a winner of the National Book Award. *The Light around the Body* is considered a critique and meditation on the Vietnam War. Yet critics often took Bly's position as a general one that could apply to everyone. As one person wrote, "The despair in this volume is a despair that is more general. It is general *all over America*."[26] Once again, we can see that Bly's Midwest-encoded, white masculine gaze is central but unexamined as such.[27] This gaze was premised on an aestheticized Midwestness, with a "sense of movement across vast stretches of waste" that guided the poetic condemnations of war.[28] For critic Paul A. Lacey, this also means that Bly's work evokes an affecting kind of insularity from the problems of the world: "The *Light Around the Body* is a despairing book. The solitude Bly invited in his earlier works has given way to isolation; the natural world which he celebrated and through which he saw a spiritual, inner world . . . have gone, and only a pale compensation for the outer world gleams through. . . . Bly keeps faith in an inner world, but it stands in judgment on this life rather than infusing it with moral energy."[29] The inner world or state of mind of Midwestness is more than a resource or a refuge for Bly. It allows him to stand in judgment of history, especially the wounds that history inflicts on the (privileged white male) self. As another critic has noted, "Signs of Midwest agribusiness frequently mar Bly's pastoral landscapes," but his early poems on this theme are more about the inscription of "industrial references on the body."[30] But whose body is inscribed upon here, to despair at history's failures? The body that would concern Bly most, it was made clear in his later writing and perhaps was anticipated by his inner journey, was a white and male one. The privilege of occupying the settler colonial landscape as if it were historyless is not one available to all, as indigenous accounts of American landscapes make clear (see chapter 2).

If the whiteness of Bly's poetic insularity is evident, as well as the whiteness of the Midwest that was his alleged muse and source of self, some of these connections become explicit in his later poems, which embraced the men's movement. For Bly, this was a response to what was perceived as a spiritual attack on white, male inwardness from outside (once again coding a necessary escape from the feminizing influence of the Eastern, cosmopolitan, and urban). This account of white male spiritual loss is found explicitly in *Iron John*, which is ostensibly Bly's search for a new set of myths to help inspire a lost generation of young men. The masculinism of this project could not be clearer, but its racial aspect has been less remarked upon. To associate Bly's later career with whiteness, it is helpful to refer to literary theorist Kalpana Seshadri-Crooks, who asserts that "the incalculability of the subject . . . can serve as an alibi for race to articulate itself with and as sex."[31] Put differently, the inward-searching poet does not leave the world of racial prejudice or race pride behind by diving within himself. What they do accomplish, by appealing to the infinite depths of Jungian subjectivity, is to offer an "alibi" that allows for influential articulations of race and sex to move or affect others.

The connection between whiteness and Bly's inwardly focused mythopoetics is more than merely symbolic or incidental. Cultural critic David Savran, most notably, compares white supremacy with Bly's men's movement in terms of their iconography and the contemporary tensions they appeal to: "For what is perhaps most remarkable about Bly's rhetoric of 'the deep masculine' is its stress on a primordial and untouchable inwardness, its ability to produce a pure and fantasmatic virility that will accord with polite social norms while leaving unsullied 'the Wild Man' within."[32] That virility, or wildness, is worth situating, again, in settler colonial fantasies of contact and conflict, which can be imagined as a lost frontier to prove one's virtue and worth. Savran agrees, "Bly seems oblivious to the deeply racist cast of his theory of masculinity. For despite the participation of a few African-American men in the men's movement . . . Bly's 'mythopoetics' remains firmly rooted in imperialistic fantasies."[33] Indeed, Bly is explicit in his appropriation of vaguely characterized "African" rituals of male initiation to show a way forward for his presumably white audience. Savran is worth quoting again here: "And all the better that this lesson should be taught the white American male by African bodies, by black bodies who, in Bly's imperialist fantasy, approximate "the deep masculine" far more effectively than the white Western subject, marooned as he is in a feminized culture."[34] The very idea that "African" rituals are to be copied and adopted, of course, suggests a primordial dimension to Black, male wildness, echoing centuries of imperial and colonial sentiments that would identify non-Western, and especially African, people as atavistic representations of a less developed form of humanity (associated also with spiritual practices, see chapter 2). Trying to openly appropriate this wildness, Savran argues, does not disavow a desire to be white, but becomes a central part of the men's movement's struggle to be white when surrounded by people who claim diverse gender and racial identities and, as Savran puts it, are thought to threaten the project of white masculinity through their otherness.

While they are not identical in aims or membership, both white supremacist and men's movement activists appeal to people with similar anxieties about being victimized by "others."[35] The white power movement is very explicit about the imperiled white race that needs to be redeemed, while the mythopoetic men's movement of Bly's imagining is similarly focused on a historical wounding of unmarked (white, male) subjectivity. For both active white supremacists and "merely" spiritually lost whites, white maleness as an identity is permanently under threat from others.[36] Moreover, both accounts of white grievance involve a romanticization of the past, one that is suitably vague enough so as not to trouble conceptions of white virtue and of nostalgic loss, for example "honoring 'fathers' and male ancestors" or endorsing a "turn to the rules and laws of our fathers, and our fathers' times, to solve the problems of the present."[37] Wiping landscapes clear of history and of nonwhite presence, as discussed in earlier chapters, arguably facilitates this inward journey into an imagined way we never were. Bly himself need not be a white supremacist in order for the discourses he has contributed to and drawn upon to be caught up in fantasies of desirable, yet ultimately inaccessible, white masculinity. In Iron John, women are not blamed for this, but Bly suggests they have already gained by the 1970s what men sorely need, such as the "ability really to say what they want."[38] Furthering this line of thought, Bly argues instead that "men are suffering right now—young men especially" and for this reason they need to self-improve by finding the "Wild Man" within.[39] Sociologist Abby Ferber is quite clear on the connection between this "mythopoetic men's movement" and white supremacy in that both start with male loss and female gain. Ferber argues that both white supremacists and Bly imagine an inward-looking subject who has been wounded by women and feminists in particular, blaming them for their having been emasculated. Bly's conviction that women had already achieved a state of self-fulfillment is less antagonistic, perhaps, but still represents a gendered, zero-sum game of female empowerment and male wounding.

Being inward facing is not merely an aesthetic orientation, but a way of feeling and doing politics. It can move people to realize specific political projects, including policy, as with immigration restrictions or economic tariffs, or more generically relate local discontent with unseen global powers and conspiracies. These are the political consequences of inward or insular aesthetics.[40] The subtle, affective politics of interiority, associated with Bly, also play out on a greater scale, where projecting insularity onto others is meant to radicalize groups into action. This form of inwardness is also relational, precisely because it is juxtaposed with a world beyond that threatens oneself. This is not the accusation of insularity as non-cosmopolitanism (as in the first sense) or an inward project of self-analysis like Bly's (as in the second). Rather, it is a projected interiority linked with global forces and that conflates security with sameness and an outward-looking suspicion. This last form of insularity is familiar in guises that translate intolerance into race pride and anxiety.

B. The Transcultural Aesthetics of German and American Nazis

A self-divided heart in its inward turning generates the dream of an unattainable object which would completely fulfill it. When this project fails, feeling collapses back into itself.

—Walter Albert Davis, 1989: 73

Identifying the relationship between Midwestern regionalism and specific racial projects of white supremacy helps to demonstrate how Midwestern tropes have historically served as both a way to identify with the nation and exclude others from doing so. Insularity can work in more than one way to this end. Some of these white supremacist imaginings link insularity and Midwestness together. Consider a set of German-US connections of the late nineteenth and early twentieth century. On the one hand, this subject challenges a prevailing stereotype of the Midwest region that insulates the region's people and places, emptying them of specificity and identifying them with land-locked, "middle America" (in that sense, our analysis is anti-insular). At the same time, the benefit of specifying a particular path of transcultural exchange, in this case, German American, also limits the generic scope of white supremacy, cutting it down to size, as it were. Just as the racial projects we consider are about more than "the Midwest" they are also less than "the whole World," yet they arguably impact ideas and experiences of both.

Celebrated tropes of industrialism possess often hidden linkages with the social production of whiteness. Even as the Midwest region paradoxically fulfilled national narratives of old-fashioned agrarianism and cutting-edge industrial work, as we have argued, these seemingly opposed values coalesced in their promotion of particular ideals of economic production that were often coded as white (see chapters 1 and 2). Frequently these narratives of regional economic character or economic progress invoke celebratory stories of early twentieth-century Fordist manufacturing that made the Midwest "the world's premier industrial zone."[41] By contrast, the world of "today" never seems as great as that idealized past, and that is partly because white virtue is thought to have withered since the closing of the frontier. Insularity can function here by providing familiar and frightening images that *feel like* they explain what happened. This is where politics meets aesthetics (a connection we develop more fully in chapter 5).

Narratives of industrial growth and prosperity, which hold an important place in conceptions of the Midwest, ideologically separate economic production from particular projects of social reproduction, making it less possible for whites to see how these circulating ideas about Midwestern economies were or continue to be racialized. This was especially true with the life and schemes of automaker Henry Ford. At the same time as the assembly line was globalized, Ford was actively involved in personally and financially globalizing white supremacist discourse and ideology—a subject that has often received separate attention by scholars and journalists discussing Fordism.[42] Ford's newspaper the *Dearborn Independent*, which was distributed at Ford dealerships and sent to schools and libraries all over the United States, published numerous articles between 1920 and 1925 that named individual Jewish Americans and characterized them as actors in a global plot to overthrow foreign governments.[43] This anti-Semitic wave of publishing, financed by Ford even though the paper was losing money, stoked racist thinking toward Jews at a time when Jews were gaining prominence but were regarded as not quite white or as racially other. Perhaps unsurprisingly, other articles in Ford's *Independent* extolled the virtues of the family farm, racial homogeneity, Christianity, and American presidents Thomas Jefferson and Abraham Lincoln.[44]

Ford's publications appeared around the same time that rural populist efforts sought to destabilize the "informational hegemony" of cosmopolitan centers like New York, establishing Midwestern historical societies.[45] Set in the context of post-Gilded Age inequality and broader mistrust of media organizations (which obviously continues to this day), anti-Semitic conspiracy theories scapegoated Jewish Americans and other racial minorities for the economic conditions of the time, catalyzing white resentment around "foreign" interference. As Tanner writes, "Ford's view of the world was constructed basically the same way as one of his famous model Ts: he assembled the spare parts of anti-semitism, angst and fear of the anonymous market into a suggestive narrative that fit the desire for an overarching narrative for all of the—at first sight—incomprehensible phenomena in an increasingly complex world. The idea that economic strength was of the utmost importance for political power and cultural influence was constitutive for his argument."[46] Ford's anti-Semitic publishing was part of a rising tide of white supremacist nativism that sought to seed doubts about the citizenship of Catholics, Greek Orthodox, and other non-Protestants. He went on to issue a series of pamphlets titled *The International Jew* and, in one of his more mild-mannered allegations, claimed that Jews who supported farmer cooperatives were part of a "front" to financially control farmers.[47] These ideas were not limited to Ford's in-house publications but gained national traction when they were reproduced in the *Christian Science Monitor* and *Chicago Tribune*.[48]

Anti-Semitic and anti-immigrant sentiments were cultivated in Ford's publications by leveling the accusation of insularity against people they deemed "foreign" and "un-American." Rather than seeing their own activities as insular, Ford's publications at the time sought to characterize the groups they targeted as unwilling to adopt particular "American values." This form of racial exclusion remains relatively common. In order to see the role of insularity in these projections, it helps to briefly consider the ways immigrant communities have been imagined and governed over the last century. In histories of migration as they have occurred in and around the Midwest, for instance, new migrants were frequently accused of being insular, that is, of failing to acclimate as part of the ideological myth of the American "Melting Pot." Traced to Israel Zangwill's 1908 play of the same name, the idea of the melting pot became popular in the early twentieth century, partly because of the possibilities and anxieties it expressed. Ever since, the melting pot has offered a shared myth about what it takes to become an American, but at the same time has been used to exclude and violently assimilate others.[49] Zangwill's play was not well received by all at the time, especially by opponents of migration, for whom it was an overly sanguine portrait of a form of assimilation that could never do away with fundamental differences of racial stock. The avid imperialist and white supremacist Theodore Roosevelt was a big fan of the play, however, in that it placed a uniquely American spin on the British idea of the white man's burden. It was the goal of good government to help assimilate communities who, without a guiding hand, might otherwise remain insular and detached from their immediate neighbors. Even more dangerous, this insularity, in which immigrant communities supposedly remained in homogeneous enclaves, could be taken as a sign of real allegiance to other foreign parties and homelands abroad.

In this way, insularity—to cultivate inwardness, to be closed-minded and/or closed off—can paradoxically be associated with pronounced forms of attachment or detachment from a locale. This is clearly part of the projection of insularity onto migrant communities who are seen to constitute a closed off group that imitates the "homeland" they left behind and erects boundaries, refusing access, for example, to fellow (white) Americans. In Ford's anti-Semitic publications, for instance, Jewish communities were assumed to be ethnically enclaved, separate by choice, with their own customs and speech, neighborhoods, and global networks—a set of assumptions that ignored centuries of active marginalization and dispossession of Jewish communities in Europe and elsewhere. In what constitutes a reversal of ethical judgment, reactions among non-inclusive, white communities are projected back on those whom they bound and rendered unequal in various ways. The allegation of migrant insularity can be seen as a way for dominant groups to maintain the dominance of their values and sensibilities or, alternately, fabricate a self-serving logic that justifies denying resources or forms of civic participation to those migrant communities.[50]

In the early twentieth century United States, Ford's literature promoted white nationalist discourses that projected a kind of "global" insularity on Jews and other minority communities (communities who were thought to be closed off and unassimilable due to their secret global ties to foreign interests). This was one of the many ways that racism and white supremacy were homegrown in the United States—tied to the landscape and economic production of the imagined Midwest, as we have suggested—and disseminated globally, as was the Midwest settlement model discussed in the previous chapter. This was the case because the invented Midwest was imagined as the most American of regions, thought to best exemplify white virtues. Henry Ford, meanwhile, not only spread these myths but also was himself seen as a figure of mythic proportion, essentially emblematic of Midwestness *and* Americanness, and not just for people in the United States, for people around the world as well.

Ford's pamphlets *The International Jew* and the anti-Semitic, fictitious text *The Protocols*, endorsed and reprinted by Ford in the *Independent* in the early 1920s, were published in new editions in Europe and South America in the 1930s and 1940s. But the *Protocols* were especially sought-after in Germany after 1933.[51] As many scholars have traced, connections between American forms of racism in the 1920s and the Third Reich are not merely speculative. By 1931, Adolf Hitler, then a politician increasing in prominence, even had a sizable oil painting of Henry Ford hanging over his desk in Munich. When asked about the portrait, Hitler told a visiting *Detroit News* reporter pursuing coverage of German affairs for Detroit's substantial German American population, as translated by the journalist: "I regard Henry Ford as my inspiration."[52] It should be mentioned that a number of historians have been hesitant to link Ford's ideas with American Nazis or German Nazi government policies with American ones (for example Jim Crow segregation).[53] Our approach is to shed light on mutually informing events that bear shared impulses, even when they may have somewhat different origins and outcomes. It is important, in particular, to reconnect images of economic strength and productivity linked to the Midwest region with the sometimes less perceptible—and other times fully apparent—work of white supremacy that they help to fuel.

These transcultural connections between American and German forms of Nazism were not limited to the European consumption of American anti-Semitic publications. In the 1920s, with the formation of the Nazi party in Germany, Hitler cultivated these linkages to the Midwest by selecting the region as the place to spread Nazism in the United States. Specifically, Ohio was chosen as the best place to begin. As Cikraji notes,

> American Nazism was born in Cleveland. Coming to the United States in the early 1920s, Walter Kappe, a man undercover as a culturally-concerned, German newspaperman, arrived in Cleveland and founded the Teutonia Society, a group of tightly knit German-Americans that were the first to promote the values of the emerging Nazi ideology in the U.S. In fact, Oberleutnant Walter Kappe was

actually a German Nazi officer on a secret propaganda and espionage mission. As an official in the Third Reich's "Ausland Institute," and an operator through Berlin's "Abwehr-II" spy center, his first tasks were to spread propaganda through America, and get foreigners to join the Nazi party.[54]

The Midwest was not chosen as a first US site for spreading Nazi ideology solely because of Ford, of course. From 1880 to 1920, Germany led all nations in the number of immigrants coming into the United States, and most of them ended up in the Midwest, especially the so-called "German Triangle" between St. Louis, Cincinnati, and Milwaukee.[55] Therefore, first the Nazi movement and later the Third Reich chose the Midwest to recruit recent immigrants to their cause, ironically because they assumed this migrant community would maintain insular loyalties to the homeland, in an inversion of Fordist anti-Semitic conspiracy theory. As Cikraji observes, "Being a major Midwestern hub, Cleveland was chosen to begin the American Nazi infiltration. Although leaving, over time, Kappe kept an eye on Cleveland, occasionally stopping by to give a speech praising Hitler and smearing Jews. In one such 1935 Cleveland meeting, Kappe discussed the boycott on German goods."[56] In keeping with the literary tradition that Ford had earlier exported to a German audience, this boycott was blamed on an international Jewish conspiracy. Society meetings bolstered the written ideologies of Nazism, rousing and organizing a transnational, aggrieved white audience to the cause. According to the Nazi ideology promoted by Kappe and others, it was because of insular Jews conspiring against America that insular German Americans should sympathize with and be moved to work to stabilize white control around the world, but beginning in the United States.

Though the circulation of Nazi propaganda loosely connected white sympathizers in the United States, Germany, and elsewhere, the racial animosity incited by them was carefully calibrated to, and fed by, regional and local conditions.[57] By 1933, the Third Reich was in power and the Nazi propaganda effort shifted to holding up Germany's growing economy as an example to follow in order to recover from the Great Depression. Meanwhile, internecine conflict between American Nazi factions left a power vacuum that German-directed organizers could take advantage of.[58]

Despite these differences in the political conditions informing Nazism, several similarities are also worth noting. It would seem that the most well-known German form of Nazism that took hold in 1924–1941 was very much in keeping with Ford's ideas about whiteness at risk. In Ford's hands, white supremacy was only implicitly about maintaining the white race in isolation; rather, it hinged on conspiracy theories about supposed Jewish control of the world economy, that is, about insular others conspiring to take advantage of unsuspecting and hardworking whites.

American Nazis, for their own part, combined the transcultural tradition of anti-Semitic conspiracism with an already well-established fear of immigration most clearly expressed in the 1924 National Origins Act. This Act tightened US government policy on immigration, but conspicuously only applied to migrants from outside the Western Hemisphere. The 1924 Act did not end the debate on immigration restriction, in other words, but intensified it.[59] The growth of Nazi sympathies in the United States was not only a product of German influence, furthermore, but also fit well with white supremacist promises and anxieties that had long been at work in the settler colony.

The Ford-Hitler exchange of ideas, though indirect and complex, played an important role in clarifying and consolidating the terms of white supremacy as anti-globalist and anti-Semitic, which would continue to shape future projects along these same lines (as in conspiracy theories today about George Soros, for example). This specific white supremacist project is worth mentioning, in part because it reveals transnational connections through which the Midwest played a specific role. It also demonstrates a distinct line of ideas about white vulnerability and insularity, where closed off communities domestically reflected secret powers abroad, who represent the greatest threat.[60]

If, as we have claimed, heartland Midwestness served as a uniquely banal, unspectacular exception to the rest of America, then it could also be made to signify the "safe space" most under threat from global machinations (or internal threats from within, as we discuss in chapter 4). This is not to say that Nazis or other white supremacists have been or are more common in this part of the world, to be clear, but that—as the indirect Ford and Hitler "exchange" shows—the regional mythos provides a useful anchor for ideas about "real" Americans, isolated and at risk from insular foreigners at home and those unseen others whose interests they serve. More specifically, protection of an imagined Heartland becomes a rallying cry for newly politicized, proudly insular people.[61] Overcoming all estrangement requires having shared norms, and we have argued that foremost among them in American history has been the phantom figure of white virtue. Though it seems counterintuitive, insularity or inwardness as an aesthetic politics, when taken to an extreme, can lead to greater global ambition, not lesser. This is so even if that phantom of whiteness seems almost unattainable. If by hard work and tenacity one cannot achieve the American Dream, then who is to blame and how can they be stopped? Here the Midwest trope's association with whiteness takes on an even more frightening guise. Isolationism, always an anachronistic concept, is thus effectively globalized and, for some, it only feels right that it should be.

IV. CONCLUSION

What do they know of England, who only England know?

—Rudyard Kipling (1942)

What do they know of cricket, who only cricket know?

—C. L. R. James (1963)

What empire, nation, and region have in common is that they all can be made to work across many scales.[62] Insularity is one tool that enables this political work. The function of projecting insularity onto others is clear in the Rudyard Kipling quote above. In it, Kipling is bemoaning insular Englishmen who do not give a thought to the world outside of the one familiar to them (i.e., the local). Kipling, a proud servant of the empire, is not concerned with their intolerance, per se, but rather with their lack of commitment and appreciation of the British imperial project and what it has done for them. Insularity, here, accounts for their lack of appreciation for and their ignorance about how seemingly distinct scales (global, local) are connected. What Kipling does not seem to consider, however, is that projecting insularity on his compatriots presumes that the national and global are naturally opposed and mutually distinguishable levels or scales (the British Empire over here, downtown Croydon over there), or at least that they appear to be that simple and divisible from the perspective of those duped into seeing the world in a distorted and fragmented way.[63] If we lay aside the troubling elitism of such a view, one thing that it obscures is the extent to which imperialists are also making a categorical mistake—they imagine economic trade deals and colonial policy as naturally separate from projects of white power and privilege. This is, in fact, a key dimension of how imperialism redounds "at home" as well as "abroad," which can include accusing insular others of being the real intolerant and unenlightened ones. To avoid this error, Kipling would have to reflect on what whiteness does for him that it also does for the most isolated, closed-off and closed-minded Englishman, and therefore how it binds and distorts relations of scale.

When you add a generic spatial scale, like region, to the mix, what that does is to offer another alibi for these kinds of debates and tensions, so that there is yet another stage on which they can play out ideas and feelings about whiteness. One tendency in Midwestern literature has been to posit the Midwest as categorically fixed. We might therefore conclude that literary acts, whether poems or anti-Semitic pamphlets, can also be insulating insofar as they bound regions from one another, from the nation, from the world as a whole. This form of insulation might create a viable aesthetic or scientific discourse, but it also furthers the fiction that such a thing as Midwestness truly exists as a distinct way of being in the world and writing about it. Conflating regional images and tropes with actual experiences impoverishes not only our understanding of the lives of people who live in places considered "Midwestern," but also the cultural and political work of regionalism—that is, its effects on the world. As with insularity, imputed characteristics about any specific region are never about an ahistorical, essential quality, but always a relational and historical one, meaning regional tropes and identities are always in flux, never permanent.[64] Projections of insularity, making use of the Midwest, therefore occur on multiple levels.

Insularity is particularly good at coding whiteness for exactly this reason. The Midwest is imagined as paradigmatically insular, not only because of an implicit or explicit rejection of difference, for example of LGBTQ persons and Black and indigenous people of color, but also because Midwesterners are therefore also distinct from unmarked people who are more open to difference as a result of this three-way relationship (marked other–insular bigot–cosmopolitan self). By definition, it would seem that insularity surreptitiously produces a white self that is unwelcoming of difference and a white self that makes room for difference. The problem is that, imagined in this way, insularity not only denies real difference as it is part of the lives of communities so labeled, but also resists recognition of the fact that the "nonwhite other/(bigoted/cosmopolitan) white self" complex is also part of a settler colonial system of racial hierarchies.[65]

Trinidadian historian C. L. R. James made this clear in his own take on the Kipling quote, "What do they know of cricket who only cricket know?"

in his book on that sport, and much more, *Beyond a Boundary*. More specifically, James's autobiographical account delves into his own experiences growing up on English games, literature, and education. He finds that those who know "of cricket" in the West Indies know more about the role of the game in colonial operations and assertions of racial difference than even white supremacists as purportedly globally aware as Kipling (or, we might add, Roosevelt and Ford). What people in James's native Trinidad knew of cricket was that it was a game that was forced on them from abroad and yet sucked them in, drove them to win and moved them to care about the outcome. "I was an actor on a stage in which the parts were set in advance," James later wrote about his childhood.[66] He continues: "I would not deny that early influences I could know nothing about had cast me in a certain mould. . . . As far back as I can trace my consciousness the original found itself and came to maturity within a system that was the result of centuries of development in another land, was transplanted as a hot-house flower is transplanted and bore some strange fruit."[67] What people knew of cricket in the West Indies or at least knew best of all colonial exports, was that they were not insular but always already implicated in global systems of racial hierarchy, a rigged and ongoing competition. As James put it, "Cricket had plunged me into politics long before I was aware of it. When I did turn to politics, I did not have much to learn."[68]

James suggests an alternative observation about insularity, encouraging reflection on the different uses that could be put to a deep awareness of local conditions. Inwardly focused storytelling—James's autobiography for instance—is just as capable of moving people to resist colonial and racial exploitation as it is of animating white supremacists or nationalists to defend those social projects. Insularity and inwardness need not mean being uninterested in the world if they start from the premise that self and world are always already thoroughly interwoven, not least because skin color remains a powerful global currency and source of power.

REFLECTIONS 3

The Midwest never seemed insular to me growing up. It was only much later, as I traveled and talked with people from many walks of life, that I grew aware that many people were convinced that "it" was. My non-insular view was partly because I had immediate family and friends who hadn't grown up in Michigan, the Midwest, or the United States. When my aunt, uncle, and cousins from Sweden visited us, usually every seven or eight years after saving up money, they'd refer to Lake Michigan as "the sea," because it conjured images for them of the Baltic. But there were always "global" linkages around me in more seemingly mundane ways. For as long as I can remember, my dad went to the same barber, a white sixty-something-year-old man whom I'll call Frank. Though Frank ran a part-time barber shop out of his house, his day job was as a technician at the local power plant. When he retired from that job, he decided to raise emus—the large land birds—full-time. This might seem strange, but he'd been doing research about emus for a decade prior. It was the early 1990s. Everyone it seemed was worried about cholesterol. Emu meat was championed as the next big thing: a lean, healthy alternative to beef. The only problem was that emus were endemic to Australia. Getting the eggs shipped to Michigan was a hassle. But even more, Frank had a terrible time acclimating his emu chicks to the hard Michigan winters and spent hours and hours setting up heat lamps for them. Each time my dad got a haircut, we'd spend the entire dinner afterward discussing Frank's emu troubles. The emus' rough ecological adjustment to western Michigan was just one of many, many small ways I glimpsed ties between where I was to places near and far.

—Halvorson

The people I met in rural Michigan, who were the subject of my doctoral thesis and first book, rarely described themselves as "rural" or "from Michigan," let alone as being "Midwestern." This was true even when there was arguably direct incentive to do so. The Don't Trash Michigan political campaign began having a local presence (in the form of road signs) around 2004, dedicated to halting Canadian trash from being dumped in landfills in Michigan. But when I talked to local activists and politicians, they were just as likely to talk about the environmental importance of the Great Lakes as they were to reference either the state or region. I never heard the term

"Michigander" that I can remember, and "American" was the only routine point of geographical reference for activists and landfill workers alike. People who ordinarily avoided going to the city really cared if the Detroit-based Pistons or Redwings won the NBA or NHL championships, respectively. People who never went to college, let alone the University of Michigan, rooted for the Ann Arbor–based Wolverines, particularly against hated Ohio State. In fact, when I would go door to door trying to meet people who lived near the landfill, the closest thing to there being a test to see if I really was who I said I was (a student from the university) would be to ask me about the team. Insular identification with one's "own" town, state, and regions happened, and likely still does, I would guess, but this is not always the most obvious or salient point of felt connection for anyone.

—Reno

CHAPTER 4

No Place Like Home

The "Ordinary" Midwest through
Popular Fiction and Fantasy

COAUTHORED WITH JADA BASDEO

Perhaps it now occurs to him that in this need to establish himself in relation to his past he is most American, that this depthless alienation from oneself and one's people is, in sum, the American experience.

—James Baldwin (*Notes on a Native Son,* 127)

I. INTRODUCTION

The Midwest is sometimes represented and reproduced as if it were painfully *ordinary*, all in service of nationalist fantasies. It is as if the Midwest were the country's (and sometimes the world's) safe space. This is not always or even often a positive valuation. For instance, their perceived ordinariness can make a Midwestern person or community seem insular and closedminded. The Midwest has been and continues to be represented as both a negative and a positive standard, but it is a standard all the same of "middle America." We do not wish to give credence to these representations just because they are dominant; though the fact that they are dominant does have serious social and cultural effects. At the same time, representations of Midwestness as ordinary can also generate anxieties and uncertainties, precisely because they do not align with lived realities, with how we sense things actually are. Claims of ordinariness produce anxious reflections on the strange or alien, and vice versa, in the form of popular fiction and fantasy. At issue here is not only otherness, in the abstract, but *intimate others,* that is, those close to "us" who are not as they ought to be or appear to be.

But once again this is a relational category. If the intimate others are challenging, they also could be said to bring that "us" into being.

Intimacy is a complex notion, both because it varies throughout history, as well as across and within societies, and because it is part of human affective domains and thus not easily represented in analytical discourse. At the same time, intimacy plays a crucial role in binding individual identities to imagined collectivities, like race and the nation. If felt attachment to an identity, place, or people can be shared, furthermore, this intimate relation can also serve to exclude and dehumanize others as alien or unfamiliar. Intimate otherness is an intermediary phenomenon in between cultural intimacy with people regarded as the same, and oppressive exclusion of those regarded as other.[1]

Like inwardness, intimate otherness arguably plays a role in the history of Christianity broadly (as an expression of the hidden evil in our midst, capable of corrupting even the most seemingly innocent), which has had a profound influence on the migrants who settled in the United States from Europe and elsewhere. But what might be unique to the United States, and nations like it, is the relationship of the intimate other for projects of settler colonialism that tend to involve some practical and symbolic mediation or confrontation between the new and the old, the strange and the familiar. Settler colonial nations like the United States are imagined and restaged in an ongoing, collective, and creative fashion through the idealization of whiteness and heartland regions. Rather than the hallucinations of an individual mind, this threefold relationship is better understood like a play or musical performance. As with the nation, this involves an audience of relative strangers who come together to bear witness to an engrossing story; whiteness may be embodied through the actors themselves, who aim to be believable, to get the audience invested in their performance, thus making whiteness seem virtuous and desirable. For their part, the audience can only aspire to whiteness—at best, the characters performed are impossible ideals they will never live up to, even though the actors themselves are just pretending. Finally, consider the Midwest region as the "empty" stage itself, which, precisely because it appears to some to be wiped of specificity and particularity, can serve as a blank slate, a neutral setting so that any production and any characterization can be realized.

This analogy is more apt than it might seem, even when keeping in mind the limitations of the dramaturgical comparison. While one might understandably associate the economic productivity of the Midwest with commodified corn and cars, the imaginary Midwest has been *as* productive if not more so, responsible for commodified global icons as diverse as Dorothy Gale, Superman, and Freddy Krueger. Using the American Film Institute database (AFI), we found 1,669 films explicitly associated with the region, with nearly 97 percent of those labeled by the AFI as relating to the "heartland" specifically. In a separate inquiry, 1,128 films, some of the same ones as we found earlier, appeared under the search term "farm," and many had either explicit or implicit connections to the Midwest. If a film was designated within the AFI database as having to do with farms, the heartland, or the Midwest, it was unlikely to also be represented as a film about African Americans, Native Americans, or Latinx communities. In this way, ideas about region can serve racial fantasies and projects even when they circulate far beyond the Midwest or the United States proper, or even when they appear to performatively subvert the very same regional tropes they presuppose. Popular fiction and fantasy not only demonstrate the promotion of imagined ordinariness beyond the United States, but they also reveal an unexamined dimension of racial projects of global white supremacy. Insofar as these cultural products are involved in generating ideals of imaginary whiteness, they make up part of what might be called the imaginative infrastructure for the value of whiteness around the world.

One can see this through a selective history of popular, fictional representations set in the Midwest, where the region serves as a stage that facilitates figurations of whiteness and tales of nationhood. "Popular" means that they are familiar to many people, across the United States and the world. In other words, they are not for Midwesterners alone. Admittedly, popular films may not be as readily understood to signal nationalism as, for example, mytho-historical representations of national events, like military battles or ideological struggles. There are of course many popular fictional performances with clear nationalist connotations. The Broadway musical *Hamilton* (2015–present) and the film *American Sniper* (2014), are both based on popular biographical books that explicitly reference struggles associated with national service and national ideals. Moreover, these kinds of nationalist media are ordinarily situated at critical points in American history (the American Revolution and the War on Terror, respectively). But popular film and fiction can express and reproduce nationalist sentiment in more implicit or banal ways, without direct reference to national ideals and service and without direct placement at critical historical junctures. Fantasy fiction is a genre of cultural production that is ostensibly neither realist nor historicist. For this reason, fantasy fiction radically differs from the biographical, auto-biographical, and historical accounts that are more explicitly about nation-hood. If even the most surreal or unreal fictions can still signal nationalism, then the influence of nationalist ideology is simultaneously more widespread and more concealed than often assumed.

For instance, many popular fantasy films focus especially on themes involving lost or threatened children. In some cases, lost children become expressions of the power of Midwestern values and virtues, coded as white, as with Dorothy Gale and Clark Kent. However, insofar as these expressions are tied to projects of white supremacy and settler colonialism, they are fraught. First, this is so because there are anxieties about producing the next generation when settling and colonizing areas inhabited by "others"—that is, Native Americans or eastern elites. Second, raising deracinated children as part of colonizing a "foreign" land, detached from the places of their parent's origin, raises issues about the connection of one generation to the next. These tensions are further reflected and reproduced through popular fiction and fantasy.[2] Successive crises confronting American values are figured through what we term the intimate other, that is, children or community members who are other or become other and must be dealt with in some way. The figure of the intimate other is associated with the tensions of compulsory, idealized, and impossible standards of whiteness, represented in a tension between Midwestern communities as full of kindhearted, forthright, and welcoming people and Midwestern communities as exclusionary, isolated, and dangerous.

II. INTIMATE OTHERS I: FROM BLEEDING KANSAS TO SMALLVILLE

Generations before people all over the world began to associate Kansas with Dorothy Gale and Clark Kent, their fictional homeland was not popularly imagined as bucolic and placid but as a site of bloody violence. While the Midwestern front of the Civil War is not normally granted the same attention as those in the North and South, the Midwest was important both before and after this conflict as a site where national tensions played out at a smaller scale. "Bleeding Kansas," as it became known, pitted pro-slavery forces against abolitionist forces—the latter represented most famously in the historical personage of John Brown. Even after the Civil War, moreover, similar episodes of vigilante justice and revenge, framed around continuing tensions between confederate/abolitionist ideology, were associated with the popular exploits of Jesse James and his gang of outlaws throughout the Midwest. These stories are more directly nationalistic, in that they involve John Brown or Jesse James epitomizing white male vigilantism against the law but in keeping with higher callings toward justice or freedom that signal ideological traits of American character, especially on the frontier. While popular accounts of John Brown and Jesse James have circulated in the time since, alongside Depression-era Midwestern vigilantes like John Dillinger, fantasy about fictional characters have been far subtler in utilizing Midwestness as a background stage to perform race and nation.

With respect to fantasy fiction, there has been much more critical discussion of the meaning of Dorothy Gale's homeland than of any of the other Midwestern settings we will discuss in this chapter. This is odd, in some ways, since Kansas makes up only a brief portion of the setting for the 1900 book, the 1902 musical, the 1910 silent film, or the well-known 1939 MGM film *The Wizard of Oz*. In the latter, it accounts for several bursts of action in the beginning (fleeing to avoid Ms. Gulch, running away from home, fleeing from the tornado) and then a very brief interior shot at the end. Yet, to appreciate the impact of *The Wizard of Oz*, religious studies scholar Paul Nathanson argues, "we must recall that it celebrates a farm in Kansas. Would a farm in Pennsylvania, Georgia, North Dakota, or California have had the same impact?"[3] The Midwest is important in this tale because, as Nathanson goes on to write, it serves as an ideological middle ground in national storytelling: "the eye of the storm, the calm center around which national life swirls." This fantastical Midwest, as a "calm center," is figuratively, if not literally, ordinary. "Consequently," Nathanson argues, "it can be filled with the dreams of all Americans. As 'Kansas,' the reality of America, a fragmented collection of rival regions, is seen as an ideal unity held together by a shared image of the agricultural frontier."[4]

And yet, this is only one reading of *The Wizard of Oz*, and not necessarily the most common. In the book and the films, Kansas is normally depicted as gray, lifeless, and boring. In Salman Rushdie's words, in an influential essay on the 1939 film, "The Kansas described . . . is a depressing place, in which everything is grey as far as the eye can see—the prairie is grey and so is the house in which Dorothy lives."[5] Here we see evidence of the marked, or negative valuation of ordinariness, as drab and uninteresting. It is not only for this reason that the protagonist dreams of escaping "somewhere, over the rainbow" for a life more liberating and more colorful. At the very start of the film Dorothy and her beloved pet are under threat. And what is even more distressing still, Auntie Em, Uncle Henry, and their staff seem unbothered by this situation, despite it being deeply troubling for young Dorothy. Not only is there no color, from her perspective there is no safety and no hope.

If the Midwest had at different times been made to stand in for the nation as a whole, America's imagined ordinary or middle standard, then Kansas during the Depression could hardly be a source of joy and freedom. Yet Kansas was no less gray in Baum's depictions at the turn of the century. Even then, the child Dorothy represented seemingly irresistible desires for something more than pastoral tedium and a closed community. Of course, Midwestern farmers had experienced economic pressures long before the stock market crash of 1929, which had partly led to the Populist movement that Baum supported and that he had partly lampooned in his children's book.[6] The cultural texts that emerge in these periods of political and economic precarity demonstrate that what counts as American becomes at these times alternatively contested and reinforced in different ways. This has often been done through mass media depictions of lost children as representations of intimate others. In the case of *The Wizard of Oz*, a child goes missing (runs away and then is taken away) because they are so unhappy with their surroundings.

Many scholars and critics seem to agree that, irrespective of the broader historical context, the central conflict in *The Wizard of Oz* is between Dorothy's desire for independence and adventure and the opposite demand and appeal of returning and staying home. For some, Dorothy betrays her true rebellious nature, and the overall theme of the tale, by returning to gray Kansas in the end after repeating the saccharine refrain, "There's no place like home." For others, this ambivalent ending makes it even more appropriate as a form of national storytelling where Americans are destined to return to our mythic origin. Ordinariness thus shifts from a negative to a positive valuation. Oz, in contrast with Kansas, is shown to represent the worst qualities of industrial, urban America: "a land of confusion, fragmentation, anxiety, and alienation. Moreover, it is a land that has been starkly polarized by good and evil."[7] This contrasts with the Midwest as ordinarily

FIGURE 7. Lobby card from the original 1939 release of *The Wizard of Oz*. MGM. Wikimedia Commons.

imagined (and as the imagined ordinary) in the hands of regionalist paint-ers, for instance, which is "a realm of order, unity, security, and happiness; the polarization between good (rural and agrarian America) and evil (urban and industrial America) has been resolved, albeit implicitly."[8]

What commentators tend not to discuss is the role of whiteness in *The Wizard of Oz*, especially a vision of white virtue embodied in the character Dorothy, who is plain-speaking amid characters who are not only fantasti-cal (a talking lion, scarecrow, and tin man) but who also do not see them-selves as they really are. If only they could see themselves objectively, they would succeed. Here Midwestern plain thought and speech is taken to be ordinary in the sense of objective—that is, in touch with the real, begin-ning with the reality of the individual and their virtuous or non-virtuous character. A similar plainness can be detected in many characterizations of Midwestern people, demonstrating an iconic resemblance or indistinction between plain people and the plains as a setting, both unassuming, both being merely what they are and nothing more. This plainness is, as we have seen in previous chapters, characteristic of idealized depictions of whiteness as unmarked and, for this reason, virtuous and desirable. Selling depictions of plain whites (in both senses of that term, ordinary whites and whites of the plains) also communicates messages about what a good person is like (pragmatic, down to earth) and looks like (white). And insofar as filmic representations have historically circulated globally, they are therefore part and parcel of a racial project of global white supremacy. Children all over the world imagine the trials and tribulations of being simple and plain-speaking, rebellious yet homesick Dorothy Gale.

It is therefore incidental, for our purposes, which interpretation of *The Wizard of Oz* is correct (whether Dorothy is a rebel who betrays her true self or a figure standing in for a pragmatic America). It is more interesting, in some ways, that a similar tension associated with intimate others can be found in other popular media set in the Midwest again and again, where lost children return to better or worsen the communities that produced and/or excluded them. This trope infuses, arguably, not only fictional narratives, but also narratives of the media moguls who produce those fictions. This is most obvious in the case of Walt Disney, who is often described as having overcome humble Midwestern origins in "the dirt and disorder" of Missouri farms, where he grew up, by scrubbing the filth out of all depictions of his animated creations, in effect insuring that there would be no place like his home.[9] Lost children can be fictions or, like the larger-than-life figure of Disney the artist, they can create new fictions, but the trope of "the ordinary" tends to stick to them in either case.

If there is a tension between interpretations of Dorothy as a rebel escaping the dreary tedium of Kansas and Dorothy realizing that she should have stayed home all along, there is also a tension over whether Superman, also known as Clark Kent or Kal-El of Krypton, made himself into a hero or was made one by his ideal upbringing. Today Kansas is famous all over the world as the place where Superman was raised. In 2013, the imagined "home" of this global icon led to a conflict over which Kansas community could rename their town "Smallville" for a day in his honor . . . and also in order to boost tourism in anticipation of new Superman films.

Beginning with the very first Action Comics in 1938, all origins of Superman begin with the destruction of his home planet of Krypton and his landing on Earth, a lost orphan in need of a home and family. But the earliest accounts left out his foster parentage and said little about where on Earth he was raised. If anything, Superman's Cleveland-based creative team, Joe Shuster and Joe Siegel, implied that he grew up in an urban setting and decided to become a hero on his own.[10] This changed as Superman's popularity grew and other writers contributed to his backstory. The earliest origin, by Siegel and Shuster, described a passing motorist who came upon a young Kal-El crawling out of a crashed ship all on his own. The definitive

Midwestern backdrop became more pronounced over time, just as the role of the Kent family became more critical in raising a superhero messiah. When Superman's adoptive father Eben Kent is introduced at the start of the novel *The Adventures of Superman*, he is no motorist. Instead, when the Kryptonian vessel lands, his horse takes off in fright, dragging the plow behind it. Gone is an anonymous motorist, replaced by a hardworking farmer. The glowing descriptions of Eben and Sarah Kent continue in these early chapters. They contrast most starkly with the first city person that Clark Kent encounters at a state fair, specifically the man who would become his boss, Perry White: "He was well-dressed and it needed but a glance to tell that he was from the city. Clark glared at the man, who returned the unfriendly stare."[11] Interestingly, in the same way that the fantastical Oz is described as a reflection of urban America, Krypton (and later Metropolis) is a troubled urban setting where the general populace ignorantly overlooks the warning signs of their own destruction.

Another critical addition to the Superman mythos comes in a chapter of the 1942 book entitled "the Death of Eben," where Clark listens intently to words of wisdom as his father slips away (a consequence of trying and failing to win a prize at a fair to save his family through a feat of strength). It is because of this pivotal encounter that Clark will become Superman. At the fair, the adopted alien had acted in anger and vengeance on behalf of his humiliated father, but after the latter's tragic death, Clark seems to gain wisdom: "Finally he sat down on the brow of a lonely hill, with nothing about him but the quiet moonlit land, he had decided definitively what he must do, what course his life must take."[12] Lowther's 1942 account is therefore a critical shift in the Superman narrative: "By the time Lowther invented Eben Kent's entreaty that Superman should always act on the 'side of law and order,' over in the comic books, the character's first years of vigilantism already had drawn to a close, and when the character's origin was retold there again in 1948 . . . his paralegal mission was once again embedded in his foster father's deathbed soliloquy."[13] This scene is repeated in nearly identical fashion again in 1961, in a definitive comic book origin story, and then in the popular 1978 film. As novelist and critic Tom De Haven notes,

> By then, and ever since, Clark Kent became Superman principally because he was instilled with the viewpoints of plain American heartlanders who stressed the value of legal authority. He has no choice but to be good and to do good, and while it surely makes him a hero, it does strip away the majesty of self-invention,

and goes against Jerry Siegel and Joe Shuster's initial creative impulse: that Superman does what he does because he chooses to; that his greatness is a matter of will rather than of expectation and a promise.[14]

In fact, Smallville is not named as the setting for Superman's childhood until the late 1940s, as part of the new series of *Superboy* comics. It is unclear when this small farming community became Kansas, but this was definitely established by the time of the 1978 film and has become official superhero canon ever since.[15]

Intimate others like Dorothy Gale and Clark Kent/Kal El/Superman represent fraught ideals of compulsory whiteness, exemplified in the contexts of settler colonial states. In these examples, "the ordinary," as imagined, reveals multiple, even opposed valences: the standard, the ideal, as well as the banal, uninteresting, dull, parochial. As protagonists from the ordinary Midwest, Dorothy and Superman simultaneously reflect positively on Midwestern communities as productive of white virtue and value, and negatively on these same settings as constraining or threatening these positive character traits and the characters that embody them. One dimension of Lowther's 1942 novelization that commentators leave out is that Eben Kent also warns his son that people will not accept him for being different and that, for this reason, he should have a secret identity. In fact, in an experience in his classroom, when a young Clark uses his X-ray vision to help his teacher, he lies to cover up his talent, showing some awareness that difference would not be tolerated. This same tension, between the Kents as kindhearted, ideal parents and the wider community and world as intolerant of difference, is echoed in more recent Superman films in 2013 and 2016, where "Jonathan Kent," now played by Kevin Costner (of *Field of Dreams* fame), warns his son that he should perhaps let people die rather than expose his alien-ness to others. The double-sided Midwest, as morally upright and as insular and unaccepting of difference, is also apparent at the very start of the 1939 *Wizard of Oz*. If anything, the fact that new iterations of Dorothy and Superman are invented to address this internal tension associated with the heartland shows that it is never finally resolved.

Not only are intimate others important to fantasy and fiction using the Midwest as ordinary homeland, but they are also linked ideologically with whiteness and nationalism. If the 1939 *Wizard* and 1978 *Superman* were full-color spectacles, then they were both distinctly lacking in people of color, whether as creators or performers. This is not merely incidental, moreover. When *The Wiz* offered a retelling of Baum's tale through Black experience and music, the 1974 book and 1975 musical maintained the Midwestern setting; yet when this became a feature film in 1978, "Kansas" was changed to "Harlem." Similarly, when Milestone Media released *Icon* in 1993, this was explicitly meant as a Black alternative with a Superman-like biography and power set. For this reason, *his spaceship* landed not in the Midwest, but on a cotton plantation of the antebellum American South. These alternatives are marked, geographically, as part of Black culture and experience, just as the white Midwest is meant to stand in as a generic backdrop of unmarked (meaning white) American existence. The imagined ordinariness of the Midwest thus reflects the invisibility of whiteness itself, offering a parable of self-creation in perpetual conflict with community obligation.[16] In both cases, self-invention (as much a frontier trope as it is a modernist one) is seen to be in tension with Midwestness, which is offered up as the origin for goodness and frankness (with the Gales and the Kents), as well as their opposites, wickedness and insular secrecy.

III. INTIMATE OTHERS II: IF YOU BUILD IT, FREDDY'S COMING FOR YOU

Certain regional images circulate globally and may even be directly critiqued or satirized in various cultural media, yet for this very reason they convey a sense of naturalness between the iconic Midwest and the region it represents. A performance can still affect us and change the way we think, paradoxically, even though we are constantly reminded of its artifice. The medium of film, in many ways, is a perfect illustration of this unusual fact.

The Midwestern trope did not go away with the economic crises of the 1970s and 1980s, rather the tensions we have identified took on even more exaggerated form. On the one hand, the goodness of the ordinary Midwest could still take form in W. P. Kinsella's novel *Shoeless Joe* or the 1989 film adaptation *Field of Dreams*. In both, an Iowa farmer hears a Noah-like call to build a baseball diamond in his failing corn fields. There, the ghosts of disgraced baseball players emerge to reclaim their lost innocence, help the farmer reconnect with his father and, it is implied at the end, give all Americans a chance to rediscover what they have lost by bearing witness to the apotheosis of their "national pastime" in its purest form. The

Oz or Krypton in this tale is Chicago, where in the early twentieth century the infamous Black Sox scandal ostensibly marred the purity of the game of baseball through gambling and unsportsmanlike conduct. The scandal of 1919 fits directly with American nativism of the time. Specifically, the scandal emerged in the post–World War I period when gambling became associated with "foreigners" who were threatening the wholesomeness of the national sport. Nativism in the interwar period took legal form in the 1924 Immigration Act, with increased quota restrictions on migrants from non–Northern European countries. Both *Shoeless Joe* and *Field of Dreams* fail to include much discussion of the interwar, nativist context, but provide instead a meditation on the power of Midwestern faith and forgiveness to heal national wounds in the cornfields of Iowa, distant from "foreign threats" associated with the city. Of course, by the 1980s all major baseball teams were located in cities, making the desirability of an Iowa corn field emerge as a clear symbolic contrast. If there is an intimate other, a child lost and found here, it is the figure of innocence that the protagonist lost, which is restored through faith and ordinary cornfields.[17]

If the supernatural intercedes in tales like this in order to heal wounds associated with urban contamination of the spirit, then the horror films of the 1970s and '80s might appear to represent an opposing tendency. This is so for two reasons. First, horror films, it may be assumed, subvert the very norms that *Field of Dreams* promotes. This became especially pronounced after 1968, when the Hollywood censorship code was lifted, the MPAA ratings system was instituted, and a new series of more gruesome horror films emerged. Second, film critics tend to associate this genre with the presence of monsters of some kind, less so with places. When places are invoked, moreover, they are "terrible places," whether haunted houses or spaceships, tunnels to other worlds, or other worlds themselves. The place is a monster, in these instances. Despite these two tendencies in film and film criticism, the trope of terrible places is also used in order to take imagined safe havens (homes, schools, communities) and reveal them to be sources of danger. This is precisely how the Midwest tends to function in horror—as an idealized, ordinary backdrop where (white) people are meant to be safe. When this sanctity is violated, it is meant to horrify audiences even more effectively than if they were terrible places to begin with.[18]

Horror films about the Midwest are not unique, but are better understood through the prism of the ongoing tension around intimate others that has long characterized regional tropes of the Midwest and whiteness. In the popular horror film franchises *Halloween* (1978–2018), *Children of the Corn* (1984–2018), and *Nightmare on Elm Street* (1984–2010), there is a recurring tendency for the Midwestern backdrop to serve as a site of lost children. This is a product of the places they come from, which are isolated and closed communities of non-urban Illinois, Nebraska, and Ohio, respectively. The first two films share in common the clearest examples of children as evil threats. As with representations of malevolent or impossible infants in horror and fantasy, children who kill are frightening, arguably, because the future they promise is undesirable or unimaginable. The idea of lost children is in fact a recurring trope in our settler-colonial society, even if it takes different forms over time. Moreover, all of these children are white, despite the fact that anxieties about nonwhite children as an ungovernable and immoral threat to the social fabric are a far more dominant discourse in settler colonial societies like the United States, and long have been.[19]

As opposed to marked others in American media, Black men and boys most obviously, intimate others in horror films may be represented as inexplicably evil—and therefore truly representative of evil in the abstract, because they are racially "ordinary." *Halloween* began as a premise known as "the Babysitter Murders," which it was believed would unsettle and titillate audiences because people had memories of being watched by other people as children as well as memories of watching other people's children. The monster in *Halloween* not only attacks and threatens children, but begins the film as a child. The first perspective we adopt is that of Michael Myers as a boy, who puts a mask on his face, grabs a knife and brutally murders his sister and her male companion. What became the successful film franchise *Halloween* "reminded audiences that, *even in the most civilized and domesticated parts of America, there are eruptions of disorder.* The town of Haddonfield looks safe enough, with its cookie-cutter houses and its neatly manicured lawns, but the slow-moving camera reminds us that there is something lurking in the shadows during the characters' most vulnerable moments."[20]

The tagline for the posters and trailers in post-production for *Halloween* was "the night he came home," which could be taken as a direct subversion of "no place like home," from *The Wizard of Oz*, revealing through this juxtaposition unsettled anxieties associated with the intimate other. *Halloween* was credited for "shattering the illusion of safety in suburbia for middle-class Americans," yet it did so by drawing upon a fear of children who are inexplicably born killers in those same, seemingly ideal settings.[21] This internal contradiction (idyllic/horrific) inspired pioneering *Halloween* producer Debra Hill to move the location from her childhood town in New Jersey to Illinois:

> I wanted a Midwest, sleepy town. . . . What's so interesting to me about horror movies is they take place in small towns where they don't have a huge police force. You put the story in a sleepy town, really beautiful homes, nice full trees, it seems safe. You think nothing could go wrong there and nothing could be further from the truth. Every town has a secret, every town has that lore of something that went horribly wrong with it. . . . The idea of pulling off the veneer and seeing what lies beneath has always intrigued me.[22]

Director John Carpenter echoed Hill's sentiments: "It could be any place in the Midwest."[23] *Halloween* was shot in California, as *Wizard of Oz* had been, but it created its fantasy by utilizing the seemingly neutral stage of the Midwest as ideally ordinary, as anywhere and everywhere, because it was homogenous and white. Many film critics made much of the film's apparent punishment of teenage sexuality as expressing puritanical values, or anxiety about child sexuality. But for Carpenter the neutrality of the setting, its ordinariness, also meant it was devoid of "social statements" of any kind.[24] Whiteness and Midwestness are both key ingredients here, the figures and stage, respectively, that secure the impression that the cultural content is "empty" of deeper meaning and therefore pure entertainment. This is a social statement, that whiteness is ordinary and ideal, all the more so because it is assumed not to be.

These tensions are developed more explicitly in the *Children of the Corn* franchise, where the homogeneity and idyllic nature of the setting is the real monster. This began as a short story in a collection by noted horror author Stephen King, but was later turned into a film of the same name, spanning multiple sequels. The basic story is of a small, seemingly idyllic Nebraska farm community which descends into terror in the opening scene as the children are corrupted by an unseen spirit that emerges from the corn fields. A twisted subversion of the *Field of Dreams* premise, the endless rows of corn, the generic, homogenous, mono-cropped landscape becomes a source of fear and punishment rather than hope and forgiveness, concealing some kind of demon that corrupts children and threatens civilization. If you build it, he will come indeed.

While taking place in a suburb, not unlike that of *Halloween*, *Nightmare on Elm Street* resembles *Children of the Corn* in that the very imagined Midwestness of the setting is arguably responsible for the monster in the first place. The villain of the *Nightmare* franchise is Freddy Krueger, an undead, grinning, fedora-wearing, badly burned murderer with a glove of knives. Unlike other monsters, Freddy attacks white children in their dreams, while they are tucked under the covers in their suburban homes. In the first film, we learn that this demon was not lurking in between rows of corn, but was created when otherwise seemingly ordinary parents engaged in vigilante justice against a suspected child molester, burning him alive. Another successful franchise, "Freddy would continue to dominate impressionable teens—acting the part of a maniacal father figure. . . . According to [the writer Wes] Craven, much of this 'father figure' subtext was part of his original concept of the monsters."[25] As Craven put it, "It's a sickness where youth is hated. Childhood and innocence are hated."[26] But Freddy Krueger's hatred of children is not a mystery because it appears at the very beginning of the film, like murderous Michael Myers or murderous Nebraskan children. The real mystery of *Elm Street* is the curious indifference and denial on the part of the parents of the children Freddy is terrorizing and killing. They are not in denial merely because they cannot believe and cannot admit that children could be at risk while asleep in their beds, where "we" are all meant to be safe, but because the parents of *Elm Street* actually know who Freddy is and helped create him. The two sides of seemingly idyllic communities come through here, ideal homogeneity and safety made possible through the insular repression and refusal of difference. Michael Myers comes home, despite being locked away and forgotten, and Freddy reappears in the fantasy realm of dreams, despite his murder having been covered up and kept secret. The masked and scarred appearances of these two monsters are, in a sense, the literal mark of their difference as "monsters" and a result of their banishment. In *Children of the Corn*, the young take on that role themselves, identifying all adults as threats.

One could reasonably argue that many places in the United States have been used as sites of horror and fantasy, and have recycled the trope of intimate others we have described. Perhaps the same stories could be told in any American region and the Midwest is merely incidental in this regard. The kinds of cultural work performed in these films is not only done with reference to the Midwest, nor could it only be done in this fashion. Rather there is a dominant tendency to imagine the Midwest as a neutral, empty, or unmarked backdrop, as ordinary, which makes it critical for banal or subtle representations of race and nation. The ordinary may be made aesthetically appealing, as with Dorothy Gale (once back home) or the Kents, by selectively emphasizing morally virtuous features like realness, plainness, earnestness, or straightforwardness—the 1978, celluloid Superman informs Lois Lane that he cannot tell a lie. It might also be made horrible and horrific, as in the examples we have considered in this section. What they share in common is a reliance upon and reproduction of imagined ordinariness, which is apparent despite varied and multivalent applications in popular fantasy.

From another point of view, it makes perfect sense that the Midwest should be home to fictional monsters. After all, episodic Midwestern violence did not stop with Bleeding Kansas and John Dillinger. Some of the most well-known American serial killers come from this region. This includes two of the first documented in American history (setting aside the legacy of settler colonial violence, that is), H. H. Holmes (from Chicago) and Ed Gein (rural Wisconsin), followed by John Wayne Gacey (suburban Illinois), Jeffrey Dahmer ("the Milwaukee Monster") and the BTK killer (Wichita, Kansas). These real-life "monsters" have inspired various fictional characters, though, curiously, their fictionalized counterparts *do not tend to be from the Midwest*. Ed Gein famously inspired the 1959 book *Psycho* by Robert Bloch (who lived not far from where Gein's crimes occurred) as well as the *Psycho* film franchise (1960–1998) and the *Bates Motel* TV series (2013–2017), none of which take place in the Midwest. Gein also inspired the *Texas Chainsaw Massacre* film franchise (1974–2017). Similarly, Gein and Dahmer helped inspire the character of Hannibal Lecter in the Thomas Harris books, and the films and TV series based on them, but these are set in Baltimore, primarily. The BTK killer's story was controversially reproduced in a fictional Stephen King 2010 novella, *A Good Marriage*, and the 2014 film of the same name, is placed in Maine along with most of his stories.

There is one obvious exception to this pattern, Truman Capote's true crime bestseller *In Cold Blood* (1966) and the movie of the same name released the year after it was published. Yet this exception proves the rule— the ordinary, unassuming pastoral setting is what makes the Midwestern victims vulnerable to violent outsiders. As Tibbets puts it, "Both book and film employed that quintessential feature of the midwestern landscape, the vanishing point—the convergence of those archetypal elements of the prairie, the highway and the farmhouse—as a metaphor for the fatal intersection of the nomadic killers and the peacefully domestic Clutter family" (2003: 426). One of the two killers (an intimate other) actually came from Kansas too, though this does not prevent both Capote and the filmmakers from imagining a tension between the bucolic farm setting and a violent "outside." This is clear, for instance, in how Capote characterizes the murdered Clutter family, beginning with its patriarch: "Always certain of what he wanted from the world, Mr. Clutter had in large measure obtained it. On his left hand, on what remained of a finger once mangled by a piece of farm machinery, he wore a plain gold band, which was the symbol, a quarter-century old, of his marriage to the person he had wished to marry."[27] Precisely because of the, here virtuous, ordinariness of the Clutters and their Midwestern world, there is something unpredictable and uncharacteristic about the murders that result, "as sudden and inscrutable as a prairie lightning strike."[28]

It would appear that, generally, when monsters are imagined to exist in the Midwest, they are paradoxically not based on real life. These real-life "monsters" instead become associated with other parts of the country and "return" in a two-part process. First, the Midwest is scrubbed of stories that might contaminate visions of heartland wholesomeness and white virtue. Second, those stories are displaced to other settings where they somehow seem to belong. As a consequence, we get ironic developments whereby crimes that take place in the Midwest—those of Ed Gein—are reimagined elsewhere—as in *Psycho*—only to be reimported into the Midwest as *Halloween* which is chosen as a setting where (mostly white) people would not expect such horror. Consequently, commentators and critics do not attribute the fantasy figure of Michael Myers directly to Gein, but instead refer to Hitchcock and Bloch's influence on John Carpenter. In some ways, this is about how film lore develops apart from "real life" in general. Yet these processes also reflect the idealized ordinariness, homogeneity, and whiteness of the Midwest as a national standard. Horrible things just don't happen there, even when they do.

This is also evident in the very origins of Freddy Kreuger. What initially inspired Wes Craven to develop the idea of a monster killing people in their sleep was the experience of Hmong refugees in Minnesota, not far from where he was living at the time. "Since the first reported death, which occurred in July 1977, more than 100 persons of various Southeast Asian ethnic groups have died from the mysterious disorder that is now known as SUNDS, the Sudden Unexpected Nocturnal Death Syndrome. The sudden deaths have an unusually high incidence among Laotians, particularly male Hmong refugees. The rate of death from SUNDS among Laotian-Hmong men has reached alarming proportions."[29] Craven read about the stories at the time, but to attract a mass audience he made the sufferers white Midwestern teens rather than Hmong Midwestern refugees. This whitened narrative proved very effective as mass entertainment but did nothing to increase attention to the plight of refugees of Southeast Asian violence, or the relationship of US militarism to the alleged posttraumatic stress disorder they suffered. Instead, their suffering and the literally deadly nightmares it led to was appropriated to reproduce representations of whiteness, lost children, and Midwestern tensions going back more than a century.[30]

The Midwest was chosen for these horror franchises, not because of its history of bloodshed but because of its imagined and metaphorically loaded emptiness as America's heartland. That this generic stage for telling stories about America is also white is clear not only in how these films are cast, with overwhelmingly white monsters and victims, parents, and professionals. It is also clear in the translation of real-life events into fantasy.

IV. CONCLUSION

In the late spring of 2019, a genre-mixing film, or mash-up, was released called *Brightburn*. Created by a director of mainstream blockbuster superhero franchises, like *Guardians of the Galaxy* (2014 and 2017), *Brightburn* deliberately mixes the hopeful and horrific sides of the intimate other trope with a coming-of-age story about a lost child growing up in the Midwest. Nearly identical to the Superman origin story, a young boy in a spacecraft crashes to Earth in the backyard of a white and kindhearted Kansas couple. Only instead of using his godlike powers for good, as they try to instruct him and as viewers have come to expect from the Superman mythos, the boy instead becomes a murderous monster. *Brightburn* is a familiar genre film, but also adds a new dimension to the long-standing Superman story, one where his alien origins are a source of suspicion and fear, and his father's death instead sets him on a path toward evil. In fact, in an early scene of the film, the young alien is compared to a parasitic wasp having invaded another insect's nest. In previous Superman stories, going all the way back to the

1940s, it was ordinary Americans, represented by Midwesterners, who were to be feared for not understanding the way in which he was different. Similarly, it is the exclusionary enforcement of homogeneity, in *Children of the Corn*, *Halloween*, and *Nightmare on Elm Street*, that leads to the creation of monsters. Perhaps *Brightburn* is reimagining the Superman story in an era of intense debate and suspicion of migrants. As the first celebrated undocumented "alien," Superman would seem to be a key character to express this anxiety in the Trump era.

Clearly, mutations in theme continue to occur in popular fantasy taking place in the Midwest. Yet these tend to be organized around recurring tropes associated with generation and regeneration. Specifically, these tensions are tied to the compulsory and enforced nature of these attributes of whiteness—their ongoing contestation and exclusion—which raises the possibility of resistance, or the return of the repressed. Put differently, those who are productively excluded in order to secure white standards may return to contaminate the vision of a perfect and homogeneous community. In these cases, lost children may become monsters who expose the repression and exclusion upon which compulsory whiteness depends. The theme of rejected or marginalized difference in some of the films is also a practice of bordering, in other words, one which replicates in a recursive fashion some of the nationalist and racializing work that happens in other sites discussed in this book.

Despite coming from different historical periods and distinct genres, fictional portrayals of the Midwest tend to reproduce tensions associated with the heartland as ordinary, white, empty, and homogeneous. That image in question is as much global as national, circulating far beyond the United States; it is also aided as much by fictitious tales as realist ones. In fact, the supernatural or fantasy element of the popular fiction we considered in this chapter serves the regional trope very directly. In all cases, supernatural elements allow characters to go from one reality, or planet, to another; moreover, such journeys to and from alternative worlds typically provide a deliberate contrast with the homogeneously drab, ordinary "Middle American" settings the characters inhabit. On the one hand, there are literary and filmic representations of endless fields and small, isolated farming communities, from the Kansas of Oz and Superman to the Nebraska of *Children of the Corn* or the Iowa of *Field of Dreams*. On the other hand, there are the small, friendly towns with a repressed secret in *Halloween* (1978), *Nightmare on Elm Street* (1984) and *Pleasantville* (1998).

That the ordinary could provide passage to the fantastic is a common phenomenon around the world with religious and, in particular, Christian dimensions. This no doubt accounts for the resonance of the iconography and symbolism of some of the films we mentioned. The idea that familiar faces might turn out to be "wolves in sheep's clothing" can be a way of describing moderate acts of hypocrisy or betrayal (as in the case of Judas of course) or more Satan-inspired forms of demon possession. Among evangelicals in the United States during the 1980s, there was an intense panic about Satan worship and killing, particularly among corrupted teenagers and young adults thought to be controlled by evil forces (which resulted in the actual trial, imprisonment, and later acquittal of the West Memphis Three, among many others). Another Christian religious thread is the "messiah"-like dimensions of Superman who, like Jesus, has part-human, part-alien/nonhuman elements; descends to earth and ascends to aid humankind; is marginalized or poorly understood; and often sacrifices his own bodily integrity to help others.[31] Finally, as one other Christian religious association, in *The Wizard of Oz* and *Field of Dreams*, belief and faith play a significant role in manifesting dreams, which could be analyzed as a nationalist (and Christian) trope. Arguably, in these and other ways, the narrative frameworks of these films and fictions take Christianity as part of the complex of unmarked forms that were being indirectly highlighted as white and American and worthy of social renewal.

At the same time, the Midwest is not an absence or emptiness we can take for granted, against which the fantastic appears even more so. The Midwest's perceived connection to homogeneity, whiteness, and nostalgia is a fiction that has to be actively produced and, furthermore, is productive of conceptions of nationalism and racial projects of white supremacy. In many fictional accounts, there is a return to the Midwest as a productively ordinary center that belies its relegation to a merely negative or empty non-space. This is especially clear with the recurring trope of intimate others, exemplified by lost and threatened children. This trope is by no means exclusive to fictional portrayals of the Midwest. That being said, there are good reasons to suggest that the symbolic resonance of lost children, as a parable of compulsory whiteness, is sufficiently powerful within the realm of Midwestern fictions that it tends to overwrite other kinds of horrors and mysteries that might well have gone on to represent the Midwest in popular imaginations. Bleeding Kansas, Jesse James, John Dillinger, Ed Gein, John Wayne Gacey, and

Jeffrey Dahmer could just as easily have been the focal point of a representation of the Midwest as a literal house of horrors, painfully ordinary indeed. Instead, those fictional monsters that were filmed—from Michael Myers to Freddy and now the supervillain child in *Brightburn*—proceed from the assumption that they are challenging the typical image of the Midwest as white, homogenous, serene, and bucolic. Even when that regional paradise is lost, through violence against or the corruption of intimate others, the audience is still meant to mourn that loss. A filmgoer need not explicitly ally themselves with white grievance politics today, of a far or alt-right sort, to be moved by a sense of grief for a world, coded white, that is no more, and a sense of alienation from a younger generation of intimate others who may sometimes appear unfamiliar, alien, or even monstrous.

My childhood in Muskegon, Michigan was a time when many of the sub-
sidiary parts manufacturers—our town made piston rings and camshafts—
declined as the Big Three moved their suppliers overseas. Starting when I was
ten or eleven years old, some of the town's hulking brick factories suddenly
became empty, with whole city blocks vacated and the parking lots fenced in.
I knew the history of the city's manufacturers through unusual, odd details:
for a sixth-grade biology project, I had to canvass the city and collect leaves
of different tree species. The city's only two gingko trees had grandly lined
the entranceway of the Campbell-Wyant and Cannon foundry. By then an
empty shell, I recall having my parents stop our car outside on the street,
running up the overgrown sidewalk to the chain-linked front doors, and
pulling two pristine gingko leaves from the trees. Our biology teacher told
us the trees had been a gift of visiting dignitaries from China. The factory
and trees have since been razed and a strip mall, dollar store, and Rite Aid
now sit on the same lot.

Even earlier in my life, there were often signs of the city's industrial
economy. Some days the air "smelled like the paper mill," a fact everyone
noted and yet took in stride. Occasionally the air quality bordered on
hazardous—we were told in the newspaper—due to the influence of Indiana's heavy industrial corridor of Hammond and Gary, which released air
emissions and particulate matter that traveled atmospherically up the lake.
If you followed the Business 31 route toward North Muskegon, you could
sometimes glimpse camouflaged tanks on jaunty runs through dirt roads, an
Orwellian parallel to the highway visible through a chain-link fence. These
were the proving grounds for the town's tank manufacturer, a company that
formed one, rather minor wing of a much larger defense contractor. The
sight of a tank could usually elicit a wry, critical comment from my father
that Muskegon always seemed to be doing the best when the country was
at war. My only tangential encounters with the toxicity and real hardships
of industrial pollution and industrial labor, let alone global imperialism, are
part and parcel of my white middle-class experience.

—Halvorson

I grew up in a house my father built, with seventy-seven acres of farm and
woodland surrounding it. Rural life was also part of family lore. One of

the first family stories I remember hearing involved my maternal great-grandfather, who was a cowboy in the Midwest. I do not remember play-acting as a cowboy, per se, but I did have a toy six-shooter and rifle, cap guns that were dear to me. I have also told the following story dozens if not hundreds of times to different people, one that lampoons white, male suffering as much as it romanticizes it. From the age of sixteen, my great-grandfather drove cattle from the Bitterroot Mountains of Montana to the stockyards near where his family lived, in Council Bluffs, Iowa, a distance of some twelve hundred miles across the Midwest. The way I heard it, one day he shot himself in the stomach while twirling his pistol (though I now hear from my mother that it was a careless neighbor that was goofing around). No matter, the story goes that the local doctor was out, so they had to load the whole family together—leaving the newborn baby alone to fend for herself on the couch, which still bothers my mother to this day—and make for the local veterinarian. My great-grandfather's suffering or heroism in the face of possible death were never the point, but the absurdity of it all. And that is how it was that the cowboy ended up with sheep intestine being used to patch up his wounded guts. And that is how I was taught to not take my white male heroes too seriously and to be respectful of guns (which I continued to play with, in cap gun form at least).

When my maternal grandfather's family moved from Iowa to Moravia, in upstate New York, the stage for family storytelling shifted with it from one of Midwestern cowboys and cattle to smaller suburban gardens and factories, and later to the Depression and World War Two. None of these stories were ever about anyone but white people.

—Reno

CHAPTER 5

Theater of Whiteness

Mass Media Discourse on the Midwest Region

COAUTHORED WITH LENA HANSCHKA

It's no secret, the middle has been a hard place to get to lately. Between red and blue, between servant and citizen, between our freedom and our fear. Now fear has never been the best of who we are.

—"The Middle" Jeep commercial, featured during the 2021 Superbowl

Media stories about race are our consistent touchstone for understanding what counts as racial. We are ardent consumers of these morality tales. . . . But we are barely conscious of the welter of assumptions, experiences, and social precedents that condition our perceptions of these stories.

—John Hartigan Jr. (2010: 10)

I. INTRODUCTION

The Midwest has gained a lot of overt media attention since 2016. Represented as a region of critical "battleground states," considerable journalistic effort is being expended to track voters' mercurial shifts between political parties, and to document the economic struggles faced by people living in those states. Yet a deeper and much more unexamined battle over the meanings of political belonging is being played out in the open through the very category and representation of the region, long a sign and symbol of whiteness. Uncritical references to the heartland and the Rust Belt can fuel nostalgia for a pastoral past that was peaceful and productive, that exhibits white, place-based morality and deservingness, that has only recently suffered the effects of globalization and economic downturn or been confronted by global migrations and cosmopolitan meanings. When region is deployed uncritically in this way, such nostalgia brings with it collective amnesia. What these contemporary tropes do is stage a collective forgetting that the Midwest region is a constructed cultural category, not a natural feature of the nation we can take for granted. In doing so, they also cast real conditions of struggle and loss as singularly traumatic and general, rather than perpetual, systemic, and uneven. By hiding in plain sight, mass-mediated discourses of the Midwest facilitate consequential realignments of race and nation founded precisely on such forgetting.

In this chapter, we explore how mass media reporting on the Midwest builds up an influential imaginary of whiteness through scripting and elaborating moral dramas of white labor.[1] The Midwest has long been a cultural repository and reference point for industrialism, not merely as a system of economic labor but, more specifically, a covertly racialized system of entitlements, opportunity structures, and narratives of progress. At a time of deindustrialization, stories of the Midwest reveal, often without close scrutiny of their whiteness, the culturally deep-seated latticework of white entitlement and expectations of social mobility long associated with industrialism. The gradual collapse of these entitlements has been made even more acute by the absence of a social safety net and government programs that would offset the job losses and downward social mobility associated with deindustrialization. Rising neoliberalism has exacerbated forms of inequality associated with deindustrialized places, not only in the American Midwest.

We are interested in what can be gained by looking across media articles to identify patterned systems of meaning making about whiteness, labor, industrialism, and the Midwest that can escape notice when only a handful of sources are consulted. In order to study the coded narratives of labor in the Midwest that underlie disparate media references, we explore how they normalize certain ways of looking upon and feeling about whiteness. Critical race theorists have described race as a "regime of looking" that attributes differential meaning and value to not only bodies but also places, gestures, speech styles, financial activities and much more.[2] By this, they mean not only that race is based on the social organization of perceived visual difference but also that racial hierarchies rely on tacit or backgrounded unifying scripts that justify and reproduce in frequently coded ways those racializing values.[3] Regimes of looking are frequently presumed to be relevant to marked racial categories subject to a dominant gaze. They are equally important to maintaining the dominance of supposedly unmarked racial forms, such as the structuring logics of whiteness and white supremacy.

Mass media discourse on the Midwest can be thought of as an affective theater or performative space of whiteness.[4] Media discourse does not merely provide a language of race, in other words, but coalesces images, bodies, and moral scripts in compelling ways to perform race.[5] Media stories are performative, not because their racial storylines are unreal or put on, but because everyone (or every American at least) is always and inescapably caught up in the doing of race, as we are the doing of gender. Yet some racial scripts become dominant and gain greater traction, visibility, and plausibility through their reinforcement across many different social sites, especially through circulated media. Approaching media discourse as performative or as caught up in the making of a reality enables a focus on its influential interweaving of body and story, representation and lived experience.[6] Media discourse about the Midwest often evokes normative scripts of whiteness and industrialism with historical dimensions. Performance is an essential feature of race and one that speaks to its embodied and scripted—or dominantly socialized—dimensions. In other words, race is rehearsed, performed, and known culturally through mass media or through an interplay of represented words, bodies, and spaces and their far-reaching material effects; these *choreographies*, in turn, selectively come to life in varying contexts.[7]

Recurring Midwestern figures enable people to look in on, reject, and imagine various ways of being white, building up patterned scripts of white experience that are implicit and therefore go frequently undisputed. Perhaps even more importantly, these figures help consolidate certain compelling and affective narratives about the white working-class in particular. The emotional center of these news stories about the Midwest is perhaps the most striking, in that they evoke deep sentiments of loss, frustration, anger, and despair at the shifting fortunes of deindustrialized communities and, most often, associate these feelings with whiteness. This occurs, for instance, when they depict the singular rather than systemic suffering of white male laborers and characterize the Midwest as generically rather than unevenly and perpetually deindustrialized. As anthropologist Bianca Williams has observed, race and gender are significant factors in how people come to experience and most importantly *feel* the world. Drawing on the work of Shaka McGlotten, Williams writes, "Personhood is not necessarily constituted by what one does, but by how one feels, and by the way one names those feelings (or doesn't) and puts them into a relationship (or doesn't) with larger social histories of difference and national belonging."[8] In this way emotions of sadness and indignation at a more glorious past and way of life gone by are both public and private experiences, filtered through and shaping how people come to know themselves and identify with much more far-reaching historical and social transformations. They are intimate, political, and social all at once, both moving people and moving them into alignment with stories that explain the unequal and often unjust world we live in. Here, the affective or emotional organization of nostalgia, empathy, and moral spectatorship in news stories *is* whiteness, that is, is critical to enabling white supremacy.

Prominent and widely circulated mass media articles are a good source for evidence of this kind of racial ideology, no matter how seemingly pithy the utterance or insignificant the speaker and audience.[9] This is especially clear in the wake of the 2016 US presidential election. In the months leading up to this event, and in the time since, traditional and new media platforms have increased their readership and viewership, a phenomenon referred to as "the Trump Bump."[10] Even at a time when confidence in "the media" is reportedly waning, media representations still play an unacknowledged role in framing ideas of collective belonging, whether or not we are consciously aware of "trusting" the source.

In order to investigate common mass media narratives of the Midwest, we performed a content analysis of 125 English-language news articles referencing the Midwest that were published between 2010 and 2019.[11] Our analysis draws upon pieces from the *New York Times, Los Angeles Times, Wall Street Journal, Boston Globe, Washington Post, Christian Science Monitor,* BBC News, Al Jazeera, Politico, Fox News, and *Huffington Post.* (See appendix B for a full list of the articles we cite in the chapter.) These mainstream news outlets exhibit a variety of political persuasions, audiences, authors, and styles of news reporting; they also often combine print, televised/video, and online platforms in an increasingly cross-referenced media landscape. We purposefully searched for references to the Midwest in articles from news outlets with varying conservative and liberal political bents, geographically dispersed readerships, and even international audiences (Al Jazeera and BBC). When we found articles that directly referenced the Midwest, we employed content analysis to identify common tropes and their erasures in media reporting.[12] In the process we explore how media discourse participates in producing historically shaped folk theories of region, race, and nation or "assumptions that operate as unexamined 'common sense' in everyday interactions."[13] Charting cultural associations and categories frequently evoked in discussions of the Midwest—often under the threshold of critical awareness—demonstrates how these mass-mediated regional images facilitate certain cultural logics of white industry.

Scrutinizing mass-mediated discourses on the Midwest, we identified three storylines of whiteness, labor, and virtue, which we analyze sequentially in the chapter. Although they engage with different styles and scripts of whiteness, they each paint scenes of worthy, industrious work and racialize them white. This is one way that talk about the Midwest is not only about the region, but becomes an affective theater or performative space in which to reference and secure forms of white supremacy associated with industrialism.

II. COLLECTIVE MEMORY, FORGOTTEN FARMS

One common trope in the media articles was that of the Midwest as a rural, pastoral heartland, a framing crucial to manifesting the character of the Midwestern farmer. This is not surprising given the deep history of the heartland trope, though the persistence of its specific features is worth exploring further. For example, in "Trump Takes His Hard Sell to the Heartland" from Politico.com (7/26/18), the article notes in the first line that President Trump was in the heartland of Iowa to "greet workers" who may have been hard-hit by his trade tariffs. Mentioning farmers a full fourteen times and featuring a photo of Trump holding a "Make Our Farmers Great Again" hat, the piece thoroughly associates the Midwest region with an "agricultural economy." Only in one later paragraph does the article mention that Trump was also making a stop in southern Illinois to celebrate the reopening of a steel mill. Other articles indirectly capitalize on the heartland imagery of stoic, morally upstanding farmers by referring to the Midwest as a "no-baloney" region (*Wall Street Journal*, 8/20/14) and, quoting Republican Wisconsin Governor Scott Walker, as a region filled with "no-nonsense kind of people" (*Wall Street Journal*, 10/15/10). The latter commentary blamed the Obama administration for ignoring the moral values that animate Midwestern communities: "The values that have long been associated with the Midwest are almost anachronistic in the Obama era.

Thrift, hard work, common sense—the messages and policies coming out of Washington seem to disregard these once-revered virtues" (*Wall Street Journal*, 10/15/10).

Even in cases where the heartland pastoral imagery and its clear political meanings were problematized, authors often still evoked the familiar trope they were seeking to move beyond, suggesting its continued significance in publicly portraying Midwestern farming. A well-researched feature-length article described particular areas of the Midwest as a "region of small towns and rural attitudes," and as having a landscape around the Mississippi that admittedly "consists of bluffs and rolling hills, scenery not commonly associated with the billiard-table images of the American heartland" (*Washington Post*, 5/10/18). Occasionally news reporting challenged the notion of the Midwest as a rural "flyover country" or cultural no-space. The author Tom Geoghegan, reporting on the books *Our Towns* by Deborah Fallows and James Fallows and *The New Localism* by Jeremy Nowak, touted the success stories of Midwestern towns flexibly responding to deindustrialization through entrepreneurship (BBC, 6/18/18). He writes, "These deep, structural changes and bursts of creativity appear to be especially evident in cities and towns in the Midwest, long derided as 'flyover country'" (BBC, 6/18/18). While such activity is undoubtedly happening and a sign of innovation long present in Midwestern communities, that the Midwest is emblematic of a "new localism" and return to "Main Street" in the national imaginary echoes well-established narratives of the region as insular, parochial, and non-global.

The term "heartland" was mentioned directly in one-tenth of the 125 articles we analyzed. Just as common was "rural" and related descriptive imagery as it came to apply to the whole region. While emphasizing the loss of manufacturing jobs and the challenges of affording health care surrounding Defiance, Ohio, one piece also described it as a place where "farmland stretches for miles between towns" (*New York Times*, 3/19/17). In an analysis of President Obama's legacy, another article notes, making a subtle association between the (non-urban) Midwest region and rural whites, "While [Obama] built a majority heavy on women and minorities in urban, coastal regions, some Democrats believe the party would be better off if it also worked harder to expand support among rural, white communities and in the Midwest" (*Los Angeles Times*, 2/19/19). Furthermore, an in-depth analysis, "A Shot at Rural America," profiles Republican organizing among South Dakotans and interweaves references to the state as "rural" or "rural America," "socially conservative," "Midwestern," with an "ag-heavy economy," and possibly echoing pitched political rhetoric, populated by "farms," "farming" and "farmers" (*New York Times*, 10/22/18). Finally, seeking to better understand Trump's election, another news article describes the "profound demographic shift among white rural voters in the northern Midwest." While noting that its Iowan interviewees include an optometrist, farmers, and former utility company employees, the piece focuses partly on the area of *American Gothic* (1930) artist Grant Wood's birth, finding "older men" there "still" in "pinstriped overalls" (*New York Times*, 1/13/17).

Collectively, repeated references to the Midwest as a pastoral heartland theatrically stage farming in public discourse as a white drama with specific moral contours.[14] As in the reference above, individual farmers in news discourse are often portrayed as older men who signal tradition or a recalcitrance to change (evoked, for instance, through the words "still" and "once-revered"). Here, Regionalist painters' artistic imagining of a white, bucolic Midwest finds its ironic realization. The farmer's moral narrative, whose outline is built up through the various coded references we have described, is a story of struggle, hard work and making something from the land; yet in spite of these efforts, the farmer receives an unjust dose of marginalization and mistreatment by the political and economic system. Such unfairness runs counter to the articles' depiction of farmers as "no-nonsense" individuals, with "rural attitudes" and "values" that paint them as worthy, hardscrabble characters in a quiet bid for recognition. By doing so, they communicate a style of whiteness oriented around the racialized rural-urban contrast and hard work, simplicity, honesty, and straightforwardness. That the farmer is frequently a gendered masculine figure can be interpreted as a white nostalgic yearning for a social order that features patriarchal white control of economic and social reproduction (e.g., making farmers "great again," as they once were). All of this is accomplished with no explicit reference to whiteness itself. Instead, activities, sensibilities, and spaces covertly racialized as white are organized through familiar arcs stringing together their storylines.

This narrative often seems specific to particular individuals in news articles and to a degree it is of course built on careful journalistic reporting on the conditions of struggling Midwestern farmers. Yet in our sample news media tends to focus on white rural farmers as prototypic Midwesterners.

In doing so, it inescapably relies on the historically formed cultural category of the Midwestern farmer and signals collective memory of empire, race, and nation, a set of cultural grooves filled in and upheld through media discourse. In chapter 2, we showed how historical portraits of Midwestern white settlers and rural landscapes, with open skies and vast, undulating, verdant fields, were never merely transparent chronicles of things as they were. Rather, they arose and were produced and circulated at specific times, such as in the 1930s, and fed populist movements that sought to redefine forms of American imperial inclusion and exclusion using images of the Midwest. By upholding the Midwest as a place of resourceful, modest, and old-fashioned white (often male) farmers, contemporary media discourse taps into these long-standing narratives of the Midwest as a repository for the essence of American citizenship and national belonging, an imagery that draws political meaning from its connections to white landholding. Primordialist stories of the Midwest, which make the region seem unchanging and old-fashioned and sometimes even a relic of tradition, enable other spaces to seem more global and cosmopolitan. But these qualities are not only made meaningful through contrast. By amplifying connections to the soil and other kinds of insularity, heartland imagery subtly shapes nativist ideologies of rootedness and belonging to the land, as well as obscures US imperial projects taking place inside and outside the territory of the state through similar racial formations.[15]

Midwestern farming and rural lifestyles are iconic of the region and for that reason the somewhat staid imagery in news discourse may appear rather one-dimensional and limited in its persuasiveness. However, we can appreciate better what these stories do if we think about cultural domination as a sequence of "scenarios" with compelling, alive, and yet repeatable or even deeply familiar stories.[16] The Midwestern farmer who attempts to make something good from the land, serve the common good, and live simply and honestly, yet who is faced with the harsh realities of the market and an indifferent American public, is such a repeated and repeatable scenario. One might even go so far as to identify it, in various manifestations, as *the* scenario of US settlement, while also bearing complex ties to racializing colonial projects abroad. Yet, because people are attuned to reading media articles as single pieces that are focused on current issues and based on discrete encounters between individuals and reporters, it is hard to perceive this background cultural work of memorializing settler colonialism. The cultural subtext is also made indistinguishable from individual people who happen to practice farming as a livelihood in the Midwest. This is precisely how media discourse, and arguably all cultural discourse in settler colonial contexts, unwittingly trades in and reinforces structuring logics of whiteness. Through imagining the particularity of experience as it is lived, audiences and readers are invited to fully buy in to the idea that, even though specific Midwestern farmers may seem old-fashioned and even caricatured, they *really* exist, effectively binding the long-running cultural icon with a real individual's story. This helps to perpetuate the seeming truthfulness of those long-running stories of whiteness, entitlement, and the Midwest. And because of its alternately positive links to virtue, hard work, and American values or negative associations with rural insularity, hyper-whiteness, and the past, the moral story of Midwestern farming may sometimes appear distant from the ongoing politics of settler colonialism.

The influential frames and associations of mass mediated images shape how collective memory is ignited and pursued, often in undetectable ways. Geographer Joshua Inwood (2016) has maintained that the concept of white innocence, of what writer James Baldwin referred to as "innocent and well-meaning people," has been central to the "permanent occupation of space" in settler colonial contexts by enabling cultural forgetting about the structural violence of white supremacy and focusing instead on individualizing qualities and values like one's work ethic.[17] And this settler logic was flexible enough to be revived in order to perform slightly different work in the service of white supremacy under varying historical and political conditions. In the Reconstruction period, the *"systemic"* qualities of slavery, or the ways Northern capitalists and industries such as ship-building and woolen mills relied heavily on economies of slavery, were actively papered over to promote the notion that the North had avoided the ethical lapse of slavery while the South had succumbed to it.[18] Political theorist Cedric Robinson writes, "As ideologues for both virtuous northern capital and a now chastened southern agrarian capital, the white intelligentsia—academician and otherwise—rewove social and historical legends that accommodated the exploitive projects of those ruling classes."[19] The independent Midwestern farmer could be seen as a (Northern) cultural counterpoint to both the aristocratic Southern white landowner and Black free laborer, a figure imagined to pursue a more small-scale, virtuous, Jeffersonian form of work foundational to the republic. This recaptured a moral logic of whiteness, whether as innocence, simplicity, honesty, or ruralness, in post–Civil War realignments of race, nation, and empire. Peasant farmers have often globally been deployed at distinct times as nationalist figures, wherein they embody the founding colonial and civilizing moves of discovery, progress, and settlement but render them humble, understated, and laudable. Such figures diffuse the edge of empire through their embodiment of innocence and purity of action.

At distinct historical times, the Midwestern farmer has also been explicitly evoked as a figure of national strength, in ways that more openly display imperial and even fascist qualities and play into complex racial politics surrounding national vigor and weakness. As we described in chapter 1, Theodore Roosevelt was influenced by and enamored with Charles Pearson's 1894 book *National Life and Character*, read by some whites at the time as an alarming text foreshadowing a future when populations of people of color would exceed whites.[20] In this context, white farming families, with many children, signaled eugenicist vigor, an image that could counter the racist worry that, with civilization, nations became weaker.[21] Roosevelt admired the hardiness and manliness of the frontier and "the pastoral stage," which he saw translated partly in his time into the modern figure of the railway man.[22] The reproduction of a white male virility was encoded in the pastoral, stitched together with the widespread knowledge of farming's harsh, literal physicality and its masculine acts of regenerating life. Farmers' rural lifestyles, requiring economic contributions of their large families, prefigured a kind of white strength in future numbers. Roosevelt's well-documented "imperial turn," characterizing US expansionism in Hawaii, Cuba, the Philippines, and Puerto Rico, was built on an explicit "battle for racial supremacy" in which he aligned the United States with Anglo-Saxon colonists elsewhere.[23] The farmer could become a symbol of these cultural projects of race, empire, and nation, embodying the economic and social reproduction of whiteness at certain moments.

What's particularly notable in this context is that the Midwestern farmers evoked across our media articles are characterized as forgotten subjects, left behind and overlooked.[24] That the farmer is a sign of the founding of the American republic, simultaneously situated in time, of the past, and in a timeless or enduring present, helps produce this orientation and sense of a forgotten or bygone figure. To be sure, individual farmers *are* forgotten structurally by large-scale agri-business and globalizing capital markets, in their struggles for economic sustainability. Increasing corporate control of food and meat processing facilities, made especially clear during the coronavirus pandemic of 2020, have decreased independent farmers' already small profit margins and determined how and if their products circulate to consumers through national distribution networks. Additionally, as anthropologist Alex Blanchette has pointed out, chemical farming methods and the corporate scaling-up of meat production has increasingly brought "poor white rural residents and migrant workers of color into disproportionate degrees of porous contact" with harmful substances, like fecal dust clouds and airborne animal antibiotics.[25] The farming of today is often an industrial and technical operation relying heavily on workers of color and worryingly transforming animal and human biology, more *Brave New World* than *Prairie Home Companion*. However, in the attempt to rally attention to their cause, media coverage subconsciously interweaves into their portrait a whole constellation of historical associations with Midwestern farming that made it a powerful trope of whiteness, nation, and empire. Therefore the farmer's forgotten-ness gets entangled with and taken up to serve a more insidious set of structures: the cultural category and its moralizing qualities facilitate the reproduction of elite white political and economic interests by being an icon of landed white industry in ways that often paradoxically disenfranchise individual farmers.

The moral logic of whiteness surrounding the cultural figure of the rural Midwestern farmer thus partakes in a retrenchment of structural inequalities of nationalism, empire, and nativism. It does so in at least three ways. First, it selectively focuses on the experiences of primarily US-born white Midwesterners, which are abstracted from wider global conditions and associations, leaving the incorrect impression that the geographic region is overwhelmingly, even exclusively agricultural, rural, and white. Second, when trading in imagery of the Midwest as a space set apart, rural, agricultural, and to an extent frozen in the past, the regional trope feeds into nativist ideologies and nostalgia for a past of "traditional values," reinforcing the social and economic relations of white heterosexual patriarchy in ways that disenfranchise variously positioned white people and individuals of color. Finally, by emphasizing the region's traditional livelihood of farming, its moralism and undulating, rural landscapes, media discourses unwittingly dramatize and perpetuate settlement as an ongoing project of securing white claims to property and resources as well as white supremacist projects at home and abroad. It is unsurprising, then, that one South Dakotan running for office did not mention his hometown or state but noted in one news story that the national Democratic Party "hasn't been relating to people in the Midwest," animating a complex set of white values and economic relations through the regional trope (*New York Times*, 10/22/18). Such tropes conceal and distort the important globalisms and migrations that have long formed part of life in the Midwest, as well as other places in the United States, amplifying a selective narrative of race, labor, and land.

III. THE RUST BELT AND WHITE INDUSTRY

Mr. Trump made large gains across rural America, helping to defeat Hillary Clinton and her urban supporters. . . . His most significant support came from counties in the industrial Midwest where whites without a college education are the majority. . . . Mrs. Clinton made gains in big metropolitan areas, but she was soundly rejected in smaller cities, especially in the industrial heartland."

—Larry Buchanan et al., *New York Times*, November 8, 2016

We don't have time to fuck around out here, money doesn't grow on trees. . . . Time to "man up" and get to work.

—Rick, twenty-seven-year-old farmhand in Kansas[26]

In the excerpt above from Buchanan et al.'s interactive *New York Times* graphic analysis of the 2016 US presidential election, we see a hybrid motif of the Midwest: the industrial heartland. The article authors identify the Midwestern voters supporting Donald Trump as white industrial workers without college educations. The notion of the industrial heartland interestingly fuses the well-established, covertly racialized white imagery of the pastoral heartland described earlier with the notion of an industrialized underclass. It is a race-class-gender formation that has been anchored in a place—the heartland or Midwest—and that derives cultural force from its regionalization. In this section, we closely analyze a second trope of whiteness and labor communicated through media coverage of the Midwest: the narrative of a hardworking, often masculine, white blue-collar worker who exhibits self-reliance, dignity, and humility by working hard and not expecting much under challenging conditions. Though this narrative paints a portrait of white economic restraint, it relies on and furthers a social compact of industrialism that assumes disproportionate white control of the social and economic benefits of industrial labor, covertly promoting specific values of industry and stewardship of financial resources that are racialized white.

In our media analysis, we strikingly found that twenty-four articles about the Midwest region referred to the "white working class." One article addressed the Republican plight of possibly alienating "older, working-class white voters" who need access to Obamacare and "live in small Midwestern cities" (*New York Times*, 3/19/17). Another pre-election piece builds on a sociologist's work to interview "white working-class voters in the Midwest" and finds that they may be put off if Trump does not pay his business debts, viewing it as a moral transgression (*Los Angeles Times*, 8/18/16). In an opinion piece, columnist Ross Douthat examines distinct economic and racial arguments for Trump's election among the "millions of working-class white voters in the Midwest" who supported Trump, concluding that in Douthat's estimation what looks like race baiting in Trump's rhetoric may actually be about economic inequality for those voters rather than white nationalism (*New York Times*, 11/11/18). This point is disputed in an opinion piece by Tamara Winfrey-Harris, also published in the *New York Times*. In this second piece, Winfrey-Harris argues that Black Midwesterners experiencing economic struggle did not find Trump's candidacy appealing and that white racism more likely compelled his election (*New York Times*, 6/16/18). Still another commentary urged Democrats seeking a new political strategy to not chase "conservative white working-class voters in the Midwest" but instead pursue white voters in battleground states who voted for third- and fourth-party independent candidates (*New York Times*, 2/21/17).

Cultural narratives of the Midwestern white working class exhibit several common features and subtexts. As mentioned earlier, white industrial workers are frequently imagined in media discourse to be individuals paying their debts to society who might view *not* doing so as a moral breach. What's notable about this is that it quietly but persistently associates whiteness, masculinity, and the working-class and, even more, characterizes a public of *millions* of white industrial workers as hardworking, responsible citizens. Their work ethic, economic struggle, and presumed ability to make do with little and not demand much in terms of public resources is part of what moralizes them *as a population* and produces a heroic story, arguably fueling forms of populism in which imagining white labor and masculine virtue in this way are central. The promotion of a Midwestern homogeneous white working-class population is not, however, a new claim, specific to the Trump era. It draws strength from a long history of creating white male laborers as a cultural category separate from Black laborers and workers of color. Building on the associative tracks laid by the moral figure of the white farmer described earlier, the Midwest region is quietly mobilized in this second narrative as an important theatrical frame for racial storytelling. The notion that the white working class simply exists in space—in the Midwest region—is a double move of whiteness, drawing strength from the historical whiteness of the Midwest category and the long-running construction of the white industrial worker as a racial category.

We can trace the notion of a racialized white, male, blue-collar worker to the eighteenth-century formation of the republic, and much further back to European state formation. Heartening and moving national stories have long been necessary, cultural theorist Lauren Berlant argues, because "the cultural expression of national fantasy is crucial for the political legitimacy of the nation: it is evidence of the nation's utopian promise to oversee a full and just integration of persons."[27] They are also critical to the economic legitimacy of capitalist systems that mete out unequal access to resources. Not all persons, after all, are imagined as part of this utopian project, and some are routinely considered obstacles to its fulfillment.

A more recent place to start in order to unravel the concept of the white blue-collar worker is the labor movement in the early twentieth century. In *Black Reconstruction*, W. E. B. Du Bois identified the "labor aristocracy" of trade unions in Germany, England, France, and the United States and argued that they provided "crucial support to the imperialism and colonialism of the late nineteenth century."[28] Though they made strides in terms of fighting for better wages and work conditions, trade unions cordoned off prestigious higher-wage jobs along white, European ethno-national racial lines and disbursed lower-wage, less desirable labor to racialized minorities and migrants within those states or through offshore production in colonial territories. This built on a much longer European history of racial discrimination toward immigrant ethnic groups that were thought not to embody the racial, historical, linguistic, and cultural qualities of the nation, such as Irish canal builders in England and Polish laborers in eastern Germany, but who were nonetheless essential to European economies.[29] In the late nineteenth century United States, labor unions often organized initially through the same channels of ethno-national trade unions among immigrant Europeans. And this continued into the Progressive movement.[30] When a segregated Black hospital was being built in St. Louis in the mid-1930s, unionized white tile setters protested the one Black laborer who had been hired until

the city relented and fired the contractor.[31] Racism fueled labor union organizing in its heyday, partly because white working-class laborers feared that
free Black workers would devalue the prestige of their jobs and erode the
white cultural capital or "wage" they gained from the company they kept.[32]

The way these racial politics played out in different sectors of manufacturing and industrial work was not always so simple as white workers blocking
Black, Latinx, and other workers of color from access to all jobs (though that
did of course also occur). Rather, the shifting labor hierarchy fed into and
reinforced the shifting racial hierarchy, often maintaining Anglo white access
to the most prestigious, well-paying jobs. In the next several paragraphs, we
map some of these important social and historical influences that shaped the
white industrial worker, bringing forward the exclusionary history left out of
contemporary news stories. The early twentieth-century meatpacking industry, for example, featured an ethnic and racial labor division that was similar across operations in Chicago, Omaha, Milwaukee, and East St. Louis.[33]
German, Irish, and Bohemian workers often took the skilled butcher work,
while Eastern Europeans did lower-skill jobs. The Great Migration of Black
workers for industrial work in northern cities changed this ethnic breakdown of meatpacking jobs and, by 1922, Black workers held one-third of
Chicago's meat industry jobs while 5.7 percent of workers were Mexican in
1928. The 1930s and 1940s saw some important multiracial union organizing,
such as through the United Packinghouse Workers of America, and this had
the effect of raising wages in the post–World War II period. However, by
the 1970s and 1980s, multiple transformations in how meat processing was
done and the move of facilities to rural areas near farms gradually worked
to dismantle the ability of unions to maintain well-paying jobs. As a result,
the hard-working, white Rust Belt worker familiar across current media
portraits is a product of nostalgia for the social and economic benefits and
lifestyles made possible by those earlier well-paying jobs, as well as a cultural
figure that historically helped maintain unequal access to them.

In addition, a different but equally significant influence on the complex of
values associated with white blue-collar work can be seen in long-standing
racialized conceptions of worthy and unworthy workers. One common
trope in this vein is what scholars refer to as the derogatory notion of the
"nonindustrious Mexican," which dates to the nineteenth century but has
become part of the openly racist symbolism of the twenty-first century
United States. Cultural studies scholar Lee Bebout notes that this trope

RENDERING.

PORK PACKI

Chromo-Lithogra h of the Cartoons exhibited by the Cincinn

FIGURE 8. Pork packing in Cincinnati, 1873. The print shows four scenes in a packing house: "Killing," "Cutting," "Rendering," and "Salting." Wikimedia Commons.

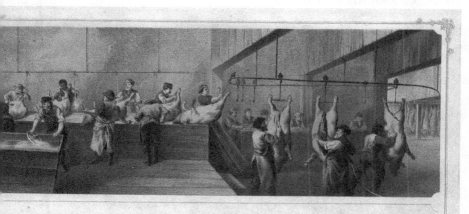

SALTING.

CINCINNATI.

FIGURE 9. Swift Brands, South Chicago, meatpacking plant, circa 1917, Wikimedia Commons.

characterizes Mexican workers as "needing a differently racialized managerial class to bring them into modernity."[34] Related cultural discourses also trade in ideas of Mexican American perpetual foreignness, even after generations of citizenship, to homogeneously characterize Mexican migrants and Mexican American laborers as "invading" and "taking American jobs."[35] When taken together, these troublingly prevalent narratives can be seen as actually related to how the humility and dignity of white industrial work is often treated by contrast in the mass media. White independent labor, self-reliance, diligence, and deservedness come forward through all of these sources because they imply time and again that white working-class laborers are facing a rigged system *as a raced and classed population* in spite of their dignified and merited efforts to secure work. They also point blame at other racialized populations, rather than engaging in a more searching way with the systemic and uneven inequalities of global capitalism that affect working people more broadly.

The historical labor conditions and exclusions of white industrial work were also upheld through a vast web of de jure (legal) restrictions that claimed to have nothing to do with race (but did). Historian Richard Rothstein points out, for example, that in order to pass Franklin Roosevelt's New Deal in 1938, which sought to establish a fair minimum wage, lawmakers had to make a concession with southern politicians that the new wage policy would exclude the agricultural industries where African Americans predominated, keeping Black wages lower than white wages.[36] When housing discrimination was formally rendered illegal through the Fair Housing Act of 1968, a raft of financial policies across the banking and insurance industries advanced racial residential segregation through redlining, thereby producing through white flight the racialized urban-rural divide referenced in current news reporting.[37] Therefore, even in cases of integrated (but often unequal) industrial workplaces, Black laborers were prevented from living in the same neighborhoods as their white coworkers. White fears of losing the value of their homes and a decline in resources for local schools if neighborhoods were racially integrated powered racist policies and narratives of homogeneous white spaces and white labor with real financial stakes, not only in the Midwest but across the nation.

And government documents and policies played a part in moralizing these urban-rural associations of race and labor in the American imagination, without honestly claiming the role of government policies in subsidizing white wealth and segregating neighborhoods in the first place. The controversial 1965 Moynihan Report, titled *The Negro Family: The Case for National Action*, set forth the idea of an undeserving urban Black underclass that presumably relied on (white) suburban and rural taxpayers and contrasted it with a deserving white working class, catalyzing white racial "opposition to social welfare policies."[38] These influential racial associations of work, space, and public resources fueled narratives of fairness and unfairness that persist to this day, making urban spaces "synonymous with Blackness and a familiar theory of Black moral failings."[39] By contrast, the cultural association of rural, flyover, heartland, and Rust Belt spaces with the white working class reinforced a durable set of connections to industrial labor and self-reliance. Yet without an open accounting of how Black laborers and workers of color were systematically blocked from the greatest financial and social benefits of industrialism and white laborers were structurally enabled, these pernicious stories endure and reinforce myths of superior white merit and deservingness.

Researchers have looked at how these complex politics of labor and race continue to play out in contemporary Midwestern communities, shedding further light on how the deepening economic inequality of deindustrialization fueled nativist white sentiments. In *Global Heartland*, scholar of globalization Faranak Miraftab describes how the neighboring towns of Beardstown and Rushville, Illinois, pursued two different strategies to gain jobs during the tumultuous deindustrialization of the 1980s. Both Illinois towns were known as "sundown towns" that had maintained their white homogeneity over the twentieth century through violence toward people of color, such as burning down the house of a Mexican family in the mid-1990s in Rushville the night before they moved in.[40] During the deindustrializing 1980s and 1990s, Rushville lobbied to be the site for a high-security prison and Beardstown, known historically as "Porkopolis," acquired a meat processing facility. While the prison industrial complex hired a white labor force, the meat industry eventually changed the racial composition of Beardstown. The company running the meatpacking plant, which by the 1990s had successfully battled unions and won, standardized the plant's slaughter work into a series of repetitive yet high-injury tasks while reducing wages and benefits. White workers used to better pay and conditions retired or looked for work elsewhere, such as in trucking. As a result of the shrinking labor pool, the company took to recruiting a transnational labor force of Mexican, Guinean, and Senegalese immigrants. Miraftab relays how, even though white workers did not want the kind of work the meat processing facility offered, immigrant workers were often treated by white residents of Beardstown as if they had "taken American jobs," leading to harassment, violence and even the resurgence of the local KKK. In spite of evidence to the contrary, some white residents fit the changing racial composition and labor practices of Beardstown into much more widely circulating exclusionary narratives about "fairness" and "American jobs" with a clear set of recurring claims to the whiteness of industrial work.[41]

In current news reporting, we can hear these white claims of fairness when industrial workers are characterized as not expecting much from the system while paying their debts to society. Sometimes, quoted Midwesterners make these unfairness narratives and their racial content explicit to reporters. In a feature-length *Wall Street Journal* profile of Midwestern voters, one sixty-nine-year-old white male agricultural instructor in eastern Iowa was asked what local residents had told him about why they voted for Trump. He was quoted as saying: "Number one, they said minority political people have been well taken care of. Small business and working people have been identified as the source of income to take care of those people" (*Wall Street Journal*, 5/13/2018). The "working people" mentioned by

FIGURE 10. Reconditioning used spark plugs for the war effort, Melrose Park, Illinois, Buick plant, July 1942, Wikimedia Commons.

the agricultural instructor is a thinly coded reference to whiteness, while "minority political people" are of course people of color. Rarely however are the references quite this explicit.

Other articles reinforce the flip side of unfairness narratives by building up the moralism of white workers through their economic austerity and scrupulousness. A young white businessman in rural Illinois commented: "This is an area [where] we try to work hard, play by the rules. It's not a fast pace, it's not a fancy pace, but we appreciate it" (*Wall Street Journal*, 5/13/2018). Another white woman in northwestern Illinois, when describing the struggles of making ends meet as a single mother earning $11 an hour, made clear to the reporter that "she declined to go on Medicaid, although she was eligible to use it. 'I've always paid my own way,' she said" (*Wall Street Journal*, 5/13/2018). Here, scrupulousness, modesty and restraint prefigure a racialization of financial thrift. De-industrial narratives of whiteness, and especially their moralizing claims, rely on an imagined Other unfairly working the system, spending ostentatiously, and gaining work without personal sacrifice. This demonstrates how much industrialism was oriented around the social reproduction of white values, sensibilities, and entitlements as much as it was an economic system. When people in Midwestern news reporting today reflect on generically white hardships, they draw upon and give new life to racial logics, which have long associated whiteness with economic and political resources or economic security. At a time of deindustrialization, those values can seem antiquated, a thing of the past, and yet for that reason they become more entrenched in a place, emblematic of both lauded, old-fashioned ways and of being stuck and unable to move on.

If industrialism was dominantly characterized by this notion of virtuous white labor, deindustrialization has often likewise been constructed as a white moral drama tied to the Rust Belt, rather than something that might be experienced differently depending on whether an industrial worker is Latinx, Arab American, Black, white, Native American, or Asian American. To some extent, narratives of deindustrialization continue the earlier work of whiteness tied to the disenfranchisements of the Reconstruction era.[42] The cultural figure of the Midwestern industrial worker is inextricably tied to the dismantling of slavery, industrialization, and the subsequent forms that the racialization of labor took in the Reconstruction period. As historian Richard Rothstein notes, when African Americans migrated to northern cities for industrial work in the early twentieth century, "federal, state, and local governments collaborated with private employers to ensure they were paid less and treated worse than whites."[43] Yet current reporting on the white working class neglects these histories. It also ignores to some degree how white supremacy has been enacted and made palpably visible through public stagings of white labor and white economic stewardship with theatrical dimensions (often ignoring how multiethnic and multiracial industrial workforces actually operated). Put another way, obscuring the complex, discriminatory history of the category of the white worker is exactly what makes the white working class available to be rediscovered with each generation as if it has been lost and forgotten, an apparent "surprise" that activates its political power.[44]

Our evidence to some degree charts a set of cultural narratives of white labor, industry, and value, linked to the downward mobility and narrowing field of opportunity of industrial communities, which played a crucial role in the 2016 election. It suggests that circulating scripts of whiteness and industrial capitalism are produced in an ongoing fashion and that seeing them reflected across a variety of sites, such as news reporting on the Midwest in the years leading up to the election (2010–2019), may have in turn increased their political influence. A mutually-reinforcing, circular process becomes visible: familiar scripts of whiteness, appearing in many forms, confirmed for some the shared struggles and values of a white working class; this idea in turn strengthened the cultural notion of the existence of a white working class with shared political and economic interests.

In the ensuing months after the 2016 election, journalists scrambled to document the white working class as an electorate with distinct needs and political persuasions, and arguably tried to make up for being blindsided by the election outcome.[45] In addition to feature stories, opinion pieces, and political analysis, scholarship on the white working class formed part of the media blitz. Sociologist Arlie Hochschild's book *Strangers in Their Own Land* on anti-regulation white Tea Party participants, though based on research in Louisiana's petrochemical corridor, became part of a media attempt to produce cultural knowledge on the white working class, now seen as an elusive and forgotten group. Other works harnessed in this project were Nancy Isenberg's *White Trash* and J. D. Vance's *Hillbilly Elegy*.[46] One National Public Radio (NPR) story on Hochschild's book, for instance, is subtitled "The Deep Story of Trump's Supporters" and suggests her work offers insight into "white, heterosexual, working-class Americans," regardless of region (NPR, 1/24/17). In her book, Hochschild portrays the Midwest and South as white, insular, and rural, at one point observing, "The rural Midwest and South need the cosmopolitan outreach to a diverse wider world."[47] Yet by homogenizing regions racially and taking for granted that a singular "white working class" exists and that journalists and scholars must only find and document it, mass media reporting took part in a more far-reaching process of racialization. It became a performative space, a stage to witness and affirm a claim of white labor with a deep and discriminatory history.

IV. WHITE SUFFERING, HAUNTED LANDSCAPES

"In Rust Belt towns that few national reporters bothered to visit, I didn't find many racists or rednecks (some, but not many). The mainstream media caricature of angry blue-collar whites turning to Trump out of racial animosity and misogyny didn't stand up to scrutiny.... Their support for him has a different explanation: respect. Trump was the first national political figure in generations who saw them, acknowledged that they have been left behind, that their cities and towns are in a state of persistent decline, and promised to help out somehow."

—John Daniel Davidson, *The Federalist*, November 10, 2016

Journalist John Daniel Davidson uses stark polemical language in this paragraph from a 2016 *Federalist* article to challenge "media caricatures" of working-class whites, though some of the ways he qualifies his statement ("some but not many") simultaneously reproduce problematic classist notions of blue-collar white voters. His somewhat subtler and more careful portrait of the Midwest region as a deindustrialized Rust Belt warrants further attention. Davidson points to the region as characterized by a period of "persistent decline," while implying that political and cultural elites have largely ignored this process. These arguments are meant to account for voter support of Trump's rhetoric and anti-globalist policies, such as trade tariffs. In our third section, we explore an emotional state visible between the lines of this portrait: white suffering.[48]

White suffering is partly communicated in media discourse through references to economic struggle and the unrelenting downturn of the economy in Midwestern communities. Pieces frequently gloss these issues in their description of the Midwest, referring to the region's "sagging economy" (*Washington Post*, 11/1/10), "economic destitution," "decay," "struggle" (*Washington Post* 1/11/11), "devastation," and lack of recovery (*Washington Post*, 5/13/18). Going into greater detail, one *Washington Post* feature article described the job losses of residents in Morrison, Illinois, where a General Electric plant had once employed four to five thousand people, then twenty-five hundred, until it closed in 2010 (*Washington Post*, 5/13/18). Morrison's mayor, a former plant manager, was quoted as saying: "We used to have three or four small mom-and-pop grocery stores. We have one major grocery store now, which we're thankful for. . . . We had women's clothing stores, men's clothing stores, shoe stores. All of that was up and down Main Street. They were the small-business people. We don't have any of those anymore. . . . We had a country club. We no longer have one." The losses described by the Morrison mayor are real and suffered across the United States in many communities as a result of neoliberal policies. However, their frequent description in Midwestern news reporting also carries substantial affective weight and makes Midwestern spaces mediums of loss itself. Combined with the whitening of industrial work, such tropes secure these losses as white and communicate white suffering without ever directly naming it (see chapter 3).

White suffering happens in media discourse not only through the descriptive arsenal of economic struggle but also through scenes of haunted, gloomy, and declining deindustrialized Midwestern spaces and through job-loss statistics. In these portraits, both numerical and figurative, the past is overwhelmingly present: hulking shells of factories, curling weeds in parking lots, and shuttered businesses tell a story of a by-gone, more glorious past.

They alert the reader's senses to a postindustrial memoryscape where meaning bubbles up to the surface. White suffering is premised on this contrast of past and present and by all of the ways the present falls short. Yet by referencing a way things were through the absent presence of what is, the racial, social, and economic order of industrialism is mourned and imagined as a superior way of life. Such "post-industrial" suffering is in fact deeply multiracial and experienced in less publicly visible, yet acute ways by workers of color. However, the affective landscape of the deindustrialized Midwest is dominantly racialized white in popular media. One could extend these ideas to note that, due to pervasive circulating representations in film, television, music, news media, fiction and other images, the affective experience of loss associated with formerly industrial Midwestern towns and factories *is* whiteness, just as the affective experiences associated in the twentieth century with "urban" spaces in the United States *make* Blackness. How we see and feel about these spaces and what they represent is a crucial part of how race works culturally in subterranean, and not-so-subterranean, ways.

Through its public performance in media discourse, Midwestern white suffering—communicated through spaces, lost jobs, and intimate portraits—also makes its audience as much as it validates widely circulating racial scripts. It helps to produce moral spectators who witness and palpably feel the struggle of some individuals and spaces, humanizing them, while forestalling empathetic identification with the hardships and communities of workers of color. Here, feeling does the work of politics: it makes white experiences relatable and worthy of compassion. And even if these scenes do not elicit compassion per se but rather a sense of distance and class distinction, they nonetheless further an association of Midwestern spaces, loss and industrialism, braiding together several cultural narratives of white labor.

The suffering subject is a familiar moral trope in international aid organizations and one that can elicit sympathy and intervention. Narratives of suffering, whether through poverty, natural disaster, civil unrest, or disease outbreak, are often used to compel a response to crisis on the part of Western donors. Frequently such narratives reproduce racialized depictions of bodily suffering, portraying through photography, illness statistics, and personal stories Brown and Black individuals in regions of Africa, Asia, and Latin America as aid recipients. As James Baldwin said about overly sentimental political novels, such as *Uncle Tom's Cabin*, they may be filled with details about wretched lives, but "far from being disturbing, [they are] an accepted and comforting aspect of the American scene, ramifying the framework we believe to be so necessary."[49] Among other things, calls to end suffering, whether in a novel or a simple request for a donation, can covertly "ramify" the role of white savior called to sweep in and relieve hardship.[50] Proliferating mass-media depictions of global suffering, some argue, are a voyeuristic outgrowth of debilitating, debt-servicing policies in former colonies as well as the rise of economic inequality in various forms around the world. Yet by making intervention a matter of individual moral compassion, fragmented aid responses maintain, rather than alleviate, the root structural causes of economic hardship and poor health care infrastructure, obscuring the colonial and neoliberal policies that have perpetuated global inequality.

When we apply these insights to postindustrial suffering in the Midwest, several significant similarities and differences become evident. First, aid agencies often promote one-dimensional portraits of aid recipients of color, which ignore their cultural and historical context and agency while magnifying white responsiveness to global inequalities. However, dominant racial forms also rely on the social production of figures of compassion, in that they similarly help consolidate white moral spectatorship and empathetic identification toward white people. Mass-mediated figures of white suffering could also be analyzed for the way they elicit sympathy and care in their audiences.

Choreographies of white suffering can be, like representations of aid recipients, rather flat and one-dimensional portraits; however, such mass-mediated depictions do not necessarily undermine white agency. Instead they uphold white supremacy by casting disproportionate attention on white economic struggle, whether through job loss statistics, haunted deindustrialized landscapes, or nostalgic yearning for the past. Secondly, such scene-setting has the similar humanitarian effect of depicting the deindustrialized Midwest as a space in crisis and ripe for intervention, a region needing people "to help out somehow," in the words of the journalist John Daniel Davidson cited earlier. As with other narratives of Midwestern white industry, these qualities build a compelling moral story that can lead to action. The humanitarian intervention strongly recommended through scenes of white suffering is one that brings jobs back or provides some kind of economic or political relief. By affectively describing the losses of deindustrialized Midwestern spaces, an overarching message—characteristic of many forms of intervention—is that action is necessary if not imperative to relieve suffering.

V. THE BACKSTAGE OF WHITE SCRIPTS

Let's return briefly to the three moral scripts of whiteness. They also carry counter-scripts or elements that remain backstage or hidden from view in the work of making whiteness, a multi-stranded and pervasive cultural project with overt and covert dimensions.[51] As a result, mass-mediated white moral dramas have many understudies or actors who prop up the production behind the scenes or who fall outside the spotlight of white myth making. These silenced or erased elements are worth analyzing because, to take the dramaturgical lens a step further, they help facilitate the production of whiteness through their very invisibility.

Most significantly, naturalizing the connection between the Midwest and white workers erases the region's ethnic and racial diversity.[52] While some pieces in our sample referred to Black voters in Michigan being "unenthused" by Hillary Clinton's candidacy (New York Times, 2/21/17), for example, only a few of our news articles commented on the broader occlusion of Midwestern racial diversity in discussions of the election, with the most prominent being "Stop Pretending Black Midwesterners Don't Exist." In this opinion piece, Indianapolis-based journalist Tamara Winfrey-Harris writes, "I am a Black woman born and raised in the space between the coasts and above the Mason-Dixon line. I am a face of the heartland, but you might not know it if you've been following the Trump-era reporting and commentary about the lives and political choices of people in the Midwest" (New York Times, 6/16/18). Winfrey-Harris goes on to observe that the region in which she lives is, in the minds of many Americans, "synonymous with whiteness." This stereotype ignores the seven million African Americans currently living in the Midwest region, more than in the West or in the Northeast, and the history of the Great Migration of African Americans seeking work in northern cities from the 1910s to the 1970s. It also perpetually whitens the working class in national discourse, when the working class is increasingly populated by people of color.[53]

These omissions in representations of labor are not the only consequences of associating the Midwest with white workers. By focusing on white struggle, mass-mediated narratives of the white industrial worker also conceal the racialized structural inequality of Midwestern towns, including residential segregation, disproportionate police profiling, incarceration rates, and employment and housing discrimination among African Americans and people of color. According to the US Office of Civil Rights, the six Great

Lakes states had the most segregated schools in the nation at the beginning of the 1990s.[54] Yet only two articles in our sample, besides Winfrey-
Harris's op-ed piece, addressed systemic racism. A *Los Angeles Times* article
reported on how various Democratic candidates for the 2020 presidential
nomination observed Martin Luther King Jr.'s birthday and hinted at a
strategic trade-off between appealing to "white working-class voters in the
Midwest" and acknowledging systemic racism (*Los Angeles Times*, 1/22/19).
Through a more in-depth and historical approach, the article "'Sundown
Towns': Midwest Confronts Its Complicated Racial Legacy" described how
Utica, Ohio, and Goshen, Indiana, among other cities like Beardstown and
Rushville, Illinois, mentioned earlier, were known as towns where African
Americans were violently denied housing and jobs from the 1890s until the
1940s, effectively manufacturing white racial homogeneity (*Christian Science
Monitor*, 3/27/17). One recent survey by the American Studies scholar David
Roediger of Kansas State University has even established that former sundown towns in Wisconsin played a decisive role in Trump's razor-thin 2016
election in that state.[55] The moral drama of the white working class thus
conceals persistent, historically rooted forms of structural inequality linked
to race and class in Midwestern communities.

With the exceptions of Trump's tariff war and the loss of manufacturing jobs through deindustrialization, news reporting also frequently elides
mention of the globalizing characteristics of Midwestern communities. As
with other US regions, historical and contemporary migrations, whether of
foreign workers, exiles, refugees, or other border crossers, have fostered complex politics of inclusion and exclusion within Midwestern communities, as
well as Midwest-based forms of diasporic belonging and identification with
places elsewhere.[56] Over the past thirty years, Midwest cities and towns have
been transformed by the "largest wave of immigration in U.S. history."[57] In
Minnesota, for example, emigres from Vietnam, Cambodia, Laos, Mexico,
Somalia, and Ethiopia have faced pervasive forms of institutionalized discrimination upon their settlement in the United States.[58] Nuer (Sudanese)
refugees in Minnesota, for instance, have struggled with racism and many of
the problems of the American working poor: the cost of living and managing
money; working jobs in meatpacking and fast-food industries with low wages
and third-shift hours; finding transportation to the locations of work in large,
urban areas; and affording child care and medical care.[59] We have found that
these issues are much less frequently reported on in national news coverage of

the Midwest region, which focus unduly on the plight and concerns of white farmers or former industrial workers. Due to the parochialism and whiteness frequently ascribed to notions of the Midwest in US history, both of the authors have experienced interlocutors expressing "surprise" to discover the multiracial migrant populations, refugees, globalizing forces, and diasporic experiences of people and places in the Midwest region.

Furthermore, as it has been deployed in contemporary media, the suffering white subject, like other kinds of humanitarian discourse, avoids deeper structural questions. The affective theater of white suffering associated with Midwest deindustrialization turns compassion into an end point and an incitement to action, while implying that global outsourcing (i.e., workers of color elsewhere) is to blame for white malaise. This narrative of white loss obscures recognition of the way people and places in other so-defined US regions, as well as elsewhere in the world, have participated in capitalist processes that invested, benefited from, lost ground to, and de-invested in Midwest manufacturing.[60] Such capitalist processes have devastated many Midwestern communities and tied them intricately to labor, production, and financial markets in other locales, both in the United States and abroad. However, these capitalist processes are fundamentally uneven and do not affect all Midwestern communities equally. As Reno argues in the context of a large landfill in rural Michigan, the transformation of neglected backwaters into literal waste sites is facilitated by the systemic unevenness of capitalist cycles of investment and divestiture. As a result, rural locales gradually emptied of human, economic, and political capital appear ripe for large and/or unpopular developments, from landfills and incinerators to casinos and wetlands.

Therefore, it is not that the entire Midwest is a Rust Belt suffering a similar fate or that the Rust Belt is a shared racial experience. Narratives of white suffering conceal class inequality and the possibility of shared class interests across racial lines. Capitalist processes in the Midwest have produced a patchy field of towns and residents that suffer incredibly, while other, neighboring areas reap the benefits of capital investment. Painting the Midwest in a unitary fashion—and associating loss only with white workers—obscures appreciation of the swift and devastating effects of capitalist processes of investment and dispossession and whose interests they ultimately serve.

Finally, the historical qualities of white moral narratives are erased in contemporary media discourse. This is especially evident in the discriminatory history of the white laborer, a category that arose in part as a point of social distinction from the free Black worker and Euro-ethnic, Mexican, Chinese, and Japanese immigrant and non-immigrant labor. Erasures are also visible regarding the history of the Midwest's participation in global markets that led to forms of inequality and struggle among Midwesterners, well before deindustrialization. Nostalgia for a glorious bygone industrial past—or an agricultural one—leaves out their always-present hardships and uncertainties. As we argued in chapter 2, the pastoral aesthetic was not a natural feature of some Midwestern landscapes, but the large-scale mono-cropping of corn was an artificial product of the Midwest's central role in worldwide agricultural markets.[61] Meatpacking was already a big cross-regional business in Chicago by 1900, when fourteen million live animals were sent on railcar for slaughter in the Northeast.[62] The later Dust Bowl, so much an icon of prairie Midwestern spaces, was blamed by some at the time on capitalist modernity and specifically on the exhausting demand of supplying wheat to Europe, which accelerated soil erosion.[63] Though it was not widely used in national discourse until the 1960s, the "Rust Belt" term is indicative of how the Midwest region was woven into broader national and global economic processes of manufacturing and industry, a process that actually began with the late nineteenth-century incorporation of the Midwest into globalizing agricultural markets.[64]

VI. CONCLUSION

All art is political in the sense that it serves someone's politics. Here in America whites have a particular view of blacks. I think my plays offer them a different way to look at black Americans. For instance, in *Fences* they see a garbage man, a person they don't really look at, although they see a garbage man every day. By looking at Troy's life, white people find out that the content of this black garbage man's life is affected by the same things—love, honor, beauty, betrayal, duty. Recognizing that these things are as much part of his life as theirs can affect how they think about and deal with black people in their lives."

—August Wilson (quoted in Lyons and Plimpton 1999)

A celebrated playwright raised in the famed (post)industrial city of Pittsburgh, August Wilson's use of the stage to portray the humanity of Black workers is vital and necessary, in part, because audiences in America and around the world are all too familiar with unstaged but no less performative scripts depicting what white workers are supposed to be like (though, there are also plenty on the stage like Willy Loman and Stanley Kowalski who immediately come to mind). Media representations of white virtues are more than just talk. Like a play you see acted in the flesh, as opposed to one you read off the page, they reach out to and move their audiences in a visceral way. Reporting on the Midwest produces just such an affective theater, in which moral dramas of white labor are defined, watched, felt, and reinforced through the interplay of represented words, images and lived realities. In particular, recent mass-mediated discourse on the Midwest amplifies the theme of white industry and the notion that white labor is persistently undervalued, a site of economic struggle, and even unjustly ignored. The implied hiddenness of white labor has the effect of making the Midwest a repository and site of a beleaguered white underclass in the mass media. To some extent, the familiarity of some of these narrative arcs, so long associated with Midwest agriculture, manufacturing, and the heavily publicized decline of opportunity in Midwestern communities, enables them to largely escape critical attention. Yet white supremacy is arguably consolidated through these disparate, compelling scripts of white labor and deservingness publicly played out in the region.

These scripts fundamentally rely on and perpetuate the historical association of the Midwest with the dominant social and racial entitlements of industrial capitalism. Reconceptualizing media discourse as a cultural practice with a complex and far-reaching historical and global spread sheds light on how the Midwest has long been a screen or stage onto which forms of global white supremacy have been sustained, reworked, performed, and influenced.[65] Seen through this lens, represented performances of whiteness in Midwest news reporting are not simply about individual identity formations of whiteness or about nationalism alone but, as Beliso-De Jesús and Pierre put it, they are about "the systematic deployment of white supremacy as a structuring logic that serves as the baseline for modernity and its cognates of liberalism, democracy, progress, and rationality."[66] Therefore, national news discourse is a space for articulating and challenging these underpinning logics of dominance, including those of race and white supremacy in particular.[67]

Newspaper articles can quietly and consistently draw from an emotional landscape that supports white nationalist viewpoints and thinking, as they have in the United States for generations.[68] Everyone in racialized societies like the United States, including journalists, are swimming in cultural narratives that promote white industry and often associate it with the Midwest.

Sometimes these narratives are critically engaged with and questioned. But most of the time they become part of the assumed backdrop of tacitly made associations and storylines and get evoked effortlessly. They can feed into journalistic tropes and areas of investigation ("Trump voters in the heartland") or discourage writing on subjects that do not fit regional associations ("Muslim Midwesterners"). And, just as feelings of white indignation, loss, and anger can pervade national storytelling, these views can also influence more extremist and violent white power organizations. For instance, in the documentary *Alt-Right: Age of Rage* (2018) white supremacist Richard Spencer discusses his fantasy of a white "ethno-nation," and, in a US map on an alt-right website, much of this post-US imaginary state is located in the Midwest—apparently Nazis still think of the region as ripe for invasion (see chapter 4). Racial storytelling can be put to many different ends, some much more violent and extremist than others. Questioning recurrent story lines in the media that equate the Midwest with whiteness is important for a generations-long cultural reckoning with structural racism. It is also one way to challenge the attempt on the part of alt-right groups to draw from and use the national myth of the white American heartland to root their ideology in a place.

Looking into how news discourse reproduces dominant narratives of race, empire, and nation is central to developing a more critical understanding of contemporary politics as they are lived in the United States. The media storylines we have outlined, precisely because they are simultaneously obvious and obscure, can quietly and cumulatively transform how people imagine such impactful subjects as who has industriously created the country we find today, who is deserving of social support, who has worked for what they have received, who is a "real American," and so on.[69] Regional references operate not only in our talk, as in overt mentions of a shared Midwest character, but frequently circulate through a variety of interwoven communicative media that combine the resources of words, images, and bodies into compelling and moving narratives. These include stereotypic cultural images of folksy or backward Midwestern people, maps and paintings, national myths, allusions to "flyover country," economic and government profiles, and that which the Midwest is imagined not to be (e.g., global, cosmopolitan, Eastern, or coastal). Considering the wide-ranging and disparate cultural field from which regional stories draw and to which they contribute is key to mapping their role in contemporary forms of global white supremacy. The risk of not doing so is to affirm the dubious claim that entire regions can make history, swing elections, or experience uniform kinds of alienation and disaffection, when such claims are actually partaking in a project of whiteness, nationalism, and empire that is far older and more insidious than is commonly acknowledged.

J: What seems challenging to you about being a white person writing about whiteness and the Midwest, in particular?

B: In this cultural moment, a lot of white people are claiming to know a lot about racism and race and how they operate in the world. So there's a real risk of writing about something that white people especially have been deeply ignorant about as a condition of American experience. People of color, Black people, and indigenous people know, feel, and live the experiences of our book—the exclusionary qualities of Midwest narratives—in a way that I have never personally experienced.

J: I agree, and that has made us more careful in choosing strategies for this book project. Our reflections, for instance, are meant to put our personal experiences front and center, so we can't hide behind facts and theory and leave aside the fact that we have had particular and very privileged experiences in some ways. At the same time, while there is discomfort that comes from being white and writing about whiteness, in this moment as you point out, it is also uncomfortable to write about oneself, especially if you are trained, like we both have been, to be social scientists. That is a different kind of discomfort, though. What has it been like for you?

B. To me, one of the goals of those reflections has been to highlight all the things we didn't know and didn't get as we were growing up—and how white supremacy is absolutely built on that partialness of white experience and all the disconnects it entails. All this takes a lifetime to uncover, to me, through a lot of unlearning, reading, listening, critical thinking, paying attention. For me, that's where the Midwest comes in, in a variety of complicated ways. Because of the inescapability of white supremacy in the United States today, I think it can be appealing for some white progressives to distance themselves from the effects of white racism by identifying other white people who don't get it or who seem simply to be bad white people, unsophisticated, closed minded and unaccepting of difference. How have you come across these issues of whiteness and the Midwest as we've been writing the book, as you've described the project to other people?

J: One thing that has happened to me on more than one occasion is that I begin talking about our book to a white friend, colleague, or family member and am unable to finish explaining what it is about before my interlocutor already begins saying something to the effect that they believe a book like this, by someone who looks like me, is necessary, presumably for someone who looks like them. Already this positions us as "good whites"—me for merely writing about white supremacy at all, no matter what I have to say about it, them as white people receptive to a book like this, in order to signal a separation from the bad whites that they assume we found associated with the Midwest. In a way, as a result of the way white supremacy works, its inescapability as you put it, you and I will gain advantages for having written it in part premised on being white and doing so. That is the part that bothers me the most, I think, not only by what right we talk about these issues, but that no matter what we say, we will gain advantage from a system that rewards white people disproportionately, including for writing on white privilege! That is the thing I am ashamed to have learned quite late in my academic career, or learned I need to unlearn as you put it, that academic life is not a lofty utopia separate from these systemic disadvantages. But that would be true whether or not we were writing about the Midwest. In your case, you are from there, have family from there. Are the stakes different for you as a result?

B: I can relate to that feeling of unease at the unearned privilege of being a white person writing about white supremacy. I have also worried about this book simply reinforcing elite whites' sense of the Midwest. I've sometimes found myself in conversations with white people who seem convinced that, finally, we'll write a great exposé about those terrible white people in the Midwest! This fairly common misperception bothers me a lot, for many reasons. One of the things I've found myself struggling against is strangely prevalent ideas from white folks I've met—most of whom have never spent time in the Midwest—about what the region is "really" like. These convictions of the Midwest as filled with disaffected and insular, unsophisticated white working-class people seem so bombastically overdrawn. They don't fit with my experiences living in mid-size Midwest cities, knowing quite a few people who did not grow up in the United States (including in my own family) and being in communities with people of different class positions and racial identities (as is the case all over the United States).

J: At the same time, I encounter more people with ideas about what Southern whites, Appalachian whites, New England whites are really like (and how racist they are). In Upstate New York, where I grew up and now live, we used to refer to people just to the south of us as from "Pennsyl-tucky" in a portmanteau that positioned (rural) Pennsylvanians as less

Eastern, more working class, less "Blue" during elections and more "Purple," less sophisticated and more Appalachian than we were even though we had family from there, my father was raised there! My point is that there is this contradictory mix of reactions that we've tried to capture in this book, about the Midwest being prototypically full of bad whites *and* it being not as bad as some other regions or places in the country, meaning less openly racially toxic. I have found that that quality, the not-as-bad or more middling character of the region, has made it just as difficult for me to write about and has also encouraged us to include writing on sundown towns and white mob violence like in Tulsa. It is hard to strike that balance, but necessary to avoid the bad white/boring white dichotomy.

B: I agree—and I think striking that balance is one of the things that has been hard in writing this book. In general, if people look for easy narratives, the one we provide is not so "easy" because it fundamentally relies on our readers being implicated in everything we write about. I'm hopeful that people will be able to see how they're caught up in everything we discuss, not separate from it.

Conclusion

In April 2020, national news outlets covered two different stories in quick succession. One focused on Sinai-Grace Hospital in Detroit, where exasperated health care workers had leaked stark images of the stored dead to show the hospital's inability to keep up with the coronavirus death toll in the nearby Black communities it serves. The very next day national news coverage shifted to the stay-at-home protests of mostly white men, women, and teens on the capitol steps in Lansing. Widely published images showed people holding signs with messages like "Set Us Free" and "Trump, Lock Up the Nazi Woman from Michigan," referring to Michigan's governor, Gretchen Whitmer. These images would return to the national spotlight in February 2021, when Congressman Jamie Raskin called the Michigan protests and later plot to kidnap Governor Whitmer a "dress rehearsal" for the January 6 mob attack at the US Capitol in Washington.

Of these two sets of images from the spring of 2020, which one is likely to be labeled and circulated as an image of the Midwest? Of America? Regardless of the intent of the person doing the labeling, regardless of their political leanings, our research suggests the latter. Whether the white folks in question are considered aggrieved and virtuous freedom-fighters or entitled and unaware of their own privilege, the imagined Midwest is taken to be their stage on which to perform. Most people in the world would likely agree that Michigan is "in the Midwest," territorially speaking, and that Detroit is "in

Michigan." Our point, throughout this book, has been that region is not only territory or, better said, that "territory" in a society indelibly shaped by settler colonialism and transatlantic slavery, is a complex and contested *claim* about the world and not a natural *property* of that world. As a result, someone can know an image is set in Detroit, in Michigan, in the Midwest, in the United States, and yet it becomes loaded with meaning that relates to those spatial correlations. A Black body does not automatically denote Midwestness and Americanness, in general, but especially when further shorn of all social context and social relations, shown without family and community to grieve the loss. Scholars of race have made similar points about the wrongful deaths of American Black people, especially boys and men, which are arguably robbed of their singular humanity when merely listed one after another, as if stacked in identical body bags with no sign of the loss suffered as a result.[1]

For the most part, this book focused on understanding dominant ideas that have become associated with Midwestness and documenting some of their troubling political effects. It is worth noting that we have both known people who would proudly identify as "Midwestern" and we are not suggesting that any such self-identification is automatically tied to forms of whiteness, nationalism, or empire. It may be that these forms have shaped what people mean by "Midwestern," but these minor acts of regionalization, as they might be termed, have not been our primary focus. A different analytical approach might have started with the day-to-day social interactions where region is tacitly or openly referred to or brought alive in various ways, and how people use it over the course of their lives to shape regional geographical belonging and exclusion. One could, for instance, attend an anti-lockdown protest or visit a hospital and see when, if at all, "region" is called upon and with what purpose. Such an approach would surely reveal important things about what talk of "region" does at a micro-social level. But insofar as everyday interactions are not merely making but made by histories and processes beyond any immediate situation, critical scholarship ought to attend to the emergence of Midwestness and other regional categories over the last century and to consider the other ideas that coalesce around them.

In this conclusion we propose that such a critical approach to region is necessary and to outline some of the directions that further work and thinking in this vein might take. First, we outline what we mean by a critical approach to region and then use that to consider what might be termed the actual Midwest. The actual Midwest is not equivalent to something like "the real America," a term that is bandied about in political discourse with no clear meaning (apart from the fact that the people of "the real America" are almost certainly imagined to be white and non-urban). Rather, what we call the actual Midwest takes the critical approach to region into account and therefore assumes that people living in a territory that has enduring and/or contested labels must exist within these regionalizing forms and forces. In particular, a critical approach to region in the settler colonial United States, and places like it, must consider the relationship of those labels to enduring and ongoing projects of white supremacy. These projects have used region and region has used them in turn.

II. A CRITICAL APPROACH TO REGION

Consider the extraordinary price, the absolutely prohibitive price, the South has paid to keep the Negro in his place; and it has not succeeded in doing that, but has succeeded in having what is almost certainly the most bewildered, demoralized white population in the Western World.

—James Baldwin ([1961] 1989: 7)

In this quote, taken from an interview conducted by Studs Terkel, James Baldwin offers a critical avenue from which to approach both whiteness and American studies, and does so through region. Importantly, his deliberately provocative argument does not begin with region as a taken-for-granted territory, whether an economic sector or one of political identification, even though his focus is on the American South; the South could certainly be seen in these conventional ways, as the site of white agrarian slave and plantation owners who collectively rebelled as the Confederacy. Rather, Baldwin uses whites in the South as exemplary of American historical experience for denying their complicity in forms of racial hierarchy. It would seem, from Baldwin's words here and writing elsewhere, that the South is not important because of how distinct it naturally is, as a political and economic regional territory, but rather because of how distinct actual people with power have tried to make it, in terms of the racial segregation and violence enforced through white supremacist projects. That common white, American experience, for Baldwin, is denial.[2] From this point of view, Baldwin almost turns W. E. B. Du Bois's concept of double consciousness on its head: if to be Black in America is to be forced to constantly reflect on how powerful (white) others perceive you, then to be white is to have partial or half-consciousness, to be in constant denial about the system of power and privilege that benefits you and threatens and harms others. When Baldwin says that white Americans do not know America like Black Americans, and thus do not really know themselves, he is flipping the uneven distribution of benefits and harms that characterizes white supremacy, making that very unevenness a source of epistemological privilege for nonwhites.[3]

We suggest that a critical approach to region must proceed as Baldwin does. Rather than assume that region conforms to seemingly natural divides in territory, political identification, and economic sector—or, indeed, that territory, identity, and class are fixed and natural—it is critical to begin with how categories of space and time are routinely filtered and distorted through uneven experiences of systemic white supremacy. If, in a settler colonial context, the question of white power and privilege does not at first appear pertinent to any analysis, or seems in fact altogether irrelevant, then it is necessary to investigate how such appearances have been produced and *for whom* they appear as such. As Baldwin suggests, a more complete historical, epistemological, and sociological reckoning of any power structure is not reliant on clever (and often white) social scientists to expose how foolish social actors (who think they know what is going on) are in fact adherents to ideology and tradition. It is plain as day to those who embody positions marginalized by dominant structures. The task, then, is to question the naturalness of territorial wholes, of whatever scale, and to challenge the assumed privilege of perspective of (often white) scholars who may appear to hold authority over the largely unseen whole. It is necessary to recognize how some people bear the burden of collective projects of belonging to a place, whether that place is a region or a nation. Region, deployed critically in this way, can help contribute to better understandings of power as it manifests in place, especially who has the power to recognize what is "really" happening.

If a critical approach to region has relevance outside of contexts like the United States, it is because white supremacy does as well. Racial capitalism is not only specific to British history, for there are clear ways in which the racial capitalism of the United States has been modeled on and developed through that of the British Empire. We have argued, in particular, that tropes of Midwestness have been and continue to be productive of American racial projects. Our analysis is partly inspired by critical Black scholarship by C. L. R. James, Cedric Robinson, and St. Clare Drake, who not only document historical African and Afro-Caribbean contributions to

civilization, capitalism, and modernity, but make clear that these contributions are so abundant and so easily documented that it took centuries of
historical labor to actively exclude and forget them (Baldwin's experiential
denial in institutional form).[4] Silencing history is an active practice, as much
as documenting it, as Michel Rolph-Trouillot argues.[5] When it comes to
representations that subtract Black people from history and culture, philosopher Charles Mills describes this as an "epistemology of ignorance"
whereby white people (including white scholars) implicitly agree to misrec-
ognize the humanity of nonwhite people.[6] Following Baldwin, this would
also mean denying a critical piece of their own humanity.

While we emphasize how global conditions helped shape the Midwest and
its relationship to projects of white supremacy, regionalism is not solely the
product of impersonal, economic forces, even in the United States, where the
ferocity of capitalist competition, between and within regions, has been historically intense. People also feel regions and feel regional. Regionalism—
in this case, the discursive and affective production and circulation of
Midwestness—is also practically achieved by social actors from the area in
question and beyond.[7] Part of what regional thinking does is help people feel
the future—both the pull of irresistible forces and the sense of imminent
threats. This is often where white supremacy is most obvious—a guiding
value and ideology that animates decisions in the present in order to avoid
imagined futures. It is not just that white people are taken to be superior,
in other words, but that existing conditions and crises of inferiority suggest
that even more dismal consequences for the white race await just over the
horizon, coupled with a sense of nostalgic loss for when things were great
that has been key to immigration policy (chapter 2) and to the more recent
men's movement (chapter 3). An embrace and projection of regional attachment is only one possible reaction to these dilemmas, but we argue it is a
common and influential one, as the case of the Midwest shows.

III. THE ACTUAL MIDWEST

What might a critical approach to region look like? We have written this
book in order to demonstrate how pervasive and enduring ideas of the Midwest have been as ways of indexing nation and empire, even as their connection to white virtue and white deplorableness have shifted over time.
Since this analysis, by definition, has involved examining ideological and

value-laden assumptions about the world and the United States, it might seem difficult to relate this critical approach to what actually happens in places that have been regionalized. In order to make this conceptual leap, we want to examine elements of what we term the actual Midwest, meaning life in contested places among people for whom projects of white supremacy are the most evident and impactful.

Specifically, when regions like "the Midwest" take on certain dominant, albeit flexible and dynamic, meanings, they can have very real consequences such as moving some people to accept or act on exclusionary racial projects that contribute to the spread and consolidation of systems of white supremacy. Understanding the actual Midwest means taking this as central to what regions really are for people without the benefit of denial. In *Barrios Norteños*, Dionicio Nodín Valdés describes how, as we discussed in chapter 2 in reference to Sujey Vega's work, contemporary portrayals of Mexicans as the "last of the immigrants" in the Midwest actually date from the early years of Chicano settlement in the 1920s in the region.[8] Valdés further links these discriminatory discourses to the mutually reinforcing labor and residential conditions Mexican migrants initially faced in the 1920s in Midwestern cities and towns, which established spatial and symbolic boundaries with European Americans. He writes: "Midwestern Mexicanos almost invariably worked separately from other groups in the sugar beet fields and commonly were isolated on the railroads, while they intermingled more often with European immigrants and African Americans, but not European Americans, in urban factories and residential neighborhoods."[9] Much later, by the 1980s, the Mexican émigré populations of southern and western Minnesota had increased substantially due to recent labor migration from Mexico. Mexican migrants provided the majority of farm labor during this time, and worked jobs in sugar beet production, the service sector, and meat and poultry slaughter and processing operations across the Midwest.[10]

This racial capitalism made possible the Midwest many think they know, but was systematically erased as a founding element. And this has continued to be the case across different time periods. If we return to the late twentieth-century labor conditions Valdés describes, the least desired manufacturing jobs in the Midwest, particularly those in meatpacking plants, increasingly sought out, and relied on, the labor of new immigrants beginning in the 1980s and 1990s, including Mexican migrants and Sudanese refugees.[11] At this time, some of the five major meat-processing firms—Cudahy, Swift,

Armour, Wilson, and Morris—shifted their production factories from cities like Chicago to smaller towns, as we saw in chapter 5. The prime reason was that they often received tax breaks, exemptions from environmental regulations and water treatment, and other incentives from those towns, who were eager to attract new businesses amid rapid deindustrialization.[12] This kind of employment, which entailed dangerous work conditions, third-shift hours, and low, entry-level wages, compounded the precarity of recent immigrants who saw it as one of few accessible lines of work.

At the same time as this was occurring, the image of the Midwest, which spread a story line of suffering and dispossessed (but never dispossessing) whites overtook the actual Midwest in the popular imagination. As Vega describes of Latinx experiences in central Indiana, dominant constructions of foreigners and "illegal immigrants" further added to recent immigrants' and long-term Spanish-speaking populations' experiences of insecurity and everyday racial animosity.[13] Valdés writes, "The political backlash [against Mexicans] was also influenced by disillusionment over declining opportunities for upward mobility among European Americans and by the long-standing stereotype that Mexicans in the region were 'migrants' and consequently not entitled to the rights of 'permanent' residents. Dominant popular culture maintained a racialized American Dream and treated many spaces as the exclusive domain of Whites, while some Mexicans spoke positively about separation."[14] A powerful dimension of white supremacy is that the way things actually are and long have been can be swallowed up and concealed by imagination with apparent ease. While economic conditions have arguably accelerated white nativist sentiments, Valdés and others importantly assert that such discourses have long existed in Midwestern communities and continue to foster exclusionary notions of citizenship and belonging. Therefore, as Valdés suggests, what is at stake is how dominant notions of the white Midwest (not the actual Midwest) actually perpetuate a much more pervasive project of white racism with a deep history. And this project is reproduced over time through the Midwest category and against the long-existing multiracial histories of Midwestern communities.[15]

Representations of the Midwest can arguably serve to hide ongoing forms of racial bordering that amplify sensibilities of fundamental difference. Put another way, Midwestern tropes can have the effect of making people (white and nonwhite) falsely appear more individually responsible for their circumstances, whether positive or negative. Meanwhile, describing actual histories and experiences of how racial capitalism is made and remade through region can be done through other means, not only writing. Regionalist paintings, described in chapter 2, helped to produce the sense of agricultural insularity frequently ascribed to white Midwesterners. Yet, in contrast with painterly erasures, a much smaller, less widely known group of Midwestern visual artists took as their subject the economic and racial inequality of early twentieth-century Midwestern communities, providing an important glimpse of the ongoing bordering practices described by Vega, Valdés, and others. For instance, Farm Security Administration photographers and writers actively documented the social conditions of Midwestern towns affected by the Great Depression. Some like Ben Shahn, who had worked as an assistant for Diego Rivera, chronicled both farm auctions and racial segregation in the country-side around Columbus, Ohio, which was his designated work zone. Shahn's black-and-white photograph "Sign on Restaurant, Lancaster, Ohio" (1938), for instance, focused on a window sign that read "We Cater to White Trade Only." Additionally, rather than present fantastically verdant landscapes, Missouri-born Joe Jones painted barren, brown farm fields as he experi-enced them in the 1930s, as in "American Farm" (1936).[16] He also completed "Roustabouts" (1936), a painting that depicted African American men lined up for work on the docks of the Mississippi while a single white male super-visor in a suit stood nearby. Such art work had what author and art curator Debra Balken calls a "subversive subcurrent" and portrayed inequalities of race and labor that had long existed in Midwest communities.[17]

While building on critical race studies that question race and ethnicity as stable or fixed cultural formations, ethnographic work has also sought to document the unique social histories of ethnically marked Midwestern populations that have historically been marginalized or poorly understood in dominant representations of the region. Consider Detroit. This city has the largest Arab-descent population outside the Middle East and shows considerable political, ethnic, religious, and national diversity, with sizeable numbers of people who self-identify as Lebanese, Yemeni, Iraqi, Syrian, and Palestinian. Though the Arab American population is often mistak-enly identified as Muslim, particularly after 9/11, Detroit's Arab-descent communities exhibit striking religious diversity, with many Christians of different denominations, particularly Maronites, Egyptian Copts, and Iraqi Chaldeans. Additionally, though there are recent migrants among the varied and diverse Arab American population, some families speak no Arabic and have lived in the Detroit metropolitan area for over three generations. In fact, anthropologists Nabeel Abraham and Andrew Shryock (2000) point out that three waves of immigration characterize Detroit's Arab American population.[18] In the 1920s, before the 1924 US Immigration Act tightened quota restrictions on immigrants from Middle East countries, Lebanese semi-skilled laborers came to Detroit for work in the auto industry. A subsequent migratory wave occurred in the late 1960s as primarily Syrian and Lebanese professionals fled civil war and settled in Detroit looking for economic advancement. Finally, the 1990s and subsequent years have seen a third wave of Arab migration to the Detroit area, primarily of Iraqis seeking asylum or resettlement as refugees. In short, scholarly work on "Arab Detroit" contravenes dominant discourses of the Midwest that homogenize ethnic and racial diversity or that seek to identify ethnic diversity as a fairly recent phenomenon, tied only to the migratory waves of the 1990s and later. Such multiethnic communities are much more foundational to manufacturing centers in the Midwest, which attracted migrants seeking work in the auto industry as was true of Lebanese and Syrian laborers in the early 1920s.

Just as cities were long constructed through racial capitalism, so was the Midwestern farm not a refuge apart from industrial modernism and diversity, but long deeply implicated in its forms and forces, as an ideological support for settler colonialism. As such, the uses and abuses of the Midwest trope demonstrate the inseparable link between modernity and colonialism.[19] By imagining the Midwest as purely or simply agricultural, the region served national longings and nostalgia for stability amid the rapid economic and political changes of industrialization, as well as the toil, inequalities, and alienation of factory labor. It also attempted to increasingly root white claims to place and nation in the landscapes and economic processes of the Midwest at a specific historical time. During the 1920s, for instance, thousands of African Americans were participating in the Great Migration from southern states to northern factory towns. Due to failed government policies and economic hardship on reservations, Native Americans were also journeying to Midwestern cities for wage work, a process that accelerated in the 1950s.[20] Narratives of white Midwestern industry at this particular time therefore destabilized Native Americans', African Americans', and many other groups' claims to place-based belonging and economic resources, not only in the Midwest but in the nation as a whole (as we discuss further in chapter 5). The Midwest regional trope, and its "heartland" corollary, thus served intertwined processes of capital intensification and white supremacy, at home and abroad.[21]

How could this be the actual Midwest, as we characterize it, and not influence dominant perceptions of region? As we have shown of the region's white pastoralist imagery (see chapter 2), ideological forces of place-making can further exclusionary nativist processes by rendering individual states, towns, and other localities symbolic repositories of "mono-cropped" ethnic identities. That is, such places can seem to effuse, and thus reinforce, their alignment with particular ethnicities, erasing ethnic and racial variation and naturalizing ethnic hierarchies. For example, as mentioned earlier, stereotypic representations of Minnesota overemphasize a connection to Scandinavian Americans and, especially, Norwegian Americans. More than eight hundred thousand Norwegians immigrated to the United States from 1860 until 1890, more than any other Scandinavian-descent group, primarily sharecroppers without access to land in class-stratified, nineteenth-century Norway.[22] Yet while Scandinavian languages, religious practices, and forms of political participation have undoubtedly shaped civic life in Minnesota, the association of Minnesota with Scandinavian-descent populations masks the violence of settler colonialism that usurped land from Ojibwe (Anishinaabeg) in northern Minnesota to enable the farming of Euro-American immigrants.[23] Smaller rural Minnesotan communities may have historically resembled the insular, more ethnically homogenous world satirized by the novel *Main Street* and more recently *A Prairie Home Companion.* Such contemporary representations, however, erase the ethnic and racial diversity of Jewish, Mexican, and African American communities that have existed in the Twin Cities since the late nineteenth century, as well as the contemporary national and ethnic diversity of Minneapolis/St. Paul. According to the 2000 US Census, the Twin Cities had the country's most diverse population in terms of national origins.[24]

Similar conditions have been discussed by scholars as transcultural or superdiverse situations associated with contemporary global migrations.[25] But insularity has rarely been the rule, either in the Midwest or arguably anywhere in human history. It is not only with contemporary migration, multiculturalism, and globalization that human interactions have been marked by super-diverse exchanges across time and space.

That "superdiverse" multiculturalism is the actual rule has proven no barrier to white supremacist imaginings. To begin with, their fantasies involve

FIGURE 11. March against Islamophobia and war, Minneapolis, September 17, 2016, photo by Fibonacci Blue, Wikimedia Commons.

a dual process whereby whiteness has been simultaneously subdivided and purified as a category of global membership. Who counts as white is never merely a descriptive labeling of one person or group because it is part of much more pervasive political projects that seek to organize and control social and economic resources and privileges on the basis of race. For this reason, determining who is "really white" is more than an exercise in racialization or identity. Rather, it is critical for establishing projects of ambivalent desire and difference characteristic of white supremacy. This involves not only determining who is essentially refused identification as white but who can flexibly claim such an identification, not only closing off but also expanding acts of racialization for political ends. Pluralizing and singularizing whiteness are ongoing and mutually implicated projects, involving many different people and places over long periods of time. In fact, the Midwest is a product of migrations going back to the earliest years of the settler colony, an inter-regional and inter-cultural process that did not cease but was overtaken by frontier narratives and the politics of insularity upon which they rely. It is more accurate to imagine the actual Midwest as one continual process and product of migrations, great and small, interrupted by occasional projects of white supremacy, with more or less success. As a result of this alternative historical framing, cosmopolitanism and globalism are simply not new and exceptional with respect to the Midwest. As demonstrated by ethnographers who position the United States within global circulations and exchanges, the real diversity of the settler colony troubles images of the Midwest proffered by essentializing and constructing whiteness.

We can see through these examples that regional narratives, in fact, rely on forms of cultural production that uphold certain social histories, anchoring them to symbolic geographies of region, nation, and world, and erase a host of other interconnections and histories that do not fit into such dominant logics of region (and the interests they serve). Both moments are critical to the construction of region as a trope: the elevation of some stories and the people they point to as paradigmatic cultural figures and the simultaneous forgetting of other narratives. Unearthing these forgotten narratives, as the scholars we selectively read have done, is arguably an act of resisting white supremacist denials and erasures. Disavowing ongoing global and transcultural processes, as they exist now and existed in the past, means denying the full humanity of persons who are otherwise imagined as excessive or incidental to history and contemporary life. Put differently, the epistemology of ignorance central to white supremacist projects is ongoing in scholarly and popular representations of places and people. Like the denial of transcultural interactions in the distant past, depictions of the Midwest rely on similar work to deny actually existing intercultural variety in favor of simplistic and reductive accounts that identify geo-cultural stagnation and isolation after the imagined closure of the frontier.

IV. A FINAL WORD ON NATIONALISM

Nationalism is arguably on the rise the world over, as more authoritarian-leaning leadership in Brazil, Hungary, India, Japan, Russia, Turkey, the Philippines, and the United States, to name but a few, wrap themselves in flags and ethnic pride. As we have argued in this book, ideological heartlands are not an obstacle to national imaginings any more than race is, but what they are and where they come from provides direct support for exclusionary and unifying nationalist images and effects. In this way, a region imagined as a territorially fixed yet symbolically "average" container for national identity can stand in for the nation as a whole and appear to represent its ideal essence.

Taken separately, region and nation may appear like nothing more than convenient fictions, particularly in settler colonial contexts as historically recent as the United States. But together, they can help express that sought-after national essence, meaning that the reality of being "American," in spirit and not only in citizenship or residency, appears all the more natural when one can also identify an entire region as middling, average, gray, ordinary, or nowhere America, as the Midwest has been. Critical awareness of region means noticing when certain places and people come to stand in for the nation as a whole, even if it is by being unremarkable, pitiable, or deplorable that they do so. All of this depends on what people do with region. In fact, the production of the Midwest trope is a double act that involves people who do not identify as "Midwestern" and those that do. In other words, not only do ideas of the Midwest *circulate* globally, but also global projects, migrations, and exchanges have paradoxically been central in *producing* localized conceptions of Midwest isolation and provincialism. In turn, these conceptions, produced from the inside out, as it were, have a recurring impact on global projects of white supremacy and imperial ambitions. Put differently, a world for whites was the new "frontier" to which historian Frederick Jackson Turner's thesis about the significance of the frontier for American life and democracy actually led. And for this project to be effective, whiteness had to be stabilized, sedimented, and insulated from processes that would otherwise pluralize differences between so-called "whites" and trivialize differences between them and "nonwhites." The global production of the white Midwest thus ties the manufacture of whiteness to geopolitical imagination.

If regional representations tend to spread and can even be co-constructed, then nationalism is no mere "local" concern or project for any one country. By this we do not mean simply that diasporic connections link people to homelands they still feel they belong to or hope to in the future. We mean that storytelling about places, like all stories, can spread far and wide. And this is so even when the subject of the story is the most seemingly banal of places—out of the way, a safe space, or a fly-over area without a stop. Such places, after all, can be the storied settings for modern gods and monsters, whether Superman or Freddy, or be held responsible for world-changing political shifts, where the Midwest makes Trump president. Nationalism at its most banal is a global business and, like nativism, not so much about oneself as about "others" who do not belong (in the case of the United States, bad whites and nonwhites). It therefore makes sense that regional dramas should attract and appall more than just their countrymen. All the better if those regions, those global heartlands, are so fascinating and fictionalized, so fundamental yet utterly forgettable as the Midwest.

Filmography in Chapter 4

American Sniper. Directed by Clint Eastwood. Burbank, CA: Warner Bros., 2014.

The Bad Seed. Directed by Mervyn LeRoy. Burbank, CA: Warner Bros., 1956.

Batman v Superman: Dawn of Justice. Directed by Zack Snyder. New York: DC Entertainment, 2016.

Brightburn. Directed by James Gunn. New York: Screen Gems, 2019.

Candyman. Directed by Bernard Rose. Los Angeles: Propaganda Films, 1992.

Children of the Corn. Directed by Fritz Kiersch. Atlanta, GA: New World Pictures, 1984.

A Clockwork Orange. Directed by Stanley Kubrick. Burbank, CA: Warner Bros., 1971.

The Exorcist. Directed by William Peter Blatty. Vancouver, BC: Hoya Productions, 1973.

Field of Dreams. Directed by Phil Alden Robinson. Cheetowaga, NY: Gordon Productions, 1989.

Get Out. Directed by Jordan Peele. Los Angeles: Blumhouse Productions, 2017.

A Good Marriage. Directed by Peter Askin. New York: Reno Productions, 2014.

Guardians of the Galaxy. Directed by James Gunn. Burbank, CA: Marvel Studios, 2014.

Guardians of the Galaxy, Vol 2. Directed by James Gunn. Burbank, CA: Marvel Studios, 2017.

Halloween. Directed by John Carpenter. Los Angeles: Compass International Pictures, 1978.

Man of Steel. Direct by Zack Snyder. New York: DC Entertainment, 2013.

A Nightmare on Elm Street. Directed by Wes Craven. Culver City, CA: Media Home Entertainment, 1984.

Pleasantville. Directed by Gary Ross. North Little Rock, AR: Larger Than Life Productions, 1998.

Psycho. Directed by Alfred Hitchcock. Shamley Green, UK: Shamley Productions, 1960.

Rebel without a Cause. Directed by Nicholas Ray. Burbank, CA: Warner Bros., 1955.

Sorry to Bother You. Directed by Boots Riley. Los Angeles: Significant Productions, 2018.

Superman. Directed by Richard Donner. London, UK: Dovemead Ltd., 1978.

Texas Chainsaw Massacre. Directed by Tobe Hooper. Austin, TX: Vortex, 1974.

The Wiz. Directed by Sidney Lumet. Los Angeles: Motown Productions, 1978.

The Wizard of Oz. Directed by Victor Leming. Beverly Hills, CA: Metro-Goldwyn-Mayer, 1939.

Bibliography of Media Articles in Chapter 5

2010

Haberman, Maggie. "Democrats Fear Midwestern Meltdown." Politico.com. September 26, 2010.

Hayes, Stephen T. "Obamanomics Paints Ohio Red." *Wall Street Journal*. October 13, 2010.

Murray, Shailagh, and Paul Kane. "Hard Times in Midwest Endanger Democrats." *Washington Post*. November 1, 2010.

Nagourney, Adam, and Monica Davey. "G.O.P. Expands a Base from South to Midwest." *New York Times*. November 4, 2010.

Connelly, Kevin. "Optimism and Virtue: What the Midwest Wants in a Leader." BBC.com. December 29, 2010.

2011

Williams, Conor. "Don't Count Out the Midwest." *Washington Post*. January 1, 2011.

Jonsson, Patrik. 2011. "Wisconsin Protests: Why 'Week of Rage' Matters to Rest of America." *Christian Science Monitor*. February 18, 2011.

Lahart, Justin. "U.S. News: Recovery's Fitful Pace Puts Brakes on Hiring." *Wall Street Journal*. June 8, 2011.

Barone, Michael. "The Fall of the Midwest Economic Model." *Wall Street Journal*. August 16, 2011.

2012

Hughes, Siobhan, and Jonathan Rockoff. "Election 2012: Santorum Returns to Campaigning after Daughter's Health Improves." *Wall Street Journal*. January 31, 2012.

Summers, Juana. "Santorum Makes Midwest Pitch." Politico.com. February 18, 2012.

Hook, Janet, and Neil King. "Election 2012: A Crucial Test for Romney." *Wall Street Journal*. February 28, 2012.

King, Neil, and Patrick O'Conner. "Romney Regains Momentum—Holds Off Santorum in Michigan, Wins Arizona with Ease." *Wall Street Journal*. February 29, 2012.

Levenson, Michael. "Romney Struggles for Blue-Collar Vote." *Boston Globe*. March 3, 2012.

Finnegan, Michael. "Campaign 2012: South's Stalwart Right Is Uneasy with Romney; Voters Would Take Him Over Obama, but Their Lack of Passion Reflects a Drag on His Campaign." *Los Angeles Times*. March 7, 2012.

Guarino, Mark. "In Midwest, Fight over Labor Unions to be at Heart of 2012 Election." *Christian Science Monitor*. July 24, 2012.

King, Neil, and Patrick O'Conner. "Election 2012: Poll: Obama Leads in Wisconsin, Iowa." *Wall Street Journal*. October 19, 2012.

"Obama and Romney Battle For Key Swing States." Al Jazeera.com. November 4, 2012.

Kind, Neil, Carol Lee, and Colleen McCain Nelson. "Election 2012: Obama Fine-Tuned 2008's Winning Formula." *Wall Street Journal*. November 7, 2012.

"Protests as Michigan Passes 'Anti-Union' Law." Al Jazeera.com. December 12, 2012.

2013

Kessler, Glenn. "Sarah Palin's Misreading of Polling Data." *Washington Post*. July 2, 2013.

"US Cities Reversing Poverty Trend." Al Jazeera.com. December 4, 2013.

2014

Lauter, David. "Local Races, Scripted in Washington; Outside Groups Can Make Candidates Seem Like Secondary Players in this Florida Contest." *Los Angeles Times*. March 9, 2014.

"Chinese Investment Revitalises US Auto Town." Al Jazeera.com. April 5, 2014.

Williamson, Elizabeth. "U.S. News: Clinton Plays Up Her Roots." *Wall Street Journal*. August 21, 2014.

Weissman, Robert. "US: The Battle to Make a Living." Al Jazeera.com. October 2, 2014.

2016

Khrushcheva, Nina. "The Marketing of the American President." Al Jazeera.com. January 29, 2016.

Bierman, Noah. "GOP Coming to Terms with Trump's Rise; Republican Leaders Continue to Resist His Candidacy, but Some Say They'd Back Him If He's the Nominee." *Los Angeles Times*. February 25, 2016.

Fisher, Alan. "Super Tuesday: Donald Trump Looks Set to Dominate Polls." Al Jazeera.com. February 28, 2016.

"Cruz, Rubio, and Sanders Plan Their Next Moves to Close Rivals' Leads." *New York Times*. March 2, 2016.

"Clinton, Trump Eye Michigan Wins as Candidates Face First Big Midwest Test." Fox News.com. March 8, 2016.

McCain Nelson, Colleen, Peter Nicholas, and Laura Meckler. "Sanders Scores Michigan Upset." *Wall Street Journal*. March 9, 2016.

"Bernie Sanders Surprises with Michigan Primary Win." Al Jazeera.com. March 9, 2016.

Haberman, Maggie. "Democratic Debate Takeaways: Tensions Rise as the Race Tightens." *New York Times*. March 10, 2016.

Chozick, Amy. "Hillary Clinton Gets Some Star Power to Help in New Ads." *New York Times*. March 11, 2016.

Jan, Tracy. "Trade Deals Haunting Clinton in Ohio." *Boston Globe*. March 14, 2016.

"Sanders Barnstorms Midwest as Clinton Lead Narrows in Several States." Fox News.com. March 14, 2016.

"Bernie Sanders Beats Hillary Clinton in Three States." Al Jazeera.com. March 27, 2016.

Rucker, Philip, Robert Costa, and Dan Balz. "Often a Trump Target, Party Elites Get Some PR." *Washington Post*. April 24, 2016.

Cohen, Michael. "Dear Liberals, Stop Panicking over Trump." *Boston Globe*. May 10, 2016.

Cohn, Nate, and Toni Monkovic. "No, The Battleground States Are Not a Terrific Fit for Donald Trump." *New York Times*. May 10, 2016.

Pindell, James. "Trump-Clinton Battle May Alter Electoral Map." *Boston Globe*. May 27, 2016.

Mehta, Seema, and Anthony Pesce, Maloy Moore, and Christine Zhang. "Election 2016: Who's Giving Sanders All Those $27 Donations?" *Los Angeles Times*. June 4, 2016.

Brooks, David. "Where America Is Working." *New York Times*. June 5, 2016.

Prasad, Monica. "When the Bills Come Due; Conservative Voters Typically Don't Like Borrowing and Debt. But Trump Does." *Los Angeles Times*. August 18, 2016.

Wagner, John, and Anne Gearan. "Clinton Sees New Opening with GOP." *Washington Post*. October 11, 2016.

Mason, Melanie. "Democrats Have Early-Voting Edge; Data Appear to Show a Major Shift Favoring Trump in Midwest." *Los Angeles Times*. October 28, 2016.

Jan, Tracy. "Trump Has a Lot to Surmount for a 'Brexit'-Like Upset." *Boston Globe*. November 2, 2016.

Levenson, Michael. "Moulton Supports Challenger to Pelosi." *Boston Globe*. November 3, 2016.

"How Trump Pushed the Electoral Map to the Right." *New York Times*. November 8, 2016.

Zurcher, Anthony. "US Election 2016 Results: Five Reasons Donald Trump Won." BBC.com. November 9, 2016.

Davidson, John Daniel. "How Trump Won the Midwest." *The Federalist*. November 10, 2016.

Ragozin, Leonid. "Trump: Putin's Best Frenemy." Al Jazeera.com. November 12, 2016.

Horowitz, Evan, and James Pindell. "Swings in State Hint at Long-Term Shift." *Boston Globe*. November 14, 2016.

Goodstein, Scott. "Donald Trump Trolled Us All. We Should Learn from It." *New York Times*. November 14, 2016.

Steinhaurer, Jennifer, and Emmarie Huetteman. "Congressional Republicans Project Unity while Democrats Scramble." *New York Times*. November 15, 2016.

Leonhardt, David. "The Democrats' Real Turnout Problem." *New York Times*. November 17, 2016.

Debenedetti, Gabriel. "Rust Belt Democrats Summon DNC Hopefuls for Midwestern Audition." Politico.com. November 29, 2016.

Martin, Jonathan, and Emmarie Huetteman. "After Democrats' Losses, Nancy Pelosi Becomes a Symbol of What Went Wrong." *New York Times*. November 29, 2016.

Rozell, Mark, and Whet Smith. "Memo to Democrats: Look to the Southwest and Southeast, Not Midwest." Politico.com. November 30, 2016.

Hughes, Siobhan. "U.S. News: Pelosi Keeps House Leader Post." *Wall Street Journal*. December 1, 2016.

Rove, Karl. "The Many Democratic Excuses for Defeat." *Wall Street Journal*. December 15, 2016.

Kiefer, Francine. "How Democrats Slowly Turned Their Backs on Rural America." *Christian Science Monitor*. December 16, 2016.

2017

Gabriel, Trip. "A Table Full of Trump Voters Who Don't Regret It One Bit." *New York Times*. January 13, 2017.

Kingsbury, Alex. "An Address with Perfectly Trumpian Tone." *Boston Globe*. January 20, 2017.

Blake, Aaron. "From This Day Forward, It's Going to Be Only America First." *Washington Post*. January 22, 2017.

Phillips, Steve. "Move Left, Democrats." *New York Times*. February 21, 2017.

Halper, Evan. "Democrats' New Leaders Moves to Unite Party; DNC's First Latino Chief Picks Progressive Rival as Deputy to Fight Trump's GOP and a Crisis of Relevance." *Los Angeles Times*. February 26, 2017.

Hessan, Diane. "How Trump Voters Feel Now." *Boston Globe*. February 27, 2017.

Goodnough, Abby, and Jonathan Martin. "G.O.P.'s Health Care Tightrope Winds through the Blue-Collar Midwest." *New York Times*. March 19, 2017.

Shuler, Jack. "'Sundown Towns': Midwest Confronts Its Complicated Racial Legacy." *Christian Science Monitor*. March 27, 2017.

Philip, Abby. "Trump Makes Rare Push to Sell His 'America First' Agenda Outside Washington." *Washington Post*. April 19, 2017.

Rubin, Jennifer. "All of Hillary Clinton's 'but for' Excuses." *Washington Post*. May 3, 2017.

Decker, Cathleen. "Analysis: In Trump's Wake, the Two Political Parties Are Adrift." *Los Angeles Times*. May 31, 2017.

Kiefer, Francine. "A Democrat Shows How to Win Over Trump Voters." *Christian Science Monitor*. June 20, 2017.

Seib, Gerald. "U.S. News—Capital Journal: Democrats' Challenge: Middle-Class Appeal." *Wall Street Journal*. June 27, 2017.

"The Constitution vs. Trump." Al Jazeera.com. June 29, 2017.

"Right-to-Work Sore Losers." *Wall Street Journal*. August 23, 2017.

Kane, Paul. "House Democrats Start Brainstorming Agenda to Regain Majority." *Washington Post*. September 14, 2017.

Shear, Michael D., and Yamiche Alcindor. "Democrats on Tightrope in Immigration Debate." *New York Times*. October 2, 2017.

Andrews, Natalie. "U.S. News: In Tour, Democrats Listen for a Message." *Wall Street Journal*. November 20, 2017.

"Trump Risks Losing What's Left of His Populist Street Cred with GOP Tax Bill." *Washington Post*. December 19, 2017.

2018

Johnston, Katie. "For Workers, Much Remains Unsettled as New Year Begins." *Boston Globe*. January 1, 2018.

Andrews, Natalie. "U.S. News: Democrats Tussle in Illinois." *Wall Street Journal*. March 17, 2018.

Balz, Dan. "Loyalty, Unease in Trump's Midwest." *Washington Post*. May 13, 2018.

Winfrey-Harris, Tamara. "Stop Pretending Black Midwesterners Don't Exist." *New York Times*. June 16, 2018.

Winfrey-Harris, Tamara. "The Invisible Black Midwesterner." *New York Times*. June 17, 2018.

Geoghegan, Tom. "The Untold Good News Story of America Today." BBC.com. June 18, 2018.

Roberts, Paul. "Seattle Flirts with 'Municipal Socialism.'" Politico.com. June 29, 2018.

Hudson, Alexandra. "No Country for Old Pretentious Titles." *Wall Street Journal*. June 30, 2018.

Zheng, Sarah. "Hollywood on the Edge of Its Seat Waiting for China Deal amid Trade Row." Politico.com. July 5, 2018.

Case Bryant, Christa. "How Young Liberals' Moves to Red America May Temper Political Divides." *Christian Science Monitor.* July 6, 2018.

Weigl, David. "In Midwest, Democrats Are Growing More Competitive." *Washington Post.* July 18, 2018.

Cadelago, Christopher, Natasha Korecki, and Andrew Restuccia. "Trump Takes His Hard Sell to the Heartland." Politico.com. July 26, 2018.

Peters, Jeremy W. "John James. Black and Republican, Thinks He Can Crack the 'Blue Wall' in Michigan." *New York Times.* August 3, 2018.

Zurcher, Anthony. "US Mid-term Elections: What the Results Mean for Trump." BBC.com. August 8, 2018.

Sider, David. "Midwest Democrats' Answer to Trump: White, Conventional and Boring." Politico.com. August 15, 2018.

Roberts, William. "Trump Weighs on House Republican as Midterm Campaign Starts." Al Jazeera.com. September 3, 2018.

Strauss, Daniel. "Dems Break Open GOP Hold on Midwest Governorships." Politico.com. September 21, 2018.

Ollstein, Alice Miranda. "Democrats Run on Pre-existing Conditions—Their Own." Politico.com. September 23, 2018.

Papenfuss, Mary. "Millionaire Sen. Chuck Grassley Applying for Trump's Farm Bailout Funds." Huffington Post.com. September 30, 2018.

McIntosh, Kriston, Ryan Nunn, and Jay Shambaugh. "The Places America's Rich and Poor Call Home." BBC.com. October 2, 2018.

Shepard, Steven. "Politico Race Ratings: Democrats Breach GOP Statehouse Walls." Politico.com. October 18, 2018.

Maher, Kris. "U.S. News: Democrats Look to Midwest—Party Aims to Reclaim Governorships in Several Tight Races That Test Regional Trump Support." *Wall Street Journal.* October 22, 2018.

Healy, Jack. "A Shot at Rural America." *New York Times.* October 22, 2018.

Strauss, Daniel. "Democrats Make Late Bid for Governorships in Deep-Red Great Plains." Politico.com. October 31, 2018.

Craig, Tim. "Democrats' State-Level Push Falters as Races for Governor Stay Tight." *Washington Post.* November 5, 2018.

Alberta, Tim. "Trump's GOP Braces for Midwest Massacre." Politico.com. November 6, 2018.

Scher, Bill. "The Midterms Message for Democrats in 2020: Go Midwestern Nice." Politico.com. November 7, 2018.

Thrush, Glenn, and Alan Pappeport. "Red-State Voters Stand by Republicans Despite Trump's Trade War Pain." *New York Times.* November 7, 2018.

Zurcher, Anthony. "Mid-term Election Results: The Lessons US Democrats Can Learn for 2020." BBC.com. November 8, 2018.

Rosenberg, Simon. "The Midterms Show Trump Might Not Get Re-elected in 2020." Al Jazeera.com. November 8, 2018.

Alberta, Tim. "The Biggest Surprises of the 2018 Midterms." Politico.com. November 9, 2018.

Douthat, Ross. "A Defeat for White Identity." *New York Times*. November 10, 2018.

Viser, Matt. "Democrats Sharpen Debate on 2020 Path." *Washington Post*. November 11, 2018.

Edsall, Thomas B. "Donald Trump's Dimming Prospects." *New York Times*. November 29, 2018.

Rodriguez, Jesus. "Biden: 'I'm the Most Qualified Person in the Country to Be President.'" Politico.com. December 4, 2018.

Herndon, Astead, and Jonathan Martin. "G.O.P.'s Midwest Power Grab May Fuel Backlash." *New York Times*. December 11, 2018.

2019

Stokols, Eli, and Janet Hook. "The Nation: Race Is Front, Center on King Holiday; Democrats Denounce Trump and Talk Frankly about Systemic Racism." *Los Angeles Times*. January 22, 2019.

Shaw, Dave. "The Case for Democrats Winning the Industrial Midwest." Politico.com. January 30, 2019.

Korecki, Natasha. "Midwestern Dems Launch Behind-the-Scenes Offensive to Land Milwaukee Convention." Politico.com. February 13, 2019.

Hook, Janet. "Election 2020: A Contest for Obama Legacy: In a Rapidly Growing Field of Democrats, Hopefuls Quietly Vie to Be Seen as Successor to His Achievements." *Los Angeles Times*. February 19, 2019.

Mair, Liz. "Has Republican Resistance to Trump Collapsed?" *New York Times*. February 19, 2019.

Strauss, Daniel. "Midwest Governors to 2020 Dems: 'Show Up.'" Politico.com. February 26, 2019.

Zurcher, Anthony. "US Election 2020: Nine Democratic Candidates. One Event. Who Shone?" BBC.com. March 12, 2019.

NOTES

INTRODUCTION

1. What we describe connects with concepts of slow death and slow violence. On slow death, see Berlant 2007 and Puar 2017 and on slow violence, see Nixon 2011. What they share in common is an emphasis on unevenly distributed, systemic harms meted out on the basis of class and race disparities.

2. As anthropologists Aisha M. Beliso-De Jesús and Jemima Pierre (2013: 5) put it, "there still remained a misrecognition that white supremacy is something that *other* (read: ignorant, poor, or uneducated) white people *do*" (italics in original). See also Sullivan 2014.

3. We therefore follow other scholars who have called to "deprovincialize Trump." See Rosa and Bonilla 2017.

4. This is apparent in many news pieces, as we discuss in subsequent chapters. As one example, see The Majority Report, "These Are the Most Disgusting Trump Supporters You'll Ever See," https://m.youtube.com/watch?v=kCjOkB8F9Us. See also Harding 1991; Coleman 2015; Lennon 2018.

5. In our reading, the Midwest is an imaginative geography, not unlike "the Orient" (Said 1978; Gregory 2004), which has a performative effect on everyday life. Put differently, with imagined geographies, including imagined regions, "certain desired truths become lived as truths, as if they were truths, thus producing material traces and evidences of these truths, despite what counterevidence may exist" (Puar 2007: 39). On uncovering understories as a method, see Kosek 2006.

6. On autoethnography as a method, see Reed-Danahay 1997 and Bochner and Ellis 2016.

7. Cuomo and Hall 1999: 9.

SECTION I: CHALLENGING IDEAS OF THE MIDWEST

1. Regionalizing commercially attractive zones was part of the active projects of global political economy that continue to this day (e.g., with references to Celtic or Asian Tigers, post-socialist societies, BRIC nations, etc.). Regionalism in this multinational form can be historically linked to nineteenth-century empire building and colonization. Colonial powers often categorized the political-economic character of various colonial territories (as "backward" for instance) in order to govern them and channel regional economies into wider systems of production and profit making. For instance, Arif Dirlik argues that the "Asian Pacific" was invented and conceptualized "in terms of a Euro-American global vision that incorporated the region's peoples into a new inventory of the world and established relationships that bound them together in a regional structure" (1992: 66).

2. On Europe as a whole, see Applegate 1999; on Sweden, Frykman and Löfgren 1987; Spain, Núñez 2001; Eastern Europe, Augusteijn and Storm 2012.

3. As Cavazza (2012: 83) notes of the Italian regionalist identity-making of Giovanni Crocioni and other intellectuals in the 1910s, "Cultural regionalism served the cause of strengthening national feeling." On Germany, see Grill 1982, and Japan, Gluck 1985.

CHAPTER I. THE MIDWEST AND WHITE VIRTUE

1. For a recent example, the website FiveThirtyEight did a survey on which states people today think are in the Midwest, highlighting the continuing ambiguity of the term: https://fivethirtyeight.com/features/what-states-are-in-the-midwest/.

2. In what follows we therefore make interpretations "against the grain" of commonsense associations (Stoler 2009), and point to how regional tropes can contribute to forms of benefit and harm on a global scale (Puar 2007, 2017).

3. See Dhingra 2009.

4. Cited in Lake and Reynolds 2008: 2.

5. As Lake and Reynolds (2008: 4) note, "The project of whiteness was thus a paradoxical politics, at once transnational in its inspiration and identifications but nationalist in its methods and goals."

6. This fiction was promoted by ignoring a variety of evidence that showed otherwise, notably the Haitian revolution (see James 1989[1938]).

7. We use the terms *people of color* (POC) and *Black, indigenous and people of color* (BIPOC) with some hesitation in this book. Both can be terms of solidarity that politically mobilize individuals of many different ethnic and racial identities. At the same time, the terms homogenize different experiences and histories of racialization, while upholding to some extent older binaries of white/color, which we discuss in this chapter. When possible, we leave aside these terms and specify the particular racialized experiences and histories on which we focus.

8. For an interpretation of Du Bois's writing alongside other Black Marxists, see Robinson 2000.

9. Writing on how anti-miscegenation laws affected inheritance and wealth transfers in early twentieth-century Louisiana, anthropologist Virginia Domínguez (1986: 89) notes, "the point is that property is not just a corollary of racial classification; it is a criterion of it." See also Harris 1993 and Lipsitz 2018[1998].

10. In making this argument, we build on a vast body of work emerging since *Wages of Whiteness* that has been devoted to the study of whiteness. "Insofar as the modern world has been foundationally shaped by European colonialism," writes Mills, "there is a sense in which white supremacy could be seen as transnational, global, the historic domination of white Europe over nonwhite non-Europe and of white settlers over nonwhite slaves and indigenous peoples" (2003: 37). Thus in her ethnography on nationalism in the Democratic Republic of Congo, anthropologist Yolanda Covington-Ward (2016: 61) could relay a conversation in which a Congolese interlocutor described how locals label plump, ripe mangos as "European" (Manga zi Mputu) and small, green ones as "black" or "Kongo" (Manga ba Ndombe or Manga zi Kongo).

11. In this way, compulsory whiteness is similar to compulsory heterosexuality (Rich 1980; Butler 1990) and compulsory able-bodiedness and able-mindedness (Kafer 2003; McRuer 2006). Our sense of compulsory whiteness is perhaps best explained by Danny Glover's character in the fantasy satire film, *Sorry to Bother You* (2018), when he is explaining to the hero how to be more successful at telemarketing by using a white voice: "It's not really a white voice. It's what they wish they sounded like. It's like what they think they're supposed to sound like."

12. On this anti-logic, see Robinson 2000: 240.

13. Whiteness has often been described using terms like "religion" (Du Bois 2013 [1935]), "folk theory" (Hill 2011), an "invisible knapsack" of structural privileges (McIntosh 1989) and a "world view" (Smedley 2018[1993]). On how this appears or feels to white people, see Di Angelo 2018 and Goldberg 1993: 92. On criticisms of Di Angelo's work in particular, see Bejan 2020 and McWhorter 2020.

14. Belew 2018: 8.

15. This affective dimension to regional tropes interests us as well, in what follows, especially as it has gripped scholars working at the intersections of queer, disability, and critical race theory (Ahmed 2006; Puar 2007, 2017; Chen 2012; Campt 2012, 2017). Jasbir Puar (2007) makes clear, in particular, how studies of US empire have tended to neglect sexuality, but the idealized white working-class subject we describe is also straight and able-bodied, to be sure.

16. Hill 2011: 177.

17. Racism without race comes from Faye Harrison (2002: 153). See also Bonilla-Silva 2010.

18. See, e.g., Jackson 2020; Sodré 2020. By contrast, the historical record attests that attempts to "pass" as white or claim whiteness among persons who were identified as Black, indigenous, and of color carried immense risks.

19. For the *Newsday* story see Young 2020.

20. As Cedric Robinson (2000: 188) puts it, quoting Du Bois, this mythology was central to the notion of the "North [as] 'the magnanimous emancipator.'"

21. See Shortridge 1989.

22. Lauck suggests that the interior territory around the Ohio and Mississippi rivers may have already entered the consciousness of Bostonians and coastal merchants as a region by the 1750s, and even that disputes over its control may have catalyzed the American revolt (2013a: 167).

23. On racialized capitalism, see Robinson 2000.

24. A commitment to the science and industry of agriculture is also evident in the network of land-grant universities established in the nineteenth-century Midwest with dedicated agricultural schools. On Fordism, see Page and Walker 1991: 308; see also Clampitt 2015: 39.

25. On the political economy of Midwestern agriculture, see Cronon 1991, Belich 2009, and Hoganson 2019. The example of Tulsa's prosperous Black neighborhoods of the early twentieth century, mentioned earlier, shows that urban settings were not only ideologically but also physically erased from the landscape. Admittedly, Oklahoma occupies an ambiguous place in the Midwest and is considered Western or Southwestern by some.

26. Pollan 2006.

27. Blanchette 2019.

28. On Wheatless Wednesdays and the Wilson administration, see Clampitt 2015: 156.

29. See Belich 2009: 192.

30. Page & Walker 1991: 282

31. Page & Walker 1991: 290.

32. Such economic diversity, as described by Shortridge (1989), holds true in those states today, as well. For example, Collins (2012: 8) reports that, in Wisconsin, "less than 2 percent of the state's gross domestic product derives from agriculture and forestry."

33. Bebout 2016: 10.

34. Cited in Lake and Reynolds 2008: 129.

35. Bebout 2016: 19.

36. Jane Hill (2011) points out that while theories of whiteness show social distinctions of white, class-based styles and sensibilities (Hartigan 1999; Bucholtz 2001), the US Census and other policies do not and tend to homogenize whiteness while applying finer and finer racial classifications to people of color. On the historical fate of different "ethnic whites," for example, see Roediger 1991; Brodkin Sacks 1998.

37. See Mullen 2015 and Lake and Reynolds 2008: 9.

38. This is argued by Lake and Reynolds 2008: 104–105.

39. On the violent American colonization of the Philippines and its historical erasure, see Balce 2016.

40. Organizers articulated their ambition as a "world movement against colonialism and imperialism as the contemporary stages of world capitalism" (Robinson 2000: 222).

41. Pierre 2013: 113.

42. Apthecker 1974[1943]: 249; see also James 1989. On the Tulsa massacre, see Snider 2003.

43. Paraphrasing Jasbir Puar, we could therefore say that this is part of the colonial-era construction of "failed and capacitated bodies" that continues in new forms today (2017: 14–15).

44. Kirschner 1970 writes about Prohibition and Olmstead 2009 about American conspiracy theory more broadly.

45. As Jason Weems argues, "The anxiety over the eclipse of rural identity in the face of consolidation by mass culture, urbanism, and industrialization inspired much of the 'regionalism' that suffused the American countryside during the 1920s and 1930s" (2015: 162). Weems relates the emergence of an ambivalent American Midwestern-ness to the rise of air travel and surveillance and to the modes of everyday perception and understanding they made possible. As people increasingly saw themselves as "Midwestern," aerially derived images and perspectives combined with existing representations and, in so doing, "fostered a set of idealized preconceptions of midwestern culture" (2015: 44). The contradiction here, of course, is that images of open fields only circulated because they were made possible by the proliferation of new technologies of transportation and photography in the heartland. On Populism and regionalism, see Jessen 2017.

46. Lewis 1961[1920].

47. Cited in Pichaske 2006: 8.

48. Pichaske 2006: 15.

49. Quoted in Shi 1985: 77.

50. For an exception, Barillas 2006: 33.

51. On the whiteness of Midwestern speech, see Hill 2011. Our position diverges from other scholars of the Midwest like Pichaske 2006: 19.

52. Hughes 1933.

CHAPTER 2. HEARTLAND HISTORIES

1. Our goal here is not to produce a history of the Midwest region (Shortridge 1989; Cayton and Onuf 1990; Cronon 1991; Cayton and Gray 2007; Belich 2009; Lauck 2013), literature (Barillas 2006; Pichaske 2006; Oler 2019; Ochonicky 2019) or visual arts (Dennis 1975; Corn 1983; Balken 2009), as other scholars have capably done, nor to claim to represent the great diversity of experiences and histories characterizing the region as it is conventionally understood.

2. Central to our inquiry, in this respect, is what Sujey Vega (2015: 148) refers to as "struggle[s] to control the meaning of belonging in space."

3. Bebout (2016: 55) calls this approach "reading tropologically," building on the work of Henry Louis Gates Jr. and Houston Baker. He similarly defines it as one of examining "multiple iterations across disparate contexts against each other simultaneously" (55).

4. See Balken 2009: 117.

5. Artists like John Steuart Curry were also illustrators for a number of national publications, such as *Saturday Evening Post, Boy's Life*, and *Country Gentleman* (Balken 2009: 82).

6. We will consider poetry in chapter 3, popular fiction and film in chapter 4, and news reporting in chapter 5.

7. See Storm 2012: 44–48.

8. Some Regionalists like Curry were aware that they were, as Balken (2009: 86) puts it, "engaged in mythmaking, spinning a view of the Midwest that was sometimes illusory." Benton produced one work, *Prodigal Son* (1939–41), which depicted the environmental devastation of the Dust Bowl in Missouri, but Balken (2009: 104) characterizes it as "anomalous" in his overall corpus.

9. Balken 2009: 81.

10. Cited in Rundstrom 2007: 72.

11. See Balken 2009: 113, 185.

12. See Brodkin Sacks 1998.

13. See Opie 1987; Hannah 2000 on the history of the Midwest.

14. Harris 1993: 1721.

15. Quoted in Barillas 2006: 26.

16. Tocqueville 1971: 383 cited in Barillas 2006: xii.

17. Jefferson's emphasis on dividing land according to line-oriented squares and rectangles has roots in the Roman centuriation and Cartesian geometry, among other influences. The United States is the only place with strict adherence to cardinal directions in its rectangular cadastral system. However, Johnson (1994: 16) suggests that the square spatial organization of land has been used globally "since antiquity, particularly in colonized regions."

18. On the 1862 Homestead Act, see Pichaske 2006: 14. On estimates of land dispossession, see Michaelsen 1995.

19. See Cayton and Onuf 1990.

20. See Robinson 2000; Lake and Reynolds 2008.

21. Quoted in Lake and Reynolds 2008: 172.

22. Locke 1980[1690]. On Locke's relationship to settler colonialism, see, e.g., Macpherson 1962; Scanlan 2005: 23–26.

23. On this point, see Michaelsen 1995.

24. Quoted in Michaelsen 1995: 54. On Locke's relationship to the slave trade, see Farr 2008.

25. Quoted in Michaelsen 1995: 56, 62.

26. On this point, see Barillas 2006: 29. As a slave owner, Jefferson furthered other systems that invested in white landholding and economic prosperity while actively divesting African Americans of those forms of capital. His famous relationship with Sally Hemings, an African American woman and one of Jefferson's slaves, and the formal illegitimacy of their children at the time also demonstrates how the color line was used legally to enforce white economic entitlement (Domínguez 1993). Quite

strikingly, some of Hemings and Jefferson's later descendants moved to the Midwest and struggled there with forms of discrimination (Stanton and Swann-Wright 1999). Despite years of denials that they were descended from Jefferson, the Hemings received vindication after DNA testing was done in 1998. They have since become culturally emblematic of the enduring legacy of slavery in African American families and of anti-racist efforts to force white Americans to come to terms with slavery (Bay 2006).

27. On treaties, see Michaelsen 1995.

28. See Belich 2009: 181–182.

29. See Kennedy 2008: ix.

30. See Child 2012.

31. See Michaelsen 1995: 66.

32. See Black Hawk 2008[1833]: 24.

33. The sub-title of this section takes inspiration from Benton 2016. On settler colonialism as an ongoing cultural process, see Simpson 2014; Wolfe 2016; Inwood and Bonds 2016; Tuck and Yang 2012.

34. See Verdery and Humphrey 2004.

35. It's worth noting, as we do elsewhere of Locke, that many of these thinkers had financial stakes in US and Caribbean colonies as well as in the slave trade. Hobbes, for example, was invested in the Virginia Company from 1622 until 1624 and in the Somers Islands Company in the settlement of Bermuda (Johnson 2011: 398f8).

36. See also Pietz (1985) on the colonial origin of the Portuguese misconception of African "fetishism," which Marx would later use to critique European relationships to commodities.

37. See Robinson 2000 on racial capitalism.

38. On this point, see also Bosworth 2018.

39. For an important exception, see Vincent 1999 on Black farming in the Midwest.

40. Quoted in Johnson 2011: 404.

41. See Lauck 2013: 173.

42. Bushman (1992: 387), for instance, describes how the eighteenth-century "West," which included what is now the Midwest, was imagined by elite New Englanders as uncivilized, wild, and rough, in ways that could elicit comparison to supposedly uncivilized places and people around the world.

43. See Belich 2009.

44. Belich 2009: 190. Colonization as a form of warfare is also apparent through the fact that, before the Commissioner of Indian Affairs was moved to the US Interior Department in the 1870s—the time when treaty-making ceased with Native Americans (1871)—it was part of the War Department, or what is now the Defense Department (Wildenthal and O'Neil 2000).

45. See Belich 2009: 190.

46. Cited in Mills 2003: 37.

47. See Lake and Reynolds 2008.

48. Quoted in Lake and Reynolds 2008: 130.

49. See Bigham 1987: 5.

50. Bigham 1987: 44.

51. Political theorist Joel Olson (2004: xx) makes clear these connections between race and citizenship: "In the formative years of American democracy, citizenship was in a very real sense proof that one was not and could not become a slave. Given the racial character of chattel slavery in the United States, its antitheses, citizenship, was also racialized."

52. Vega 2015: 60.

53. Bebout 2016: 45.

54. Bebout 2016: 44.

55. The Boston-based United Fruit Company (UFC) had already been involved in Colombia in the early twentieth century, infamously resulting in the UFC-supported 1928 massacre of striking banana workers (Lorek 2013: 285).

56. See Lorek 2013: 285.

57. See Lorek 2013: 295. Smith taught at Louisiana State University but said he gained three years of "first-hand experience of life and labor in the great dairy farming areas of Wisconsin" (295).

58. See Lorek 2013: 295. The imperial spectacle of Midwestern settlement, the dominant racial economies of the time, and a hegemonic (white Protestant) American vision of the world were spatially commingled in the 1893 and 1904 World's Fairs, which were held in Chicago and St. Louis respectively.

59. Hudson 2017: 21.

60. Hoganson 2019: 96–104.

61. Hudson 2017: 14.

62. See Belich 2009: 335–336.

63. See Green 2007: xi.

64. On this point, see Green 2007: 53.

65. Cited in Pichaske 2006: 191–192.

66. See Shortridge 1989: 83.

67. Rothstein 2017: 127–128.

68. Rothstein 2017: 176.

69. On this point, see Finney 2014; Mills 2001.

70. See Weems 2015: 216–217.

71. Quoted in Mignolo 2011: 161; see also Quijano 1991.

72. See Weems 2015: 160–161.

73. On the relationship between the Midwest and other regions, see Lauck 2013: 170–172.

CHAPTER 3. INSIDE OUT: THE GLOBAL PRODUCTION OF INSULAR WHITENESS

1. Lam 2018: 34. Here he draws on Richard Wright's conception of the white lumpenproletariat.

2. The Stefon sketch fits with what Jasbir Puar calls homonationalism, one form of which can involve "the inclusion of gay and queer subjectivities that are encouraged in liberal discourses of multiculturalism and diversity but are produced through racial and national difference" (2007: 77).

3. Butler 2004: 125–126.

4. Ochonicky 2020: 2.

5. See Seshadri-Crooks 2000: 9.

6. Like the absent (but ever-present) Midwestern other, the radical queer other (whom Stefon represents) is not really present and never fully inhabited by the white, straight, cis-male performer. No actor fully inhabits their character insofar as they are perceived as acting, of course. But this role distance is especially marked in the Stefon sketch—another popular dimension of the Stefon comedy bit is that Bill Hader frequently breaks character and laughs during the segment, covering his face when he does so. This became so expected that the audience would laugh and cheer even louder when it happened. It demonstrates a further reflexive angle, an enjoyment of watching Stefon and an enjoyment of Hader breaking from playing the character because of just how extreme and absurd the character is.

7. Clinton 2017: 414.

8. Ochonicky 2020: 7.

9. Hoganson 2019: 31.

10. Hoganson 2019: 31.

11. Martinot 2010: 65.

12. Martinot 2010: 59.

13. See Postel 2007.

14. On Protestant and Pietist history, see Haeri 2017 and Meyer 1999; for connections between these traditions and more secular accounts of interiority, see Taylor 1989.

15. It is debated whether Rilke fits in with the "existentializing" interpretations of American poet-critics or is an early example of the "end of the Subject" (Powell 2008: 88; Pfau 2019).

16. Peseroff 1992.

17. Peseroff 1992: 22.

18. Ignatow 1981: 183.

19. Simpson 1992: 21.

20. Kalaidjian 1992: 194–195.

21. Mitchell 1992: 73.

22. Mitchell 1992: 70.

23. Matthews 1992: 25. Put differently, and again echoing an older Christian Pietist tradition in American life, there is an elective affinity between the "far country" (Davis 1984: 91) or "dark region" (Sugg 1986: 3) of the psyche that is a central theme in many of Bly's books, and the extraordinary countryside of the Midwest.

24. Howard 1992: 41.

25. Molesworth 1992: 193. This insular aesthetic is also evident in Bly's later poetry and its focus on the nonhuman world: "Water, tree, hills, grass, shells, tumbleweed, wind, rain, a bird's nest, tidal pools draw his reflective gaze and stir his imagination toward dream" (Mills 1992: 183).

26. Zinnes 1992: 42; italics in original.

27. This is the "something more than the subject" that Seshadri-Crooks (2000: 9) refers to as key to the desirability of whiteness.

28. Mazzocco 1992: 50.

29. Lacey 1992: 126.

30. Kalaidjian 1992: 196.

31. Seshadri-Crooks 2000: 44.

32. Savran 1996: 8.

33. Savran 1996: 15.

34. Savran 1996: 15.

35. See Ferber 2000: 37.

36. Or "always at risk and never secure," as Ferber 2000: 40 puts it.

37. Ferber 2000: 52.

38. Bly 2004: 27.

39. Bly 2004: 27.

40. Here we follow Jef Huysmans (2006), who considers insular inwardness in terms of its geopolitical ramifications for global security regimes. For Huysmans, the politics of exception is made worse through an existential dynamic associated with inwardness: "The intensification of inwardness that is particularly problematic in this context is an anti-diplomatic inwardness. Anti-diplomacy is a practice by which one seeks to transcend political estrangement by constructing the world into a mirror image of oneself" (2006: 21).

41. Page and Walker 1991: 281.

42. One notable exception is Baldwin 2001.

43. These articles were ripe for libel lawsuits, and Woeste (2004) tells the story of the 1927 lawsuit *Sapiro vs. Ford*, which ended in a mistrial. Ford attempted to dispense with the whole affair by issuing a nationally publicized apology. What has been kept secret until Woeste's (2004) analysis was that Ford hired a Jewish man to write his apology and thus the wording according to Woeste represented the prominent Jewish leader Louis Marshall's aims for Jewish acceptance rather than necessarily Ford's own contrition.

44. On the nonwhiteness of Jews at this time, see Woeste 2004; Brodkin Sacks 1998.

45. See Lauck 2013a: 176.

46. Tanner 2008: 59–60.

47. Woeste 2004: 883–891.

48. See Wallace 2003: 14.

49. Paul 2014: 259.

50. In a related way, Jasbir Puar (2007) examines how projecting homophobia onto the (similarly imagined) "Middle-Eastern" world region, is used by liberal regimes to justify and underwrite settler colonial and imperialist violence abroad.

51. See Woeste 2004.

52. Quoted in Wallace 2003: 2. Other work has alleged that Ford's company collaborated, under his direction, with Nazis until 1942, placing a Nazi sympathizer as the head of German Ford, producing military vehicles there, and profiting handsomely from the war (Silverstein 2000). As Silverstein (2000) strikingly states, "Of the 350,000 trucks used by the motorized German Army as of 1942, roughly one-third were Ford-made."

53. Diamond 1974 is in the former camp. James Whitman associates this tendency with problematic assumptions about historical influence: "Our literature has taken a crass interpretive tack: it has assumed that we can speak of 'influence' only where we find direct and unmodified, even verbatim, imitation" (Whitman 2017: 13).

54. Cikraji 2014: 18.

55. See Rodriguez-Pose and Berlepsch 2015 and Daniels 1990, respectively to back up these claims.

56. Cikraji 2014: 18.

57. Sander Diamond has argued that American Nazis did not commit to the movement because they were drawn to white supremacist ideology, per se—which he associates with the narrow desire to create a population of racially pure supermen—but due to the effect that the Great Depression had on their lives (1974: 151–152).

58. Diamond 1974: 115.

59. This angered nativists who "believed that the act's restrictions had created a new immigration problem while solving the old one" (Mapes 2004: 66). One of the architects of immigration restrictions, Madison Grant, opined, "It is not logical to limit the number of Europeans while we throw the country open without limitation to Negroes, Indians and half breeds" (quoted in Mapes 2004: 66).

60. This was not entirely new; after all Know Nothings had warned of a global "Roman" conspiracy to overthrow the government and some Populists blamed secret cabals of money lenders that feared a shift to silver coinage (Olmstead 2009). The content of the conspiracism was not new but the distinct efforts of Ford and the Third Reich represent a specific transnational project, with identifiable consequences for the future of white supremacist ideas, images, and efforts. Interestingly, a very different attempt at global networking around race, the Pacific Movement of the Eastern World (PMEW), has received far more attention than the case we consider. According to Lipsitz, PMEW leadership encouraged some Black Garveyites in the Midwest to prepare to rise up in insurrection in support of "non-white" Japan if war broke out, in acknowledgment of shared opposition to white supremacy (2018: 207).

61. As Huysmans (2006: 17) puts it, "Such an existential rendition of the exception can be a rationale for an extremely aggressive security policy that combines an inward turn cutting away international institutional and symbolic frameworks with a global

projection of one's own political identity." Paradoxically, this kind of insularity is used in order to advance more aggressive and globalist policies in the name of protection and security. In other words, as we have described of Teddy Roosevelt's earlier "imperial turn," these sentiments help foster discrete, racial projects of white supremacy with imperial dimensions (Huysmans 2006: 21).

62. Benedict Anderson made this clear with respect to the imagined community of the nation, with its dependence on print media, especially newspapers in shared language(s) using a shared calendar. The scalar order that Anderson associated with the modern nation-state is not merely homogeneous, but homogenizing and contested from within (Silverstein 2000: 128–129). This means that any kind of standardization of collective belonging demands "continual affirmation" (Song 2010: 83).

63. See Coronil 2019 for a breakdown of the role of imperial geography in misrepresenting the world.

64. This is arguably only exacerbated with processes of uneven development within capitalist systems, as regions become associated with alternative or competing economic sectors. In the United States, for example, Ann Markusen points out how the development of sectoral economies, those dependent on the production of whole commodities or groups of similar commodities, became deeply regionalized. In other words, as oil, high technology, agricultural goods, automobiles, and steel became regionalized in specific ways, their impacts on regional economies differed, raising the possibility of awareness of such differences and reactions to them *as regional* issues (Markusen et al. 1991).

65. It is arguably an awareness of these tensions that is part of what moves some white men to join masculinist and white supremacist movements that appeal to a lost or ancestral source of spiritual wholeness; but this promise of a return to virtue fails to recognize the wounds inflicted by systems of race and gender in the first place.

66. James 1993[1963]: 40.

67. James 1993[1963]: 41–42.

68. James 1993[1963]: 65.

CHAPTER 4. NO PLACE LIKE HOME: THE "ORDINARY" MIDWEST
THROUGH POPULAR FICTION AND FANTASY

1. On the politics of intimacy, see Herzfeld 2005; Pritzker 2014; Webster 2015; and Perrino 2020.

2. As Lee Edelman argues, one strategy to deal with these tensions is to focus on what he calls *reproductive futurity*, whereby the Child gains sacred status, as the truth of the whole social order. For Edelman, the sacred (rather than horrific) Child is also mediated through fictional fantasy, through figures like Tiny Tim, for instance (Edelman 2004).

3. Nathanson 1991: 157.

4. Nathanson 1991: 157.

5. Rushdie 1992: 16.

6. On the possible political significance of Baum's tale, see Littlefield 1964.

7. Nathanson 1991: 171.

8. Nathanson 1991: 171. Nathanson compares the "mythic pastoralism" of *The Wizard* to the Regionalist painting style associated with Grant Wood and Charles Sheeler (1991: 164–165). He goes on to argue that a "common visual idiom" inspired Wood and set designers at MGM, since "this was based on cultural traditions familiar to the American public at large" (1991: 171). He also disagrees with the criticisms from Rushdie 1992 and Gilman 1995 about the film's ending.

9. On Disney and Midwestness, see Schickel 1968: 53 and Tibbetts 2003: 422.

10. On Superman's origin, see De Haven 2010: 155–161.

11. Lowther 1942: 40.

12. Lowther 1942: 58.

13. De Haven 2010: 160.

14. De Haven 2010: 161.

15. De Haven finds this unfortunate, "This time, lucky guy, Clark got the full-blown all-American family package deal, the whole megillah. Still I think I miss the passing motorist" (De Haven 2010: 162).

16. On this critical tension between self-creation and social obligation in late-liberal societies, see Povinelli 2006.

17. On the nativism associated with the scandal, see Bachin 2003.

18. This is largely due to the influence of psychoanalysis in horror interpretation, where the monster is understood to be a "return of the repressed" (Wood 1979; Grant 1996). Our own approach to horror, along with that in the book as a whole, is more tied to critics who place this genre in historical and cultural context, see Ross and Huss 1972 and Derry 1977. On terrible places as sites of horror, see Clover 1996: 78.

19. On children in horror and in visions of society's future, see Sobchack 1996: 149, and Edelman 2004, and on fear of children in American society, see Perin 1977. Joseph Grixti argues that "stereotypes and literary/cultural archetypes (like 'fantasy') do not just develop out of thin air: they form part of complex meaning-making processes which are inspired by identifiable social and psychological purposes" (1989: 174). For example, films about child monsters and home or planetary invasions "coincided with mounting awareness and concern over diminishing resources and a growing public debate about the widespread availability of effective methods of birth control, the legalization of abortion, and the long and short-term effects of pregnancy-related drugs like thalidomide and fertilization pills"(Grixti 1989: 26). Grixti goes on to mention *The Exorcist* and *A Clockwork Orange* in this period. During the McCarthy era there had also been films about frightening children, including *Rebel without a Cause* (1955) and *The Bad Seed* (1956), which Joseph Maddrey associates with "postwar paranoia" (2004: 36) of the time.

20. Maddrey 2004: 133; our emphasis.

21. Maddrey 2004: 133.

22. Quoted in Konow 2012: 253.

23. Konow 2012: 254.

24. Konow 2012: 264.

25. Maddrey 2004: 167.

26. Craven quoted in Maddrey 2004: 167. In another nod to the contradictions of Midwestness, Freddy's dream layer is industrial and mechanical, in direct contrast to the kinds of rural and suburban spaces where his victims live in the real world, a twisted and dream-like Oz or Krypton.

27. Capote 1966: 6.

28. Tibbets 2003: 426.

29. Adler 1991: 54. On Craven's inspiration, see Morgan 2018.

30. On the Hmong health crisis, see Fadiman 1997. *Candyman* (1992) is worth mentioning as a film that subverts this trope by making it partly about white supremacy, but it still makes whiteness a source of innocence purifying that past. It also subverts the relationship between audience and film: "The victim and the audience are responsible for empowering the monster" (Maddrey 2004: 84).

31. There is also a parallelism between the visual representation of Superman and portraits of Jesus done by American painters in the 1940s. One example is Warner Sallman's famous Head of Christ (which was circulated globally as devotional art). Sallman's painting and others at the time depicted Jesus as a white, tan, all-American hero, being part of what some scholars later called a 1950s "muscular Christianity." At a time when notions of whiteness were changing, Superman represents a rather particular, WASP-ish, not ethnically marked version of whiteness, as did Sallman's painting.

CHAPTER 5. THEATER OF WHITENESS: MASS MEDIA DISCOURSES ON THE MIDWEST REGION

1. Natalia Molina (2014) coined the term "racial scripts" to refer to varied messages and stories in the United States that tend to be reused over and over to discipline and dominate different racialized groups, for instance Latinx communities and African Americans. Our use of the term is similar, though we see scripts about white people as, in many ways, structuring and giving meaning to other racial scripts, as one component of projects of white supremacy.

2. Seshadri-Crooks 2000: 2.

3. As Seshadri-Crooks (2000: 5) observes, citing Teresa Brennan's *Desiring Whiteness*, "the imaginary process of fixing the other is not limited to *seeing*; it also involves naming. More accurately, naming is part of how the other is seen, as well as being part of the way out" (italics in original).

4. In an analogous way, Edward Said used theatrical motifs to explain his critique of Orientalism (Gregory 2004: 18–19). For example, Orientalism was "a theatrical stage affixed to Europe" (1978: 63). Whereas Said considered Orientalism to have an "audience, manager and actors . . . for Europe, and only for Europe" (1978: 71), we consider the audience and actors associated with the performance of the Midwest to be much broader and heterogeneous.

5. In her work *The Archive and the Repertoire* (2003: 3), performance studies scholar Diana Taylor observes, "Performances travel, challenging and influencing other performances. Yet they are, in a sense, always in situ: intelligible in the framework of the immediate environment and issues surrounding them."

6. As many scholars since J. L. Austin's speech act theory have elaborated, performances are "regulating and citational," and sometimes so ideologically normalized as to be invisible (Taylor 2003: 5; Derrida 1988).

7. In her insightful book on deindustrialization and race, *Unfinished Business*, performance studies scholar Judith Hamera (2017) develops the idea that dramatized figures synergistically link circulating media discourse, bodily gesture, and visual images in public depictions of complex affective experiences, such as Midwest deindustrialization. On race as performance, see also Jackson 2001; Johnson 2003; Cox 2015; Covington-Ward 2016. In chapter 4, we considered how fictional film media also perform whiteness and Midwestness in analogous ways.

8. Cited in Williams 2018: 38.

9. Beginning arguably with Benedict Anderson's (1991) influential study of imagined communities, social scientists have acknowledged the role of mass media in the creation of nationalist sentiments and movements. See Hall et al. 1978; Teo 2000; Law 2002; van Dijk 2011; Hodges 2015. More recently, linguistic anthropologists have argued for the importance of analyzing how media discourse does not merely reflect but produces various "publics," building influential discursive images of political community through which individuals can position, envision, and distinguish themselves (Urban 2001; Cody 2011). As Gale (2004: 324) observes, "News media, particularly newspapers, have played a crucial role in the emergence of a new language of 'race' and nation." On seemingly insignificant "public words," see Spitulnik 1996.

10. See *The Economist* 2017.

11. Analyzing media representations of the Midwest in Spanish, Arabic, French, or other languages would deepen our examination of how the Midwest is signaled and evoked, *transculturally* as it were (see chapter 3). We do not mean to suggest that American nationalism is only synonymous with English-medium publications or monolingual populations, even though the "monoglot standard" has played a significant role in American nationalist ideology (Silverstein 1996).

12. On critical discourse analysis, see Fairclough 1995, 1998; Spitulnik 1996; Talbot 2007; van Dijk 2011; and others. The news articles we have chosen do not necessarily constitute a "unified media market or information field" (Graber 2016: 184). However, they do allow us to assess recurrent themes in mass-media discussions of the Midwest region.

13. Hodges 2015: 420.

14. Compare with Vincent 1999.

15. See DeGenova 2007; Stoler and Cooper 1997.

16. Taylor 2003: 15. Taylor notes, "In other words, scenarios exist as culturally specific imaginaries—sets of possibilities, ways of conceiving conflict, crisis, or resolution—activated with more or less theatricality."

17. Cited in Inwood 2016: 2; see also Simpson 2014.

18. Robinson 2000: 200, italics in original.

19. Robinson 2000: 186.

20. Lake and Reynolds 2008.

21. Lake and Reynolds 2008: 112.

22. Lake and Reynolds 2008: 103.

23. Lake and Reynolds 2008: 104.

24. See also Cramer 2016: 109 on rural white Wisconsinites' feelings of being ignored.

25. Blanchette 2019: 83.

26. Cited in Gahman 2020: 159.

27. Berlant 1991: 21.

28. This quoted passage reflects the words of Cedric Robinson 2000: 201.

29. See Robinson 2000: 24.

30. Creating separate, segregated labor unions was one way Black workers were eventually included in unions, until the practice was formally banned by the government in 1962.

31. Rothstein 2017: 156.

32. On the "wage of whiteness," see Roediger 1991. It was not until Lenin suggested it at the Second Congress of the Communist International in 1920 that American Communists began recruiting Black workers in 1921, well over fifty years after the start of Reconstruction (Robinson 2000: 219).

33. This example comes from Miraftab 2016: 45–46.

34. Bebout 2016: 65.

35. Miraftab 2016.

36. Rothstein 2017: 4.

37. See Rothstein 2017.

38. Walker and Bennett 2015: 186.

39. Walker and Bennett 2015: 182. On whiteness and unfairness narratives, see Hochschild 2015.

40. This material comes from Miraftab 2016: 27–53.

41. This white racial portrait of the working-class conceals how the US economy is actually reliant on, and maintains, a workforce of "unregulated, low wage work performed . . . by immigrant agricultural laborers, short-order cooks, porters, bellhops, janitors, pool cleaners, domestic servants, nannies, gardeners, and construction workers" (Lipsitz 2018[1998]: 57). As sociologist George Lipsitz has shown, white outrage at immigrant workers supposedly taking "American jobs" helps facilitate this underground system of poor wages and work conditions because it incites fear and prevents immigrant workers from organizing and calling for state enforcement of labor laws. Therefore, in many ways, white feelings about unfairness, whether resentment, anger, despair, or frustration, are actually not separate from but a part of the way economic inequality gets reinforced along racial and ethnic lines—and has for generations.

42. In *Unfinished Business*, Judith Hamera characterizes "the deindustrial" as a period and structure of feeling that reflects configurations of race, work, and capital stemming from chattel slavery (2017: 5). She writes that deindustrialization's "folk model" pivots around "hard-working if disaffected white industrial heroes left out or left behind by structural change" (Hamera 2017: 7). On deindustrialization as a folk model, see di Leonardo 1985.

43. Rothstein 2017: 155.

44. As Seshadri-Crooks points out, race "must therefore disavow or deny knowledge of its own historicity . . . or risk surrendering to the discourse of wholeness and supremacy" (2000: 8).

45. Ta-Nehisi Coates (2017), among others, has argued against this theory of the election; he points out that the median household income of the Trump voter is actually $72,000 per year, indicating that white voters with more sizeable and less working-class incomes played a significant role in his election. Among other factors, pre-election Gallup pollsters Jonathan Rothwell and Pablo Diego-Rosell found that living in a primarily white neighborhood was a better indicator of Trump support than income.

46. Isenberg 2016. *Hillbilly Elegy* (Vance 2016) has been critiqued for the way it embraces a pull-yourself-up-by-your-bootstraps approach to Appalachian poverty, placing blame on individuals for forms of structural inequality and ignoring the long-standing presence of extractive industries and corporate profit-making in the region. A recent pushback to the book and its widespread cultural appeal, including its critically acclaimed Hollywood movie version, was issued by a group of Appalachian writers who contributed to Harkins and McCarroll's *Appalachian Reckoning* (2019).

47. Hochschild 2015: 233.

48. On social suffering as a dimension of power relations in various societies, see Kleinman, Das, and Lock 1997.

49. Baldwin 2012 [1955]: 19.

50. See e.g., Kleinman and Kleinman 1996; Butt 2002; Benton 2016; Cole 2012.

51. On counterscript, see Molina 2014.

52. On this point, see the recent volume *Black in the Middle* (Williamson 2020).

53. Winfrey-Harris cites an Economic Policy Institute study that projects that by 2032 the working class in the United States will have a majority of people of color (*New York Times*, 6/16/18).

54. Valdés 2000: 241.

55. Roediger and Robinson 2016; see Loewen 2018 [2005].

56. See, e.g., Abdi 2014; Croegaert 2010; Shryock and Howell 2003.

57. Foner 2000: ix–x. In 1965, the US government lifted quota restrictions on immigration per country that had severely limited US settlement for people from countries outside Western Europe and Canada (Gordon 1998). Although numerical restrictions were still in place concerning the number of migrants per year after 1965, these limits were raised incrementally in 1990 for professionals and skilled workers. Additionally, the 1980 Refugee Act distinguished the category of refugees from immigrants and,

though under threat by the Trump administration, provided the policy mechanisms for humanitarian resettlement of refugee populations.

58. Martin 2007: 1167; Gordon 1998.

59. See Holtzman 2000.

60. See Walley 2013.

61. See Clampitt 2015.

62. Belich 2009: 341. Curing techniques in the 1820s and later railway refrigeration beginning in the 1870s had already sent meat from what was then known as the Old Northwest to the Northeast (Belich 2009: 207). See also Hoganson (2019) on the global and imperial Midwestern meat industry.

63. Balken 2009: 167.

64. Supporting the idea of regional designations as comparable, scalar units, the Rust Belt term, which originated in the United States in the 1960s, has since been applied to industrial areas of northeastern China, England's "Pauperized Belts," coal and steel towns in northern France, and the Ruhr Valley in Germany (Campbell 2007: 80). On the Midwest and global agricultural markets, see Lipsey 1994.

65. Diverging in important ways from Benedict Anderson's influential theory of nationalism as imagined community, performative approaches tend to foreground the bodily, discursive, ritual, and other resources marshaled in the everyday work of making, identifying with, and critiquing forms of nationalism, race, and empire. See, e.g., Ong 1996 and Covington-Ward 2016.

66. Beliso-De Jesús and Pierre 2019: 3.

67. On media as discursive struggle, see Hall 1996; Fairclough 1998.

68. See Bebout 2016: xvii; also Miraftab 2016.

69. Billig 1995: 14.

CONCLUSION

1. We draw especially on the writing of Curry 2017.

2. We would add that it is also common to many people around the world who are not American but who either adopt or reflect on what they imagine to be "American" models and racial projects with similar denials about white supremacy.

3. One could compare this to Fanon's conception of the sociogenic principle as elaborated by Sylvia Wynter (see Wynter 2001; Hantel 2018), or the liberation theology of martyred Jesuit priest and philosopher Ignacio Ellacuría (1990). In both cases, ontology, or the world as it is, can only be understood through the lives of people suffering the most from it and, therefore, who represent the promise of the world that could be.

4. James 1989[1938]; Robinson 2000; Drake 1987.

5. See Rolph-Trouillot 1995.

6. Mills 1997: 96–97.

7. As Markusen (1987) makes clear, regions are not imagined out of thin air, but are the culmination, first, of what actually happens historically, including what

ordinary social actors actually do and, second, of dominant representations of these events and actions, including what this means for the people to come.

8. Valdés, 2000: 18.

9. Valdés 2000: 72.

10. Valdés 2000: 224–225.

11. On Mexican immigrants, see Valdés 2000, and on Sudanese refugees, see Holtzman 1999.

12. Valdés 2000: 227.

13. Vega 2015.

14. Valdés 2000: 270.

15. See, for example, Hartigan 1999; De Genova 2005; Cox 2015; Vega 2015. Through these mechanisms, Midwest regionalisms contribute to bordering as an ongoing cultural process (see Khosravi 2010) and produce a multitude of internal "borderlands" (Vega 2015, 148).

16. Our interpretation of Joe Jones comes from Balken 2009: 128–154.

17. Balken 2009: 162.

18. Abraham and Shryock 2000; Abraham, Howell, and Shryock 2011.

19. On the relationship between modernity and coloniality, see Quijano 1991; Mignolo 2011.

20. See Jackson 2002.

21. This forms what Shortridge calls a "depositor[y] for various national values" (1989: 135).

22. See Gjerde and Qualey 2002: 2; Gjerde 1985.

23. See LaDuke 2005.

24. On Minnesota's multiracial history, see Green 2007; Wingerd 2003; Valdés 2000.

25. On transcultural, see Ortiz 1995[1940] and on superdiverse, see Vertovec 2007, 2009; Bloomaert 2010. Superdiverse places in this view are "characterized by an increase of migrants belonging to many nationalities and ethnic groups, speaking many languages and having diverse past histories, migration paths, and religious beliefs" (Perrino 2020: 14).

REFERENCES

Abdi, Cawo. 2014. "Threatened Identities and Gendered Opportunities: Somali Migration to America." *Signs: Journal of Women in Culture and Society* 39(21): 459–483.

Abraham, Nabeel, Sally Howell, and Andrew Shryock, eds. 2011. *Arab Detroit 9/11: Life in the Terror Decade.* Detroit: Wayne State University Press.

Abraham, Nabeel, and Andrew Shryock, eds. 2000. *Arab Detroit: From Margin to Mainstream.* Detroit: Wayne State University Press.

Adler, Shelley R. 1991. "Sudden Unexpected Nocturnal Death Syndrome among Hmong Immigrants: Examining the Role of the 'Nightmare.'" *Journal of American Folklore* 104(411): 54–71.

Ahmed, Sara. 2006. *Queer Phenomenology: Orientations, Objects, Others.* Durham, NC: Duke University Press.

Anderson, Benedict. 1991. *Imagined Communities: Reflections on the Origin and Spread of Nationalism.* London: Verso.

Applegate, Celia. 1999. "A Europe of Regions: Reflections on the Historiography of Sub-national Places in Modern Times." *American Historical Review* 104(4): 1157–1182.

Aptheker, Herbert. 1974[1949]. *American Negro Slave Revolts.* New York: International Publishers.

Augusteijn, Joost, and Eric Storm. 2012. "Introduction: Region and State." In *Region and State in Nineteenth-Century Europe: Nation-Building, Regional Identities and Separatism.* Joost Augusteijn and Eric Storm, eds. Pp. 1–9. London: Palgrave Macmillan.

Bachin, Robin Faith. "At the Nexus of Labor and Leisure: Baseball, Nativism, and the 1919 Black Sox Scandal." *Journal of Social History* 36(4): 941–962.

Balce, Nerissa. 2016. *Body Parts of Empire: Visual Abjection, Filipino Images, and the American Archive*. Ann Arbor: University of Michigan Press.

Baldwin, James. 1989 [1961]. *Conversations with James Baldwin*. Edited by Fred L. Standley and Louis H. Pratt. Jackson: University Press of Mississippi.

———. 2012 [1955]. *Notes on a Native Son*. Boston: Beacon Press.

Baldwin, Neil. 2001. *Henry Ford and the Jews: The Mass Production of Hate*. New York: PublicAffairs.

Balken, Debra. 2009. *After Many Springs: Regionalism, Modernism, and the Midwest*. New Haven, CT: Yale University Press.

Barillas, William David. 2006. *The Midwestern Pastoral: Place and Landscape in Literature of the American Heartland*. Athens: Ohio University Press.

Bay, Mia. 2006. "In Search of Sally Hemings in the Post-DNA Era." *Reviews in American History* 34(4): 407–426.

Bebout, Lee. 2016. *Whiteness on the Border: Mapping the U.S. Racial Imagination in Brown and White*. New York: New York University Press.

Bejan, Raluca. 2020. "Robin Di Angelo's *White Fragility* Ignores the Differences within Whiteness." *The Conversation*. August 27, 2020. Available online: https://theconversation.com/robin-diangelos-white-fragility-ignores-the-differences-within-whiteness-143728.

Belew, Kathleen. 2019. *Bring the War Home: The White Power Movement and Paramilitary America*. Cambridge, MA: Harvard University Press.

Belich, James. 2009. *Replenishing the Earth: The Settler Revolution and the Rise of the Anglo-World, 1783–1939*. Oxford: Oxford University Press.

Beliso-De Jesús, Aisha, and Jemima Pierre. 2019. "Introduction: Anthropology of White Supremacy." *American Anthropologist* 122(1): 1–11.

Benton, Adia. 2016. "African Expatriates and Race in the Anthropology of Humanitarianism." *Critical African Studies* 8(3): 266–277.

Berlant, Lauren. 1991. *The Anatomy of National Fantasy*. Chicago: University of Chicago Press.

———. 2007. "Slow Death (Sovereignty, Obesity, Lateral Agency)." *Critical Inquiry* 33: 754–780.

Bigham, Darrell. 1987. *We Ask Only a Fair Trial: A History of the Black Community of Evansville, Indiana*. Bloomington: Indiana University Press.

Billig, Michael. 1995. *Banal Nationalism*. London: Sage Publications.

Black Hawk. 2008 [1833]. *Life of Black Hawk, or Mà-ka-tai-me-she-kià-kiàk. Dictated by Himself*. Edited by J. Gerald Kennedy. New York: Penguin Classics.

Blanchette, Alex. 2019. "Living Waste and the Labor of Toxic Health on American Factory Farms." *Medical Anthropology Quarterly* 33(1): 80–100.

Blommaert, Jan. 2010. *The Sociolinguistics of Globalization*. Cambridge: Cambridge University Press.

Bly, Robert. 2004 [1990]. *Iron John: A Book about Men*. Cambridge, MA: Da Capo.

Bochner, Arthur P., and Carolyn Ellis, 2016. *Evocative Autoethnography: Writing Lives and Telling Stories*. New York: Routledge.

Bonds, Anne, and Joshua Inwood. 2016. "Beyond White Privilege: Geographies of White Supremacy and Settler Colonialism." *Progress in Human Geography* 40(6): 715–733.

Bonilla-Silva, Eduardo. 2010. *Racism without Racists: Color-Blind Racism and Racial Inequality in Contemporary America*. Third edition. Lanham, MD: Rowman & Littlefield.

Bosworth, Kai. 2018. "'They're Treating Us Like Indians!': Political Ecologies of Property and Race in North American Pipeline." *Antipode* early view. Available Online: https://onlinelibrary.wiley.com/doi/full/10.1111/anti.12426.

Brodkin Sacks, Karen. 1998. *How Jews Became White Folks and What That Says about Race in America*. New Brunswick, NJ: Rutgers University Press.

Bucholtz, Mary. 2001. "The Whiteness of Nerds: Superstandard English and Racial Markedness." *Journal of Linguistic Anthropology* 11(1): 84–100.

Bushman, Richard L. 1992. *The Refinement of America: Persons, Houses, Cities*. New York: Vintage Books.

Butler, Judith. 1990. *Gender Trouble: Feminism and the Subversion of Identity*. New York: Routledge.

———. 2004. *Undoing Gender*. New York: Routledge.

Butt, Leslie. 2002. "The Suffering Stranger: Medical Anthropology and International Morality." *Medical Anthropology* 1: 1–24.

Campbell, Craig S. 2007. "Rust Belt." In *The American Midwest: An Interpretive Encyclopedia*. Andrew R. L. Cayton, Richard Sisson, and Chris Zacher, eds. Pp. 78–80. Bloomington: Indiana University Press.

Campt, Tina. 2012. *Image Matters: Archive, Photography and the African Diaspora in Europe*. Durham, NC: Duke University Press.

———. 2017. *Listening to Images*. Durham, NC: Duke University Press.

Capote, Truman. 1966. *In Cold Blood*. New York: Random House.

Cavazza, Stephen. 2012. "Regionalism in Italy: A Critique." In *Region and State in Nineteenth-Century Europe: Nation-Building, Regional Identities and Separatism*. Joost Augusteijn and Eric Storm, eds. Pp. 69–89. New York: Palgrave Macmillan.

Cayton, Andrew R. L., and Susan Gray, eds. 2007. *The Identity of the American Midwest: Essays on Regional History*. Bloomington: Indiana University Press.

Cayton, Andrew R. L., and Peter S. Onuf. 1990. *The Midwest and the Nation: Rethinking the History of an American Region*. Bloomington: Indiana University Press.

Chen, Mel Y. 2012. *Animacies: Biopolitics, Racial Mattering and Queer Affect*. Durham, NC: Duke University Press.

Child, Brenda J. 1998. *Boarding School Seasons: American Indian Families, 1900–1940*. Lincoln: University of Nebraska Press.

———. 2012. *Holding Our World Together: Ojibwe Women and the Survival of Community*. New York: Penguin Books.

Cikraji, Michael. 2014. *The History of the Cleveland Nazis, 1933–1945*. Cleveland, OH: Erfindung Company.

Clampitt, Cynthia. 2015. *Midwest Maize: How Corn Shaped the U.S. Heartland.* Urbana-Champaign: University of Illinois Press.

Clinton, Hilary. 2017. *What Happened.* New York: Simon & Schuster.

Clover, Carol J. 1996. "Her Body, Himself: Gender in the Slasher Film." In *The Dread of Difference: Gender and the Horror Film,* B. K. Grant, ed. Pp. 68–115. Austin: University of Texas Press.

Coates, Ta-Nehisi. 2017. "The First White President." *The Atlantic.* Accessed Online: https://www.theatlantic.com/magazine/archive/2017/10/the-first-white -president-ta-nehisi-coates/537909/.

Cody, Francis. 2011. "Publics and Politics." *Annual Review of Anthropology* 40: 37–52.

Cole, Teju. 2012. "The White Savior Industrial Complex." *The Atlantic.* Accessed online: https://www.theatlantic.com/international/archive/2012/03/the-white -savior-industrial-complex/254843/.

Coleman, Simon. 2015. "Borderlands: Ethics, Ethnography and 'Repugnant' Christianity." *HAU: Journal of Ethnographic Theory* 5(2): 275–300.

Collins, Jane. 2012. "Theorizing Wisconsin's 2011 Protests: Community-Based Unionism Confronts Accumulation by Dispossession." *American Ethnologist* 39(1): 6–20.

Corn, Joseph C. 1983. *The Winged Gospel: America's Romance with Aviation, 1900–1950.* Baltimore: Johns Hopkins University Press.

Coronil, Fernando. 2019. *The Fernando Coronil Reader: The Struggle for Life Is the Matter.* Durham, NC: Duke University Press.

Covington-Ward, Yolanda. 2016. *Gesture and Power: Religion, Nationalism, and Everyday Performance in Congo.* Durham, NC: Duke University Press.

Cox, Aimee Meredith. 2015. *Shapeshifters: Black Girls and the Choreography of Citizenship.* Durham, NC: Duke University Press.

Cramer, Katherine. 2016. *The Politics of Resentment: Rural Consciousness in Wisconsin and the Rise of Scott Walker.* Chicago: University of Chicago Press.

Croegaert, Ana. 2010. "Global Dramas in the Midwest Metropolis: Representations, Dilemmas, and Decisions about Violence among Bosnian Refugees in Chicago." *Identities* 17: 131–153.

Cronon, William. 1991. *Nature's Metropolis: Chicago and the Great West.* New York: W.W. Norton.

Cuomo, Chris J., and Kim Q. Hall. 1999. "Introduction: Reflections on Whiteness." In *Whiteness: Feminist Philosophical Reflections.* C. J. Cuomo and K. Q. Hall, eds. Pp. 1–14. Lanham, MD: Rowman & Littlefield.

Curry, Tommy. 2017. *The Man-Not: Race, Class, Genre and the Dilemmas of Black Manhood.* Philadelphia: Temple University Press.

Daniels, Roger. 1990. *Coming to America. A History of Immigration and Ethnicity in American Life.* New York: Harper Perennial.

Davis, Kenneth S. 1984. *Kansas: A History.* New York: W.W. Norton and Company.

Davis, Walter Albert. 1989. *Inwardness and Existence: Subjectivity in/and Hegel, Heidegger, Marx, and Freud.* Madison: University of Wisconsin Press.

De Genova, Nicholas. 2005. *Working the Boundaries: Race, Space, and "Illegality" in Mexican Chicago*. Durham, NC: Duke University Press.

————. 2007. "The Stakes of an Anthropology of the United States." *CR: The New Centennial Review* 7(2): 231–277.

De Haven, Tom. 2010. *Our Hero: Superman on Earth*. New Haven, CT: Yale University Press.

Dennis, James M. 1975. *Grant Wood: A Study in American Art and Culture*. New York: Viking Press.

Derrida, Jacques. 1988. *Limited Inc*. Evanston, IL: Northwestern University Press.

Derry, Charles. 1977. *Dark Dreams: A Psychological History of the Modern Horror Film*. South Brunswick, NJ: AS Barnes.

De Tocqueville, Alexis. 1971. *Journey to America*. J. P. Mayer, ed. George Lawrence, trans. Revised Edition. New York: Doubleday.

Dhingra, Pawan. 2009. "Introduction to Special Issue on the Midwest." *Journal of Asian American Studies* 12(3): 239–246.

Diamond, Sander. 1974. *The Nazi Movement in the United States, 1924–1941*. Ithaca, NY: Cornell University Press.

Di Angelo, Robin. 2018. *White Fragility: Why It's So Hard for White People to Talk about Racism*. Boston: Beacon Press.

Di Leonardo, Micaela. 1985. "Deindustrialization as a Folk Model." *Urban Anthropology and Studies of Cultural Systems and World Economic Development* 14(1–3): 237–257.

Dirlik, Arif. 1992. "The Asia-Pacific Idea: Reality and Representation in the Invention of a Regional Structure." *Journal of World History* 3(1): 55–79.

Domínguez, Virginia. 1993. *White by Definition: Social Classification in Creole Louisiana*. New Brunswick, NJ: Rutgers University Press.

Drake, St. Clare. 1987. *Black Folk Here and There: An Essay in History and Anthropology*. Berkeley: University of California Press.

Du Bois, W. E. B. 2013 [1935]. *Black Reconstruction in America: Toward a History of the Part Which Black Folk Played in the Attempt to Reconstruct Democracy in America, 1860–1880*. New Brunswick, NJ: Transaction Publishers.

The Economist. 2017. "Traditional Media Firms Are Enjoying a Trump Bump." Accessed Online, August 19, 2017. https://www.economist.com/news/business /21717107-making-americas-august-news-groups-great-again-traditional-media -firms-are-enjoying-trump-bump.

Edelman, Lee. 2004. *No Future: Queer Theory and the Death Drive*. Durham, NC: Duke University Press.

Ellacuría, Ignacio, 1990. *Filosofía de la Realidad Histórica*. San Salvador: UCA Editores.

Fadiman, Anne. 1997. *The Spirit Catches You and You Fall Down*. New York: Farrar, Straus and Giroux.

Fairclough, Norman. 1995. *Media Discourse*. London: Edward Arnold.

————. 1998. "Political Discourse in the Media: An Analytical Framework." In *Approaches to Media Discourse*. Allan Bell and Peter Garrett, eds. Pp. 142–162. Oxford: Blackwell.

Farr, James. 2008. "Locke, Natural Law, and New World Slavery." *Political Theory* 36 (4): 495–522.

Ferber, Abby L. 2000. "Racial Warriors and Weekend Warriors: the Construction of Masculinity in Mythopoetic and White Supremacist Discourse." *Men and Masculinities* 3(1): 30–56.

Finney, Carolyn. 2014. *Black Faces, White Spaces: Reimagining the Relationship of African Americans to the Great Outdoors.* Chapel Hill: University of North Carolina Press.

Foner, Nancy. 2000. "Preface." In Jon D. Holtzman, *Nuer Journeys, Nuer Lives: Sudanese Refugees in Minnesota.* London: Pearson.

Frykman, Jonas, and Orvar Löfgren. 1987. *Culture Builders: A Historical Anthropology of Middle-Class Life.* Translated by Alan Crozier. New Brunswick, NJ: Rutgers University Press.

Gahman, Levi. 2020. *Land, God and Guns: Settler Colonialism and Masculinity in the American Heartland.* New York: Zed Books.

Gale, Peter. 2004. "The Refugee Crisis and Fear: Populist Politics and Media Discourse." *Journal of Sociology* 40(4): 321–340.

Gilman, Todd S. 1995. "'Aunt Em: Hate You! Hate Kansas! Taking the Dog. Dorothy': Conscious and Unconscious Desire in *The Wizard of Oz*." *Children's Literature Association Quarterly* 20(4): 161–167.

Gjerde, Jon. 1985. *From Peasants to Farmers: The Migration from Balestrand, Norway, to the Upper Middle West.* Cambridge: Cambridge University Press.

Gjerde, Jon, and Carlton C. Qualey. 2002. *Norwegians in Minnesota.* St. Paul: Minnesota Historical Society Press.

Gluck, Carol. 1985. *Japan's Modern Myths: Ideology in the Late Meiji Period.* Princeton, NJ: Princeton University Press.

Goldberg, David Theo. 1993. *Racist Culture: Philosophy and the Politics of Meaning.* Oxford: Wiley Blackwell.

Gordon, April. 1998. "The New Diaspora: African Immigration to the United States." *Journal of Third World Studies* 15(1): 79–104.

Graber, Kathryn E. 2016. "The All-Buriat 'Ray of Light': Independence and Identity in Native-Language Media." *Region* 1(1): 175–200.

Grant, Barry K., ed. 1996. *The Dread of Difference: Gender and the Horror Film.* Austin: University of Texas Press.

Green, William D. 2007. *A Peculiar Imbalance: The Rise and Fall of Racial Equality in Early Minnesota.* St. Paul: Minnesota Historical Society Press.

Gregory, Derek. 2004. *The Colonial Present: Afghanistan, Palestine, Iraq.* Oxford: Wiley Blackwell.

Grill, Johnpeter Horst. 1982. "The Nazi Party's Rural Propaganda before 1928." *Central European History* 15(2): 149–185.

Grixti, Joseph. 1989.*Terrors of Uncertainty: Horror and Helplessness in Contemporary Bestsellers.* New York: Routledge.

Haeri, Niloofar. 2017. "Unbundling Sincerity: Language, Mediation, and Interiority in Comparative Perspective." *HAU: Journal of Ethnographic Theory* 7(1): 123–138.

Hall, Stuart. 1996. "Race, Articulation, and Societies Structured in Dominance." In *Black British Cultural Studies: A Reader*. Houston A. Baker Jr., Manthia Diawara, and Ruth H. Lindeborg, eds. Pp. 16–60. Chicago: University of Chicago Press.

Hall, Stuart, C. Critcher, T. Jefferson, J. Clarke, and B. Roberts. 1978. *Policing the Crisis: Mugging, the State, and Law and Order*. London: Macmillan.

Hamera, Judith. 2017. *Unfinished Business: Michael Jackson, Detroit & the Figural Economy of American Deindustrialization*. Oxford: Oxford University Press.

Hannah, Matthew G. 2000. *Governmentality and the Mastery of Territory in Nineteenth Century America*. New York: Cambridge University Press.

Hantel, Max. 2018. "What Is It Like to Be a Human? Sylvia Wynter on Autopoiesis." *philoSOPHIA* 8(1): 61–79.

Harding, Susan. 1991. "Representing Fundamentalism: The Problem of the Repugnant Cultural Other." *Social Research* 58(2): 373–393.

Harkins, Anthony, and Meredith McCarroll, eds. 2019. *Appalachian Reckoning: A Region Responds to Hillbilly Elegy*. Morgantown, WV: West Virginia University Press.

Harris, Cheryl I. 1993. "Whiteness as Property." *Harvard Law Review* 106(8): 1707–1791.

Harrison, Faye V. 2002. "Unraveling 'Race' for the Twenty-First Century." In *Exotic No More: Anthropology on the Front Lines*. Jeremy MacClancy, ed. Pp. 145–166. Chicago: University of Chicago Press.

Hartigan, John, Jr. 1999. *Racial Situations: Class Predicaments of Whiteness in Detroit*. Princeton, NJ: Princeton University Press.

———. 2010. *What Can You Say? America's National Conversation on Race*. Stanford: Stanford University Press.

Herzfeld, Michael. 2014. *Cultural Intimacy: Social Poetics in the Nation-State*. New York: Routledge.

Hill, Jane. 2011. *The Everyday Language of White Racism*. Malden, MA: Wiley Blackwell.

Hixson, Walter L. 2013. *Settler Colonialism: An American History*. New York: Palgrave Macmillan.

Hochschild, Arlie. 2015. *Strangers in Their Own Land: Anger and Mourning on the American Right*. New York: The New Press.

Hodges, Adam. 2015. "Ideologies of Language and Race in US Media Discourse about the Trayvon Martin Shooting." *Language in Society* 44: 401–423.

Hoganson, Kristin. 2019. *The Heartland: An American History*. New York: Penguin.

Holtzman, Jon. 2000. *Nuer Journeys, Nuer Lives: Sudanese Refugees in Minnesota*. London: Pearson.

Howard, Richard. 1992. "Poetry Chronicle [Review of *Silence in the Snowy Fields*]." In William V. Davis, ed. Pp. 40–41. *Critical Essays on Robert Bly*. New York: G.K. Hall and Co.

Hudson, Peter James. 2017. *Bankers and Empire: How Wall Street Colonized the Caribbean*. Chicago: University of Chicago Press.

Hughes, Langston. 1990[1933]. *The Ways of White Folks*. Vintage Books.

Huysmans, Jef. 2006. "International Politics of Insecurity: Normativity, Inwardness and the Exception." *Security Dialogue* 37(1): 11–29.

Ignatow, David. 1981. "Reflections on the Past with Robert Bly." In *Of Solitude and Silence: Writings on Robert Bly*. Richard Jones and Kate Daniels, eds. Pp. 182–191. Boston: Beacon Press.

Inwood, Joshua. 2016. "It is the Innocence Which Constitutes the Crime": Political Geographies of White Supremacy, the Construction of White Innocence, and the Flint Water Crisis." *Geography Compass* 2018: 12:e12361.

Isenberg, Nancy. 2016. *White Trash: The 400-Year-Old Untold History of Class in America*. New York: Viking.

Jackson, Deborah Davis. 2002. *Our Elders Lived It: American Indian Identity in the City*. Dekalb: Northern Illinois University Press.

Jackson, John L. Jr. 2001. *Harlemworld: Doing Race and Class in Contemporary Black America*. Chicago: University of Chicago Press.

Jackson, Lauren Michelle. 2020. "The Layered Deceptions of Jessica Krug, the Black Studies Professor Who Hid That She Is White." *New Yorker*. 12 September 2020. Available online: https://www.newyorker.com/culture/cultural-comment/the-layered-deceptions-of-jessica-krug-the-black-studies-professor-who-hid-that-she-is-white.

James, C. L. R. 1989 [1938]. *The Black Jacobins: Toussaint L'Ouverture and the San Domingo Revolution*. New York: Vintage.

———. 1993 [1963]. *Beyond a Boundary*. Durham, NC: Duke University Press.

Jessen, Nathan. 2017. *Populism and Imperialism: Politics, Culture, and Foreign Policy in the American West, 1890–1900*. Lawrence: University Press of Kansas.

Johnson, E. Patrick. 2003. *Appropriating Blackness: Performance and the Politics of Authenticity*. Durham, NC: Duke University Press.

Johnson, Hildegard Binder. 1994. "Chapter 7, Toward a National Landscape." In *The Making of the American Landscape*. Michael P. Conzen, ed. Pp. 127–144. New York: Routledge.

Johnson, Paul Christopher. 2011. "An Atlantic Genealogy of Spirit Possession." *Comparative Studies in Society and History* 53(2): 393–425.

Kafer, Alison. 2003. *Feminist, Queer, Crip*. Bloomington: Indiana University Press.

Kalaidjian, Walter. 1992. "From Silence to Subversion: Robert Bly's Political Surrealism." In *Critical Essays on Robert Bly*. William V. Davis, ed. Pp. 194–211. New York: G.K. Hall & Co.

Kennedy, J. Gerald. 2008. "Introduction." In *Life of Black Hawk, or Mà-ka-tai-me-she-kià-kiàk. Dictated by Himself*. J. Gerald Kennedy, ed. Pp. vii–xxviii. New York: Penguin Classics.

Khosravi, Shahram. 2010. *"Illegal" Traveler: An Auto-Ethnography of Borders*. New York: Palgrave Macmillan.

Kirschner, Don S. 1970. *City and Country: Rural Responses to Urbanization in the 1920s*. Westport, CT: Greenwood Publishing.

Kleinman, Arthur, Veena Das, and Margaret Lock, eds. 1997. *Social Suffering*. Berkeley: University of California Press.

Kleinman, Arthur, and Joan Kleinman. 1996. "The Appeal of Experience; the Dismay of Images: Cultural Appropriations of Suffering in Our Times." *Daedalus* 125(1): 1–23.

Konow, David. 2012. *Reel Terror: The Scary, Bloody, Gory, Hundred Year History of Classic Horror Films*. New York: St. Martin's Griffin.

Kosek, Jake. 2006. *Understories: The Political Life of Forests in Northern New Mexico*. Durham, NC: Duke University Press.

Lacey, Paul A. 1992. "The Live World." In *Critical Essays on Robert Bly*. William V. Davis, ed. Pp. 114–134. New York: G.K. Hall and Co.

LaDuke, Winona. 2005. *Recovering the Sacred: The Power of Naming and Claiming*. Cambridge, MA: South End Press.

Lake, Marilyn, and Henry Reynolds. 2008. *Drawing the Global Color Line: White Men's Countries and the International Challenge of Racial Equality*. Cambridge: Cambridge University Press.

Lam, Joshua. 2018. "Richard Wright's 'Basket of Deplorables': The Return of the Lumpenproletariat in U.S. Political Discourse." *Journal of Foreign Languages and Cultures* 2(2): 31–44.

Lauck, Jon. 2013a. "Why the Midwest Matters." *The Midwest Quarterly* 54(2): 165–185.

———. 2013b. *The Lost Region: Toward a Revival of Midwestern History*. Iowa City: University of Iowa Press.

Law, Ian. 2002. *Race in the News*. New York: Palgrave.

Lennon, Myles. 2018. "Revisiting 'the Repugnant Other' in the Era of Trump." *HAU: Journal of Ethnographic Theory* 8(3): 439–454.

Lewis, Sinclair. 1961[1920]. *Main Street*. New York: New American Library.

Lipsey, Robert E. 1994. "U.S. Foreign Trade and the Balance of Payments, 1800–1913." Working Paper No. 4710. Cambridge, MA: National Bureau of Economic Research.

Lipsitz, George. 2018[1998]. *The Possessive Investment in Whiteness: How White People Profit from Identity Politics*. Revised Edition. Philadelphia: Temple University Press.

Littlefield, Henry. 1964. "The Wizard of Oz: Parable on Populism." *American Quarterly* 16(1): 47–58.

Locke, John. 1980 [1690]. *Second Treatise of Government*. Edited by C. B. Macpherson. Indianapolis: Hackett Classics.

Loewen, James W. 2018 [2005]. *Sundown Towns: A Hidden Dimension of American Racism*. The New Press.

Lorek, Timothy W. 2013. "Imagining the Midwest in Latin America: U.S. Advisors and the Envisioning of an Agricultural Middle Class in Colombia's Cauca Valley, 1943–1946." *The Historian* 75(2): 283–305.

Lowther, George Francis. 1942. *Superman*. New York: Random House.

Lyons, Bonnie, and George Plimpton. 1999. "August Wilson, The Art of Theater No. 14." *Paris Review* 153. Accessed January 10th, 2021. Available online: https://www.theparisreview.org/interviews/839/the-art-of-theater-no-14-august-wilson.

Macpherson, C. B. 1962. *The Political Theory of Possessive Individualism.* New York: Oxford University Press.

Maddrey, Joseph. 2004. *Nightmares in Red, White and Blue: The Evolution of the American Horror Film.* Jefferson, NC: McFarland & Company Inc.

Mapes, Kathleen. 2004. "'A Special Class of Labor': Mexican (Im)Migrants, Immigration Debate, and Industrial Agriculture in the Rural Midwest." *Labor: Studies in Working-Class History of the Americas* 1(2): 65–88.

Markusen, Ann. 1987. *Regions: The Economics and Politics of Territory.* Lanham, MD: Rowman & Littlefield.

Markusen, Ann, Peter Hall, Scott Campbell, and Sabina Deitrick. 1991. *The Rise of the Gunbelt: The Military Remapping of Industrial America.* New York: Oxford University Press.

Martin, Judith A. 2007. "Minneapolis and St. Paul, Minnesota." In *The American Midwest: An Interpretive Encyclopedia.* Andrew R. L. Cayton, Richard Sisson, and Chris Zacher, eds. Pp. 1167–1168. Bloomington: Indiana University Press.

Martinot, Steven. 2010. *The Machinery of Whiteness: Studies in the Structure of Racialization.* Philadelphia: Temple University Press.

Matthews, William. 1992. "Thinking about Robert Bly." In William V. Davis, ed. *Critical Essays on Robert Bly.* Pp. 23–26. New York: G.K. Hall and Co.

Mazzocco, Robert. 1992. "Jeremiads at Half-Mast." In *Critical Essays on Robert Bly.* William V Davis, ed. Pp. 46–50. New York: G.K. Hall & Co.

McIntosh, Peggy. 1989. "White Privilege: Unpacking the Invisible Knapsack." *Peace and Freedom Magazine* (July/August): 10–12.

McRuer, Robert. 2006. *Crip Theory: Cultural Signs of Queerness and Disability.* New York: New York University Press.

McWhorter, John. 2020. "The Dehumanizing Condescension of *White Fragility.*" *The Atlantic.* July 15, 2020. Available online: https://www.theatlantic.com/ideas/archive/2020/07/dehumanizing-condescension-white-fragility/614146/.

Metzl, Jonathan. 2019. *Dying of Whiteness: How the Politics of Racial Resentment Is Killing America's Heartland.* New York: Basic Books.

Meyer, Birgit. 1999. *Translating the Devil. Religion and Modernity among the Ewe in Ghana.* Edinburgh: Edinburgh University Press.

Michaelsen, Robert. 1995. "Dirt in the Courtroom: Indian Land Claims and American Property Rights." In *American Sacred Space.* David Chidester and Edward T. Linenthal, eds. Pp. 43–96. Bloomington: Indiana University Press.

Mignolo, Walter. 2011. *The Darker Side of Western Modernity: Global Futures, Decolonial Options.* Durham, NC: Duke University Press.

Mills, Charles W. 1997. *The Racial Contract.* Ithaca, NY: Cornell University Press.

———. 2001. "Black Trash." In *Faces of Environmental Racism.* Laura Westra and Bill E. Lawson, eds. Pp. 73–91. Lanham, MD: Rowman and Littlefield.

———. 2003. *From Class to Race: Essays in White Marxism and Black Radicalism.* Lanham, MD: Rowman & Littlefield.

Mills, Ralph J. Jr. 1992. "'The Body with the Lamp Lit Inside': Robert Bly's New Poems." In *Critical Essays on Robert Bly.* William V. Davis, ed. Pp. 176–185. New York: G.K. Hall & Co

Miraftab, Faranak. 2016. *Global Heartland: Displaced Labor, Transnational Lives and Local Placemaking.* Bloomington: Indiana University Press.

Mitchell, Roger. 1992. "Robert Bly and the Trouble with American Poetry." In *Critical Essays on Robert Bly.* William V. Davis, ed. Pp. 70–74. New York: G.K. Hall and Co.

Molesworth, Charles. 1992 "Domesticating the Sublime: Bly's Latest Poems." In *Critical Essays on Robert Bly.* William V. Davis, ed. Pp. 185–193. New York: G.K. Hall and Co.

Molina, Natalia. 2014. *How Race Is Made in America: Immigration, Citizenship, and the Historical Power of Racial Scripts.* Berkeley: University of California Press.

Morgan, Thad. 2018. "How a Terrifying Wave of Unexplained Deaths Led to 'A Nightmare on Elm Street.'" History.com. Accessed online: https://www.history .com/news/nightmare-on-elm-street-real-inspiration-hmong-death.

Mullen, Bill V. 2015. *Un-American: W. E. B. Du Bois and the Century of World Revolution.* Philadelphia: Temple University Press.

Nathanson, Paul. 1991. *Over the Rainbow: "The Wizard of Oz" as a Secular Myth of America.* Albany: State University of New York Press.

Nixon, Rob. 2011. *Slow Violence and the Environmentalism of the Poor.* Cambridge, MA: Harvard University Press.

Núñez, Xosé-Manoel. 2001. "The Region as Essence of the Fatherland: Regionalist Variants of Spanish Nationalism (1840–1936)." *European History Quarterly* 31(4): 483–518.

Ochonicky, Adam. 2020. *The American Midwest in Film and Literature: Nostalgia, Violence and Regionalism.* Bloomington: Indiana University Press.

Oler, Andy. 2019. *Old-Fashioned Modernism: Rural Masculinity and Midwestern Literature.* Baton Rouge: Louisiana State University Press.

Olmstead, Kathryn S. 2009. *Real Enemies: Conspiracy Theories and American Democracy, from World War I to 9/11.* Oxford: Oxford University Press.

Olson, Joel. 2004. *The Abolition of White Democracy.* Minneapolis: University of Minnesota Press.

Ong, Aihwa. 1996. "Cultural Citizenship as Subject-Making: Immigrants Negotiate Racial and Cultural Boundaries in the U.S." *Cultural Anthropology* 37(5): 737–762.

Opie, John. 1987. *The Law of the Land: Two Hundred Years of American Farmland Policy.* Lincoln: University of Nebraska Press.

Ortiz, Fernando. 1995[1940]. *Cuban Counterpoint: Tobacco and Sugar.* Durham, NC: Duke University Press.

Page, Brian, and Richard Walker. 1991. "From Settlement to Fordism: The Agro-Industrial Revolution in the American Midwest." *Economic Geography* 67(4): 281–315.

Paul, Heike. 2014. *The Myths That Made America: An Introduction to American Studies*. Bielefeld: transcript Verlag.

Perin, Constance. 1977. *Everything in Its Place: Land Use and Social Order in America*. Princeton, NJ: Princeton University Press.

Perrino, Sabina. 2019. *Narrating Migration: Intimacies of Exclusion in Northern Italy*. New York: Routledge.

Peseroff, Joyce. 1992. "Minnesota Transcendentalist." In *Critical Essays on Robert Bly*. William V. Davis, ed. Pp. 89–91. New York: G.K. Hall and Co.

Pfau, Thomas. 2019. "'Superabundant Being': Disambiguating Rilke and Heidegger." *Modern Theology* 35(1):23–42.

Pichaske, David R. 2006. *Rooted: Seven Midwest Writers of Place*. Iowa City: University of Iowa Press.

Pierre, Jemima. 2013. *The Predicament of Blackness: Postcolonial Ghana and the Politics of Race*. Chicago: University of Chicago Press.

Pietz, William. 1985. "The Problem of the Fetish, I." *Res: Anthropology and Aesthetics* 9: 5–17.

Pollan, Michael. 2006. *The Omnivore's Dilemma: A Natural History of Four Meals*. New York: Penguin Books.

Postel, Charles. 2007. *The Populist Vision*. Oxford: Oxford University Press.

Povinelli, Elizabeth. 2006. *Empire of Love: Toward a Theory of Intimacy, Genealogy, and Carnality*. Durham, NC: Duke University Press.

Powell, Larson. 2008. *The Technological Unconscious in German Modernist Literature: Nature in Rilke, Benn, Brecht, and Döblin*. Rochester, NY: Camden House.

Pritzker, Sonya. 2014. *Living Translation: Language and the Search for Resonance in Chinese Medicine*. New York: Berghahn.

Puar, Jasbir. 2007. *Terrorist Assemblages: Homonationalism in Queer Times*. Durham, NC: Duke University Press.

———. 2017. *The Right to Maim: Debility, Capacity, Disability*. Durham, NC: Duke University Press.

Quijano, Aníbal. 1991. "Colonialidad y Racionalidad/Modernidad." *Peru Indigena* 29: 11–29.

Reed-Danahay, Deborah. 1997. *Auto/ethnography*. New York: Berg.

Rich, Adrienne. 1980. "Compulsory Heterosexuality and Lesbian Existence." *Signs: Journal of Women in Culture and Society* 5(4): 631–660.

Robinson, Cedric. 2000. *Black Marxism: The Making of the Black Radical Tradition*. Second Edition. Chapel Hill: University of North Carolina Press.

Rodríguez-Pose, Andrés, and Viola von Berlepsch. 2015. "European Migration, National Origin and Long-Term Economic Development in the United States." *Economic Geography* 91(4): 393–424.

Roediger, David. 1991. *Wages of Whiteness: Race and the Making of the American Working Class*. New York: Verso.

Roediger, David, and Kathryn Robinson. 2016. "The Sundown Town Vote in Wisconsin: Race-ing the Trump Victory." Counterpunch.com. Accessed online: https://

www.counterpunch.org/2016/11/29/the-sundown-town-vote-in-wisconsin-race-ing -the-trump-victory/.

Rolph-Trouillot, Michel. 1995. *Silencing the Past: Power and the Production of History.* Boston: Beacon Press.

Rosa, Jonathan, and Yarimar Bonilla. 2017. "Deprovincializing Trump, Decolonizing Diversity, and Unsettling Anthropology." *American Ethnologist* 44(2): 201–208.

Ross, Theodore, and Roy Huss. 1972. *Focus on the Horror Film.* Englewood Cliffs, NJ: Prentice Hall.

Rothstein, Richard. 2017. *The Color of Law: A Forgotten History of How Our Government Segregated America.* New York: Liveright.

Rundstrom, Robert. 2007. "Heartland." In *The American Midwest: An Interpretive Encyclopedia.* Andrew R. L. Cayton, Richard Sisson, and Chris Zacher, eds. Pp. 71–73. Bloomington: Indiana University Press.

Rushdie, Salman. 1992. *The Wizard of Oz.* New York: Macmillan.

Said, Edward. 1978. *Orientalism.* New York: Vintage.

Scanlan, John. 2005. *On Garbage.* New York: Reaktion Press.

Schickel, Richard. 1968. *The Disney Version.* New York: Simon and Schuster.

Seshadri-Crooks, Kalpana. 2000. *Desiring Whiteness: A Lacanian Analysis of Race.* New York: Routledge.

Shi, David E. 1985. *The Simple Life: Plain Living and High Thinking in American Culture.* New York: Oxford University Press.

Shortridge, James. 1989. *The Middle West: Its Meaning in American Culture.* Lawrence: University Press of Kansas.

Shryock, Andrew, and Sally Howell. 2003. "Cracking Down on Diaspora: Arab Detroit and America's 'War on Terror.'" *Anthropological Quarterly* 76(3): 443–462.

Silverstein, Ken. 2000. "Ford and the Führur." *The Nation,* January 6, 2000. Accessed online: July 31, 2019.

Silverstein, Michael. 1996. "Monoglot 'Standard' in America: Standardization and Metaphors of Linguistic Hegemony." In *The Matrix of Language: Contemporary Linguistic Anthropology.* Donald Brenneis, ed. Pp. 284-306. Boulder, CO: Westview Press.

———. 2000. "Whorfianism and the Linguistic Imagination of Nationality." In *Regimes of Language: Ideologies, Polities, and Identities.* Paul Kroskrity, ed. Pp. 85–138. Santa Fe: SAR Press.

Simpson, Audra. 2014. *Mohawk Interruptus: Political Life across the Borders of Settler States.* Durham, NC: Duke University Press.

Simpson, Louis. 1992. "Thinking about Robert Bly." In *Critical Essays on Robert Bly.* William V. Davis, ed. Pp. 21–33. New York: G.K. Hall and Co.

Smarsh, Sarah. 2019. *Heartland: A Memoir of Working Hard and Being Broke in the Richest Country on Earth.* New York: Scribner.

Smedley, Audrey. 2018 [1993]. *Race in North America: Origin and Evolution of a Worldview.* London: Routledge.

Snider, Jill D. 2003. "'Great Shadow in the Sky': The Airplane in the Tulsa Race Riot of 1921 and the Development of African American Visions of Aviation, 1921-1926." In *The Airplane in American Culture*. Dominick A. Pisano, ed. Pp. 105–146. Ann Arbor: University of Michigan Press.

Sobchack, Vivian. 1996, "Bringing It All Back Home: Family Economy and Generic Exchange." In *The Dread of Difference: Gender and the Horror Film*. Barry Keith Grant, ed. Pp. 171–191. Austin: University of Texas Press.

Sodré, João Gabriel Rabello. 2020. "How Jessica Krug Appropriated Not Just an Identity, But a History." *Georgetown Voice*, 19 November 2020. Available Online: https://georgetownvoice.com/2020/11/19/how-jessica-krug-appropriated-not-just-an-identity-but-a-history/.

Song, Hoon. 2010. *Pigeon Trouble: Bestiary Biopolitics in a Deindustrialized America*. Philadelphia: University of Pennsylvania Press.

Spitulnik, Debra. 1996. "The Social Circulation of Media Discourse." *Journal of Linguistic Anthropology* 6(2): 161–187.

Stanton, Lucia, and Dianne Swann-Wright. 1999. "Bonds of Memory: Identity and the Hemings Family." In *Sally Hemings & Thomas Jefferson: History, Memory, and Civic Culture*. Jan Lewis and Peter S. Onuf, eds. Pp. 161–186. Charlottesville: University of Virginia Press.

Stoler, Ann. 2009. *Along the Archival Grain: Thinking through Colonial Ontologies*. Princeton, NJ: Princeton University Press.

Stoler, Ann Laura, and Frederick Cooper. 1997. "Between Metropole and Colony: Rethinking a Research Agenda." In *Tensions of Empire: Colonial Cultures in a Bourgeois World*. Ann Laura Stoler and Frederick Cooper, eds. Pp. 1–58. Berkeley: University of California Press.

Storm, Eric. 2012. "The Birth of Regionalism and the Crisis of Reason: France, Germany, and Spain." In *Region and State in Nineteenth-Century Europe: Nation-Building, Regional Identities and Separatism*. Joost Augusteijn and Eric Storm, eds. Pp. 36–54. New York: Palgrave Macmillan.

Sugg, Richard P. 1986. *Robert Bly*. New York: Twayne.

Sullivan, Shannon. 2014. *Good White People: The Problem with Middle-Class White Anti-Racism*. Albany: State University of New York Press.

Talbot, Mary. 2007. *Media Discourse: Representation and Interaction*. Edinburgh: Edinburgh University Press.

Tanner, Jakob. 2008. "The Conspiracy of the Invisible Hand: Anonymous Market Mechanisms and Dark Powers." *New German Critique* 103.35(1): 51–64.

Taylor, Charles. 1989. *Sources of the Self: The Making of the Modern Identity*. Cambridge: Cambridge University Press.

Taylor, Diana. 2003. *The Archive and the Repertoire: Performing Cultural Memory in the Americas*. Durham, NC: Duke University Press.

Teo, Peter. 2000. "Racism in the News: A Critical Discourse Analysis of News Reporting in Two Australian Newspapers." *Discourse & Society* 11(1): 7–49.

Tibbetts, John C. 2003. "The Midwest." In *The Columbia Companion to American History on Film*. Peter C. Rollins, ed. Pp. 421–429. New York: Columbia University Press.

Tuck, Eve, and K. Wayne Yang. 2012. "Decolonization Is Not a Metaphor." *Decolonization: Indigeneity, Education & Society* 1(1): 1–40.

Urban, Greg. 2001. *Metaculture: How Culture Moves through the World*. Minneapolis: University of Minnesota Press.

Valdés, Dionicio Nodín. 2000. *Barrios Norteños: St. Paul and Midwestern Mexican Communities in the Twentieth Century*. Austin: University of Texas Press.

Vance, J.D. 2016. *Hillbilly Elegy: A Memoir of a Family and Culture in Crisis*. New York: HarperCollins.

Van Dijk, Teun. 2011. *Discourse and Communication: New Approaches to the Analysis of Mass Media Discourse and Communication*. New York: De Gruyter.

Vega, Sujey. 2015. *Latino Heartland: Of Borders and Belonging in the Midwest*. New York: New York University Press.

Verdery, Katherine, and Caroline Humphrey, eds. 2004. *Property in Question: Value Transformations in the Global Economy*. Oxford: Berg.

Vertovec, Steven. 2007. "Super-Diversity and Its Implications." *Ethnic and Racial Studies* 30(6): 1024–1054.

Vincent, Stephen. 1999. *Southern Seed, Northern Soil: African-American Farm Communities in the Midwest, 1765–1900*. Bloomington: Indiana University Press.

Walker, Hannah, and Dylan Bennett. 2015. "The Whiteness of Wisconsin's Wages: Racial Geography and the Defeat of Public Sector Labor Unions in Wisconsin." *New Political Science* 37(2): 181–203.

Wallace, Max. 2004. *The American Axis: Henry Ford, Charles Lindbergh and the Rise of the Third Reich*. New York: Macmillan.

Walley, Christine J. 2013. *Exit Zero: Family and Class in Postindustrial Chicago*. Chicago and London: University of Chicago Press.

Weems, Jason. 2015. *Barnstorming the Prairies: How Aerial Vision Shaped the Midwest*. Minneapolis: University of Minnesota Press.

Whitman, James Q. 2017. *Hitler's American Model: the United States and the Making of Nazi Race Law*. Princeton, NJ: Princeton University Press.

Wildenthal, Bryan H., and Patrick M. O'Neil. 2000. "Native American Religious Rights." In *Religion and American Law: An Encyclopedia*. Paul Finkelman, ed. Pp. 330–340. New York: Garland Publishing.

Williams, Bianca. 2018. *The Pursuit of Happiness: Black Women, Diasporic Dreams and the Politics of Emotional Transnationalism*. Durham, NC: Duke University Press.

Williamson, Terrion L., ed. 2020. *Black in the Middle: An Anthology of the Black Midwest*. Cleveland, OH: Belt Publishing.

Wingerd, Mary Lethert. 2003. *Claiming the City: Politics, Faith and the Power of Place in St. Paul*. Ithaca, NY: Cornell University Press.

Woeste, Victoria Saker. 2004. "Insecure Equality: Louis Marshall, Henry Ford, and the Problem of Defamatory Antisemitism, 1920–1929." *The Journal of American History* 91(3):877–905.

Wolfe, Patrick. 2016. *Traces of History: Elementary Structures of Race.* New York: Verso.

Wood, Robin. 1979. *American Nightmare: Essays on the Horror Film.* Toronto: Festival of Festivals.

Wynter, Sylvia. 2001. "Towards the Sociogenic Principle: Fanon, Identity, the Puzzle of Conscious Experience." In *National Identities and Socio-Political Changes in Latin America.* Antonio Gomez-Moriana and Mercedes F. Duran-Cogan, eds, Pp. 30–66. New York: Routledge.

Young, Cathy. 2020. "Jessica Krug's Cruel Hoax." *Newsday*, 11 September 2020. Accessed January 9, 2021. Available Online: https://www.newsday.com/opinion /columnists/cathy-young/cathy-young-jessica-krug-the-george-washington -university-black-1.49185601.

Zinnes, Harriet. 1992. "Two Languages." In *Critical Essays on Robert Bly.* William V. Davis, ed. Pp. 42–43. New York: G.K. Hall & Co.

INDEX

Abraham, Nabeel, 159
African Americans: artistic representations of, 42, 77–78, 93; citizenship and, 54–55; classism and, 31–32; immigration and, 24, 129, 159–60; industrialism and, 128–29, 133, 139; media representations and, 31–32, 128–29, 133, 139–42, 151–52; nationalism and, 25; political participation of, 55; property ownership and, 50–51, 54–55; regionalism and, 55–56, 133, 141–42; systematic racism against, 24, 42, 54–55, 142, 154–55; urbanization and, 60; whiteness and, 24–25, 31–32, 54–55
agricultural mythology. *See* pastoralism trope
Alt-Right (2018), 146
alt-right movement, 73–74, 111, 146
American Dream mythology, 86, 157
American Gothic (Wood, 1930), 41–42, 63, 121
American Indians. *See* Native Americans
American Sniper (2014), 93
Anderson, Benedict, 186n62, 189n9, 192n65
Anishinaabe. *See* Ojibwe people
Ansley, Frances Lee, 53, 71
anti-lockdown protests, 11–12, 152
anti-racism, 3–4, 18, 42
Aptheker, Herbert, 26
artistic representations: African Americans and, 42, 77–78, 93; capitalism and, 92, 103; Christianity and, 110; colonialism and, 59, 94; fantasy and, 93–95, 100, 103–11, 187n19; films, 5–6, 16, 22, 42, 93–95, 97–98, 100–111, 187n17; heartland trope

and, 43–44, 61–62, 93, 100, 107, 109, 121; identity and, 100; immigration and, 102–3, 108–9; insularity and, 71–87, 158; intimate others and, 91–92, 94, 96, 98, 100–103, 105, 108–11; landscapes and, 59; lost children and, 94; masculinity and, 95, 188n31; monsters and, 102, 105–7, 110–11, 187n19; nationalism and, 61, 93–94, 100, 110; Native Americans and, 47, 56; Nazism and, 79–86, 185nn57,60; novels, 13, 29–32, 100–101, 106, 139–40, 160; ordinariness and, 2, 4, 14, 29, 33, 44, 91–92, 96, 101, 106, 110–11, 120; overview of, 30–33, 91–94, 108–11; paintings, 6, 41–44, 47, 52, 75, 121, 158, 187n8, 188n31; pastoralism and, 13, 29–30, 41–45, 52, 60–61, 73–76, 144, 187n8; photography, 139, 158, 179n45; property ownership and, 52; regionalism and, 93, 102–3, 109–11, 156–57; Regionalism in painting and, 41–44, 47, 52, 75, 121, 158, 187n8; serial killers and, 106; vigilantism and, 95; whiteness and, 5, 12, 16, 31–32, 47, 52, 74, 92–98, 100, 103–4, 107–8; white supremacy and, 93, 98. *See also* Bly, Robert; *The Wizard of Oz; specific tropes and works*
Australia, settler colonialism in, 9, 25, 47–48, 52–54

Baldwin, James, 91, 123, 139–40, 153–55
Balken, Debra, 43–44, 158, 180n8
Barrios Norteños (Valdés), 156–58

Rockefeller Foundation, 57
Roediger, David, 15, 142
Rolph-Trouillot, Michel, 155
Roosevelt, Franklin, 132–33
Roosevelt, Theodore, 25, 82, 124, 186n61
Rothstein, Richard, 60, 132–33, 136
Rothwell, Jonathan, 191n45
Rushdie, Salman, 95
Rust Belt terminology, 9, 12, 115, 136–38, 143–44, 192n64

Said, Edward, 188n4
St. Louis' Gateway Arch, 60
Sallman, Warner, 188n31
Sauk people, 48–49
Savran, David, 77–78
Seshadri-Crooks, Kalpana, 77, 188n3, 191n44
settler colonialism. *See* colonialism and imperialism
Shahn, Ben, 42, 158
Sheeler, Charles, 187n8
Shoeless Joe (Kinsella), 101–2
Shryock, Andrew, 159
Shuster, Joe, 98, 100
Siegel, Joe, 98, 100
Silence in the Snowy Fields (Bly), 75
Silverstein, Ken, 185n52
Simpson, Louis, 73–74
Smith, T. Lynn, 57
Sorry to Bother You (2018), 177n11
South Africa, settler colonialism in, 9, 52–54
South Dakota, 19, 26, 121, 125
Stefon sketch, 65–66, 68, 183nn2,6
Stieglitz, Alfred, 41, 43
Strangers in Their Own Land (Hochschild), 137
Superman, 98–100, 106, 108–10, 188n31
systemic racism, 4, 24, 42, 54–55, 142, 154–55

Tanner, Jakob, 81
Taylor, Diana, 189n5
Terkel, Studs, 153
Texas Chainsaw Massacre (1974–2017), 106
Tibbets, John, 106
Tornado over Kansas (Curry), 42
tropes. *See* heartland trope; industrialism trope; insularity trope; pastoralism trope; regionalism
Trump, Donald J.: artistic representations and, 109; heartland trope and, 119–20; immigration and, 109, 192n57;

industrialism and, 134–35; media representations and, 126–27, 134, 137–38; supporters of, 63, 65, 69, 127, 191n45; white suffering and, 137–38; white supremacy and, 2–4. *See also* election of 2016
Tulsa race massacre (1921), 26, 150, 178n25
Turner, Frederick Jackson, 69, 163
Twain, Mark, 67

United Fruit Company (UFC), 182n55
urbanization, 60
Urban League, 42

Vega, Sujey, 13, 55–56, 156–58, 179n2

Wages of Whiteness (Roediger), 15, 177n10
Walker, Richard, 22
Walker, Scott, 119
The Ways of White Folks (Hughes), 31–32
We Ask Only a Fair Trial (Bigham), 55
Weems, Jason, 179n45
Welles, Orson, 1–2
white grievance, 73–74, 78, 111
white innocence, 123
white man's burden, 15, 25, 82
whiteness: African Americans and, 24–25, 31–32, 54–55; artistic representations and, 5, 12, 16, 31–32, 47, 52, 74, 92–98, 100, 103–4, 107–8; belonging and, 56, 115–16; capitalism and, 14–15, 19, 28, 30–32, 34, 70, 80, 136; citizenship and, 14, 24–25, 54–55; civic participation and, 49–52; colonialism and, 15, 25, 32, 49–52; compulsory whiteness, 26, 100, 109–10, 177n11; election of 2016 and, 3–4, 17, 127; ethnic whiteness, 17–18; heartland trope and, 29, 133; history of, 14–18, 24–25; identity and, 15, 17, 27, 45, 161; immigration and, 24–25, 161; industrialism and, 80, 116, 129–32, 135–36, 190n41; insularity and, 68–71, 73–77, 87–88; land policy and, 17–18, 45–49, 56; landscapes and, 59; media representations and, 5, 25, 31, 115–25, 141–45, 188n1; Mexican Americans and, 24, 56, 58; nationalism and, 16, 24, 82, 125, 127; Native Americans and, 46–47; as ordinary, 17, 30, 34, 57, 65, 74, 78; pastoralism and, 61, 121, 124; people of color contrasted with, 15, 24, 27–29, 46, 50; personal reflections on, 5–8; plain whiteness, 17–18, 28–33; property

whiteness (*continued*)
ownership and, 45–47, 49–52, 56; regionalism and, 4, 16, 18–28, 153, 163; reproduction of, 5, 15–16, 18, 59, 108, 124; scholarship on, 14–16, 24; shifting nature of, 16–18, 24–29, 68, 161, 177n13; white resentment and, 13, 81; white supremacy and, 161–62; white virtue and, 27, 74
white power movement, 16–18, 68, 73–74, 86
white pride, 68
white privilege, 72, 86, 149, 161
white speech, 28–33
white supremacy: artistic representations and, 93, 98; colonialism and, 25–26, 53–54; definition of, 53; global white supremacy, 14, 25–26, 85, 93, 98, 145–46; heartland trope and, 159–60; identity and, 78; immigration and, 54, 160–61; industrialism and, 136, 140; insularity and, 69–71, 77, 79, 81–85; media representations and, 117, 123, 140, 145; men's movement and, 78–79; Mexican Americans and, 57; nationalism and, 145; political participation and, 55; property ownership and, 51–52; regionalism and, 10–14, 16, 79, 153, 155, 159–60, 163; resistance to, 4, 26, 162; whiteness and, 161–62; white virtue and, 4, 34
white virtue: artistic representations and, 30–35, 63, 78, 97, 107; capitalism and, 27; classism and, 31; colonialism and, 27, 56;

definition of, 27; heartland and, 85–86; history of, 24; industrialism and, 136; insularity and, 80; media representations and, 119, 145; nationalism and, 14; necessity of, 24; overview of, 14–18; regionalism and, 4–5, 14–18, 27, 30–35, 83, 155; reproduction of, 34; scholarship on, 24; white man's burden and, 27; whiteness and, 27, 74; white speech and, 30; white supremacy and, 4, 34
Whitman, James, 185n53
Williams, Bianca, 117–18
Wilson, August, 144
Winfrey-Harris, Tamara, 127, 141–42
Wisconsin, 19, 22–23, 61, 142, 178n32
The Wiz (1978), 101
The Wizard of Oz (1939): artistic representation in, 95–96; Christian dimensions of, 110; color use in, 96; context of, 16, 95–96; impact of, 95–96, 103; people of color in, 100–101; regionalism in, 42, 95–98, 100, 106, 109; scholarship on, 95–98; whiteness in, 97–98, 100; white virtue in, 97
Woeste, Victoria, 184n43
Wood, Grant, 41–42, 63, 121, 187n8
Wounded Knee (1890), 26
Wright, Richard, 182n1
Wynter, Sylvia, 192n3

Zangwill, Israel, 81–82
Zuloaga, Ignacio, 42

Founded in 1893,
UNIVERSITY OF CALIFORNIA PRESS
publishes bold, progressive books and journals
on topics in the arts, humanities, social sciences,
and natural sciences—with a focus on social
justice issues—that inspire thought and action
among readers worldwide.

The UC PRESS FOUNDATION
raises funds to uphold the press's vital role
as an independent, nonprofit publisher, and
receives philanthropic support from a wide
range of individuals and institutions—and from
committed readers like you. To learn more, visit
ucpress.edu/supportus.